MULTICULTURAL

JAMES A. BANKS, *Series Editor*

(continued)

GLOBAL MIGRATION, DIVERSITY, AND CIVIC EDUCATION

Improving Policy and Practice

JAMES A. BANKS, MARCELO M. SUÁREZ-OROZCO,
AND MIRIAM BEN-PERETZ, EDITORS

SPONSORED BY THE NATIONAL ACADEMY OF EDUCATION

TEACHERS COLLEGE PRESS

TEACHERS COLLEGE | COLUMBIA UNIVERSITY
NEW YORK AND LONDON

Published by Teachers College Press, 1234 Amsterdam Avenue, New York, NY 10027

Cover design by Rebecca Lown Design. Image by NASA / GSFC / NOAA / USGS.

Figure I.1 is reprinted from "Quantifying Global International Migration Flows," by G. J. Abel and N. Sander, 2014, *Science, 343*, p. 1522. Copyright 2014 by the American Association for the Advancement of Science. Reprinted with permission.

Figure 1.1 is reprinted with the permission of James A. Banks.

Library of Congress Cataloging-in-Publication Data

Names: Banks, James A., editor. | Suâarez-Orozco, Marcelo M., 1956– editor. |
  Ben-Peretz, Miriam, editor. | National Academy of Education, sponsoring
  body.
Title: Global migration, diversity, and civic education : improving policy
  and practice / edited by James A. Banks, Marcelo Suarez-Orozco, Miriam
  Ben-Peretz.
Description: New York, NY : Teachers College Press, 2016. | Series:
  Multicultural education series | "Sponsored by the National Academy of
  Education." | Includes bibliographical references and index.
Identifiers: LCCN 2016028270 (print) | LCCN 2016038967 (ebook) | ISBN
  9780807758090 (pbk.) | ISBN 9780807775219 (ebook)
Subjects: LCSH: Education and globalization. | Immigrants—Education. |
  Multicultural education. | Civics—Study and teaching. |
  Citizenship—Study and teaching.
Classification: LCC LC191 .G54157 2016 (print) | LCC LC191 (ebook) | DDC
  370.11/5—dc23
LC record available at https://lccn.loc.gov/2016028270

ISBN 978-0-8077-5809-0 (paper)
ISBN 978-0-8077-7521-9 (ebook)

Printed on acid-free paper
Manufactured in the United States of America

23 22 21 20 19 18 17 16   8 7 6 5 4 3 2 1

Contents

Preface

Global migratory flows involve millions of people from heterogeneous ethnocultural, racial, linguistic, and religious backgrounds, as well as from diverse social statuses, ages, and mobility patterns. These flows have rapidly intensified under the ascendancy of globalization, posing new challenges to some of the constitutive principles of education systems in a diversity of national settings. Mass migration and globalization create new and deep challenges to education systems the world over. Modern education systems were established in order to build social cohesion through homogenization and to maintain social control, whether through decentralized and varied school systems, as in the United States, or in highly unified and centralized systems, as in Israel.

School design, language, culture, values, texts, codes of conduct, and curricula have been utilized as vehicles for homogenization in education, though their efficacy in promoting positive forms of social cohesion is contested. At the same time, cultural diversity and cultural sustainability pose challenges to the agenda of social cohesion both for those educators concerned with integrating diverse groups within a nation-state and for those oriented to enhancing equity and autonomy for a particular ethnic or cultural community. The question of whether or not culturally specific education (such as ethnic studies and heritage language programs) exacerbates societal fragmentation or facilitates the structural integration of diverse groups into the nation-state is an ongoing and contentious issue in pluralistic nations.

A lack of shared meanings can jeopardize coexistence and endanger future development. Creating shared meanings, while recognizing and acknowledging diversity, is a precondition to securing a peaceful world. Education that is sensitive to diversity will contribute to a shared civic vision and agenda for a variety of populations, local and global. All communities are affected by these tensions, wrestling with questions about the potential congruence or conflict between real and assumed worldviews, and loyalty to or betrayal of revered traditions and modern trends. All groups, regardless of the sociopolitical context they inhabit, interrogate the possible benefits and pitfalls of various approaches in terms of their well-being and mobility. Myriad educational solutions have been attempted with mixed results. Questions concerning which educational policies are preferable in which contexts remain open, as do the implications for their multiple potential beneficiaries (states, communities, parents, students, and teachers).

The workshop that was the genesis for this book, the Initiative on Immigration, Cultural Sustainability, and Social Cohesion, focused on these topics from multiple disciplinary perspectives in terms of both theory and methodology. The National Academy of Education, with a grant from the Spencer Foundation, convened a group of international scholars, educators, and policymakers into what the National Research Council (NRC) of the National Academies of Sciences calls a "workshop." This 2-day workshop took place March 21–22, 2014, at the National Academy of Sciences building in Washington, D.C. The individuals who participated in the workshop had dealt with issues related to immigration, cultural sustainability, and social cohesion in varied national, political, and institutional contexts. The workshop was designed to facilitate an exchange of ideas, to enrich the knowledge and insights of the workshop participants, to identify promising educational practices, and to formulate questions and issues that required further research and analysis.

The major aim of this book is to examine the theories, concepts, empirical findings, and promising practices related to education for citizenship in this age of globalization and mass migration, including issues related to immigration, cultural sustainability, structural inclusion, and social cohesion. One of the pivotal issues examined in Part I of this book—which focuses on the theoretical, conceptual, and empirical issues related to citizenship education in the age of globalization and mass migration—is how nation-states can maintain social cohesion in a context in which ethnic, racial, religious, and linguistic groups can attain structural inclusion, cultural recognition, and self-determination. Historically, social cohesion was attained and maintained by hegemonic nation-states that practiced forced assimilation, "deculturalization" (Spring, 2010) and "subtractive schooling" (Valenzuela, 1999). These practices required ethnocultural groups to surrender their family and community cultures and languages—and to experience self-alienation—in order to become structurally integrated and recognized citizens of their nation-state.

Since the ethnic revitalization movements of the 1960s and 1970s—during which ethnocultural groups demanded cultural recognition and structural inclusion—forced assimilation and deculturalization are no longer viable ways for nation-states to attain social cohesion. The chapters in Part I of this book provide a deep and critical analysis of the concept of social cohesion and examine the ways in which it relates to cultural sustainability. Several of the chapter authors question whether social cohesion and cultural sustainability are compatible concepts in this age of globalization and international migration. These authors contend that we need novel and transformative conceptions and paradigms to deal effectively with educational problems that are rooted in globalization and mass migration in the 21st century.

In Part II of this book, chapter authors apply the theories and concepts examined in Part I to two nations—the United States and Israel. We selected the United States and Israel as the context for these case studies because of their demographic trajectories and rich cultural landscapes. The United States has three times more immigrants than the second-largest country of immigration in the world, and nearly all of its demographic growth moving forward will result from children born to immigrant parents. Israel is a country that consists of immigrants from a large diversity of origin countries and has a significant community of Indigenous people—the Arabs and Druze. When Israel was founded in 1948, it had less than one million inhabitants. In 2014, the Israeli population had reached 8.3 million. This enormous demographic growth means that Israel's development is dependent on the successful integration and structural inclusion of children of immigrants and Indigenous groups. Along with the United States, the Israeli experience provides insights into the intractable challenges and complex possibilities for resolving issues related to immigration, cultural sustainability, and social cohesion in this period of globalization and mass migration. The chapters in Part II examine the education of immigrant students in the United States, narratives of success of Ethiopian immigrants in Israel, the politics of citizenship education in Israel, and the ways in which Palestinian teachers construct counternarratives to official state knowledge.

Part I of this book focuses on the theoretical, conceptual, and empirical issues related to global migration, cultural sustainability, social cohesion, and structural inclusion. The chapters in Part II apply these theories and concepts to analyze selected case studies in the United States and Israel. Part III, the last part of this book, discusses the implications of Parts I and II for practice. In Chapter 7, Gregory White and John Myers examine the changing role of civic education in this era of globalization and mass migration. Sonia Nieto in Chapter 8—the final chapter—provides a comprehensive and discerning analysis of the previous chapters and explicates their implications for preparing teachers during a period of globalization and worldwide migration.

This book is being published in the Multicultural Education Series at Teachers College Press, Columbia University. The main purpose of the Multicultural Education Series is to provide preservice educators, practicing educators, graduate students, scholars, and policymakers with an interrelated and comprehensive set of books that summarize and analyze important research, theory, and practice related to the education of ethnic, racial, cultural, and linguistic groups in the United States and other nations and the education of mainstream students about diversity. The books in the series provide research, theoretical, and practical knowledge about the behaviors and learning characteristics of students of color, language minority students, and low-income students. They also provide knowledge about ways to improve academic achievement and race relations in educational settings. This book is a significant and timely one to add to the Multicultural Education Series because the most cutting-edge issues related to diversity and citizenship education today have international dimensions and require global solutions.

ACKNOWLEDGMENTS

It takes a village to successfully implement a National Academy of Education workshop and to publish a book based on the papers written for it. We would like to acknowledge the individuals who made the workshop and this book possible. We thank the Spencer Foundation for funding this project, and especially Michael S. McPherson—who was president of the Spencer Foundation when this project was funded—and Diana Hess, who was senior vice president—for their support and encouragement. We are grateful to Gregory White, executive director of the National Academy of Education (NAEd), and to Judie Ahn—who was on the staff of the National Academy of Education when the workshop took place—for their essential staff support during the planning and implementation of the workshop.

We are indebted to Robert Floden (Michigan State University)—chair of the Research Advisory Committee of the National Academy of Education—for his support in facilitating the project that resulted in this book. We extend thanks to Judith Warren Little (University of California, Berkeley)—chair of the Standing Review Committee—for coordinating the reviews of our manuscript for the NAEd. We are also grateful to Gloria Ladson-Billings and Jacqueline J. Irvine, the NAEd members who reviewed our manuscript for the National Academy of Education. We extend deep thanks to the 27 external reviewers who prepared insightful and helpful comments on each of the chapters in this book and to the chapter authors who revised their chapters in response to feedback from the external reviewers and our editorial comments. A list of these external reviewers immediately follows this Preface.

Tao Wang, a postdoctoral research associate in the Center for Multicultural Education at the University of Washington, coordinated the peer reviews of the chapters in this book as well as helped with the initial editing of the manuscript before we submitted it to the National Academy of Education and Teachers College Press. Yiting Chu, also in the Center for Multicultural Education, assisted Tao Wang with some of the editorial work on the manuscript. We are grateful to Brian Ellerbeck and Carole Saltz at Teachers College Press for facilitating the publication of this book as a joint project of Teachers College Press and the National Academy of Education.

—*James A. Banks, Marcelo M. Suárez-Orozco, and Miriam Ben-Peretz*

REFERENCES

Spring, J. (2010). *Deculturalization and the struggle for equality: A brief history of the education of dominated cultures in the United States* (7th ed.). New York, NY: McGraw-Hill.
Valenzuela, A. (1999). *Subtractive schooling: U.S.–Mexican youth and the politics of caring.* Albany, NY: State University of New York Press.

Reviewers

Manal Yazbak Abu Ahmad, Saknin College for Teacher Education, Israel
Robert Arnove, Indiana University, USA
Aviv Cohen, Tel Aviv University; Kibbutzim College of Education, Israel
Michael Connelly, Ontario Institute for Studies in Education, University of
    Toronto, Canada
Catherine Cornbleth, University at Buffalo, The State University of New York,
    USA
Carlos E. Cortés, University of California–Riverside, USA
Dafney Blanca Dabach, University of Washington–Seattle, USA
Fabienne Doucet, New York University, USA
Chris Faltis, University of California–Davis, USA
Amanda Kibler, University of Virginia, USA
Penelope Lisi, Central Connecticut State University, USA
Merry Merryfield, Ohio State University, USA
Luanna Meyer, Victoria University of Wellington, New Zealand
Mohanad Mustafa, College for Academic Studies–Or Yehuda, Israel
Pedro Noguera, University of California–Los Angeles, USA
Carlos J. Ovando, Arizona State University, USA
Valerie Pang, San Diego State University, USA
Walter Parker, University of Washington–Seattle, USA
Francisco Ramirez, Stanford University, USA
Roxana Reichman, Gordon College of Education, Israel
Margaret Beale Spencer, University of Chicago, USA
Roni Strier, University of Haifa, Israel
Carlos Alberto Torres, University of California–Los Angeles, USA
Cynthia Tyson, Ohio State University, USA
Terrence Wiley, Center for Applied Linguistics, USA
Michalinos Zembylas, Open University of Cyprus, Cyprus
Kenneith Zeicher, University of Washington–Seattle, USA

Education for Citizenship in the Age of Globalization and Mass Migration

Marcelo M. Suárez-Orozco and Minas Michikyan

Globalization defines our era. Broadly conceived, it is "what happens when the movement of people, goods, or ideas among countries and regions accelerates" (Coatsworth, 2004, p. 38). Global, economic, demographic, and cultural exchanges have complex and contested histories. The three Ms of globalization give shape to its most current iterations: (1) *markets,* their integration and disintegration; (2) *media*, the information, communication and social media technologies that deterritorialize labor, put a premium on knowledge-intensive work, and stimulate new longings and belongings; and (3) *migration*, the mass movement of people on a planetary scale. While these dynamics are neither new nor exceptional, the rate and the depth of global change are novel. Global flows and exchanges of populations and cultures are challenging old boundaries and making the aspired coherence of the nation-state increasingly elusive. Globalization represents the most significant challenge to school systems since the origins of mass public education. Nowhere is this challenge more obvious than in civic education (see chapters by Banks and by Bekerman in this volume).

IMMIGRATION AND MIGRATION

Immigration opens new windows into the world. The global cities of the 21st century encompass growing numbers of diverse immigrants. There are now over a dozen global cities with more than a million immigrants, from Hong Kong to Melbourne, from Moscow to Singapore; and in more than two dozen global cities, inter alia, Amsterdam, Auckland, Muscat, and Perth, immigrants now account for more than one-quarter of the population (see Migration Policy Institute, 2016).

Mass migration is generating a deep demographic transformation, giving rise to the children of immigrants as the fastest growing sector of the child and youth population in a number of high- and middle-income countries across the world. The adaptation of their children at a time of growing levels of inequality (Piketty, 2014) and cultural dystopia[1] sets a challenging agenda for civic education

1

(see chapters by Banks and by White & Myers in this volume). This book examines how two countries with long, yet differing experiences of immigration—the United States and Israel—are responding to the challenge of educating students for civic literacy and participation within a pluralistic nation-state (see chapter by Ben-Peretz & Aderet-German in this volume). The lessons from the two settings are both particularistic and universal.

As we enter the second decade of the 21st century, the lives of more than a billion people are shaped by migration. All continents are involved in the massive movement of people as areas of immigration, emigration, or transit—and often all three at once. Immigration is the human face of globalization: the sounds, colors, and aromas of a miniaturized, interconnected, and fragile world. But viewed anthropologically, immigration is constitutive of the human experience. Migration is written in our genetic code and is encoded in our bodies: in our bipedalism, in our stereoscopic vision, and in our neocortex. Modern humans are the children of immigration, and migrations today are transforming humanity.

During the 2nd decade of the 21st century, 244 million people are international migrants (or 3.3% of the world's population; see United Nations, Department of Economic and Social Affairs, Population Division, 2016), approximately 750 million are internal migrants (The World Bank, 2016), and millions more are immediate relatives left behind (Papademetriou, 2005). Only China (1.36 billion) and India (1.28 billion) have larger populations than today's "immigration nation."

The largest transnational migrations now occur between South and West Asia, from Latin America to North America, and within Africa (Abel & Sander, 2014; see Figure I.1). Over three million people emigrate from countries in the Asia Pacific region every year, representing a quarter of all global migrants. According to the United Nations, "International migration in Asia-Pacific is on the rise, with 59 million documented migrants in 2013 (one in four of the world's migrants) and a high number of non-recorded migrants" (United Nations, ESCAP, n.d.).

Global migration rapidly intensified in the early 1990s (see Figure I.2). November 9, 1989—the day the Berlin Wall fell—represents a decisive turning point, ushering in a new and accelerated cycle of global migration. By September 15, 2008 (the day Lehman Brothers filed for bankruptcy and the beginning of the great recession), unauthorized immigration began to significantly slow.

In the 21st century, global migratory flows involve diverse populations from heterogeneous ethnocultural, racial, and religious backgrounds. Since the dawn of the millennium, the world has been witnessing a rapid rise in the numbers of a plurality of migrants—involuntary, internal or international, authorized or unauthorized, environmental refugees, and victims of human trafficking. These flows have intensified under the ascendancy of climate change, collapsing states, war and terror, and growing inequality. Catastrophic migrations pose new international risks to millions of migrants and challenge the institutions of sending, transiting, and receiving nations. Although immigration is normative, it has taken a dystopic turn. Worldwide, civil and ethnic wars, structural violence, environmental cataclysms, and growing inequality are the causes of the largest displace-

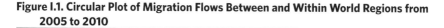

Figure I.1. Circular Plot of Migration Flows Between and Within World Regions from 2005 to 2010

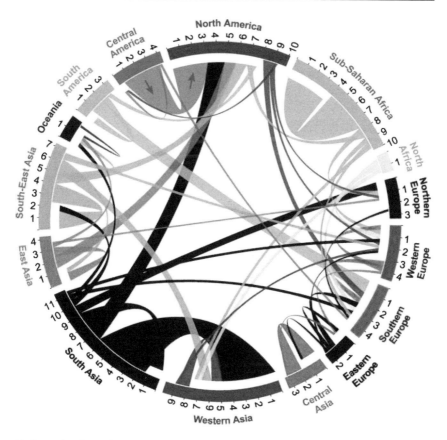

Tick marks show the number of migrants (inflows and outflows) in millions. Only flows containing at least 170,000 migrants are shown.

Note: Reprinted from "Quantifying Global International Migration Flows," by G. J. Abel and N. Sander, 2014, *Science, 343*, p. 1522. Copyright 2014 by the American Association for the Advancement of Science. Reprinted with permission.

ment of people since World War II. Of the over 5 million forcefully displaced, 23.1 million are formal refugees, over half of whom are children under the age of 18 (United Nations High Commission for Refugees, 2016).

The number of international migrants continues to grow at a steady rate and will pass the 400 million mark by 2050, "due to growing demographic disparities, the effects of environmental changes, new global political and economic dynamics, technological revolutions and social networks" (International Organization for Migration, 2010). Catastrophic migrations rooted in war and environmental collaps-

Figure I.2. Global Migration, 1990–2015

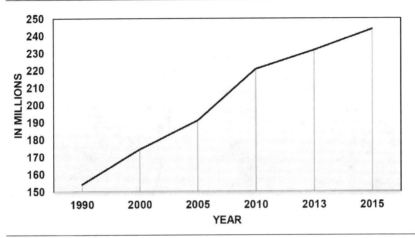

Note: United Nations Department of Economic and Social Affairs.

es, such as land degradation, desertification, rising sea levels, and inundations, are at an all-time high since the end of World War II. According to the U.N. refugee agency, the combined number of the population of concern—including refugees, asylum-seekers, stateless, and internally displaced people worldwide—now exceeds 65 million people (United Nations High Commissioner for Refugees, 2016).

The United States has the largest number of immigrants in the world. In 2016, 45 million (or approximately 14%) of people residing in the United States are foreign born (Pew Research Center, 2015a). Immigrants are very diverse and arrive in the United States from every continent on earth. The latest data tell a changing, dynamic story: Asians now surpass Latinos among those who have been in the United States for 5 years or less. Latino immigration, after peaking in the early 2000s, is now at its lowest level in 50 years. New immigration from the Caribbean now exceeds all new immigration from Europe. The number of new immigrants from "Africa grew 41% from 2000 to 2013, a sharper rise than for other major groups" (Pew Research Center, 2015b).

The children of immigrants are the fruit borne of immigration (see chapter by Suárez-Orozco & Marks in this volume). They are resilient and are an integral part of the national tapestry. In the United States, 25% of children under the age of 18, a total of 18.7 million children, have an immigrant parent. Their growth has been rapid—in 1970 the population of immigrant-origin children stood at 6% of the total population of children. It reached 20% by 2000 and is projected to be 33% by 2050 (see chapter by Suárez-Orozco & Marks in this volume). The education and well-being of these children touch a large swath of the youth population. Their story is deeply intertwined with the future of the nation.

The majority of the children of immigrants in the United States have foreign-born parents, but the children were born in the United States. They are U.S.

citizens, yet many nevertheless are growing up in the shadows of the law (see chapter by Suárez-Orozco & Marks in this volume; Suárez-Orozco, Yoshikawa, Teranishi, & Suárez-Orozco, 2011). The most recent estimates indicate that 4.5 million U.S.-born children younger than the age of 18 are living in the United States with at least one parent who is an unauthorized immigrant. The number of children who are themselves unauthorized has declined from a peak of 1.6 million in 2005 to about 775,000 in 2012 (Passel, Cohn, Krogstad, & Gonzalez-Barrera, 2014). Altogether, about 7% of all school-age children in the United States have at least one parent who is in the United States without authorization (Pew Research Center, 2015c; Suro, Suárez-Orozco, & Canizales, 2015).

For immigrants, "home"—as a cultural ideal and qua the practices of the household—now spans across national boundaries. As Banks (see chapter by Banks in this volume) suggests, new forms of citizenship education are called for in an era of long-distance familyhood, transnational identities, multilingualism, and multiple belongings. Millions of immigrant-origin children today are raised in culturally patterned long-distance family arrangements where separations and reunifications across national boundaries are normative (see chapter by Suárez-Orozco & Marks in this volume).

In a study conducted in Montreal, among 254 first- and second-generation immigrant-origin youth from the Philippines and the Caribbean, approximately 62% of the Filipino-origin participants and 38% of the Caribbean-origin participants had experienced separations during their migration (Rousseau et al., 2009). Moreover, in a nationally representative survey of 1,772 youth that restricted its sample to documented immigrants, nearly one-third of the participants between ages 6 and 18 had been transnationally separated from at least one parent for two or more years (Gindling & Poggio, 2009). Notably, the rates of separation were highest for children of Latin-American origin, which happen to be more than half of all migrants to the United States. This is a low estimate since separation rates are higher among the unauthorized or those who are in the process of regulating their documentation status.

Suárez-Orozco and Marks (see chapter in this volume) report data from the Longitudinal Immigrant Adaptation Study (LISA) that showed high rates of transnational family separations among new immigrant students. In this U.S. bicoastal interdisciplinary study, conducted with a public school sample of 400 recently arrived immigrant youth from China and the Dominican Republic, as well as from various countries in Central America, Haiti, and Mexico, Suárez-Orozco, Suárez-Orozco, and Todorova (2008) found that nearly three-quarters of the youth were separated from one or both of their parents during the migration process. Additionally, there were striking ethnic group differences in the patterns and length of family separation. For instance, the majority of Central American (88%) and Haitian (85%) children were separated from one or both of their parents compared to their Chinese (52%) counterparts. Notably, LISA also revealed that immigrant youth who underwent protracted family separations and complicated reunifications were at a higher risk than other youth to show a pattern of declining academic achievement over time once they resettled in the new country (Suárez-Orozco et al., 2010). However, it is worth noting that students whom Suárez-Orozco and Marks (see chapter in this volume) call the "Improvers," over time and with the support from mentors in schools and from community members who met their developmental needs reached nearly the same levels of achievement as the "High Achievers," those students who sustained no or short family separations and had multiple social supports and attended highest quality schools.

Furthermore, some immigrant-origin children, who researchers call "satellite children," are raised in long-distance family arrangements. These are children who are born in the United States to immigrant parents, but raised by grandparents in China. A study of immigrants in New York City estimated that more than 50% of the mothers had sent their youngsters to Fujian Province to be raised by grandparents. The mothers reported undocumented status, substantial immigration-related debt burdens, and exhausting 6-day work weeks as the main reasons for raising their children transnationally (Kwong, Chung, Sun, Chou, & Taylor-Shih, 2009; Yoshikawa, 2011). Many of these transnationally raised children, the mothers expected, would return to the United States to complete their formal education.

New research suggests that protracted family separations threaten the identity and cohesion of the family, transform well-established roles, create new loyalties and bonds, and destabilize cultural scripts of authority, reciprocity, and responsibility (Suárez-Orozco & Suárez-Orozco, 2013). Studies also suggest that, in the wake of the largest U.S. deportation campaign in recent history, over 700,000 American children are now raised in Mexico as they follow their deported parents south of the border (Jacobo-Suárez & Espinosa-Cárdenas, 2016). Even under the best of circumstances, the family is never the same after migration. One family commences the migratory journey and another, now the reconstituted family, completes it.

CIVIC EDUCATION FOR A WORLD ON THE MOVE

Schools as strategic "sites of possibilities" (Fine & Jaffe-Walter, 2007) are struggling to find ways to model immigrant and minority engagement that are culturally relevant, sustainable, and credible. In the global era of mass migration, schools the world over are pursuing multiple normative ideals: instilling 21st-century skills and competencies, fostering cohesive social relations, and crafting the tools needed for immigrants to engage as effective citizens and workers in their new societies. Others are endeavoring to disrupt gaps in achievement and language loss, as well as disengagement and alienation in the second generation. These disparate pursuits will require reimagining and re-engineering education—above all civic education—for an entirely new era.

Banks (see chapter in this volume) argues that mass migration challenges traditional civic education programs based on anachronistic and irrelevant demographic and sociocultural assumptions. If fostering civic engagement and allegiance to the nation-state was the raison d'être for civic education 1.0, the 2.0 version requires a paradigm shift. Bekerman (see chapter in this volume) reminds us that classrooms are at root spaces where knowledge, meanings, and identities—ethnic, racial, religious, cultural, and civic—are negotiated and coconstructed, and where democratic mores, attitudes, and behaviors are practiced and enacted. What is knowledge and how it is constructed and weighed is a complex flow of power and legitimacy connecting teacher and student epistemologies to classroom interactions and identities. Teachers need to be mindful of how immigrant, minority, and majority students negotiate what counts as knowledge in contested domains, how the authority of knowledge is invoked, how it is argued, and how it is contested.

Qua the development of civic identities, the question that Bekerman examines is: How do classroom discourses and practices in contemporary multicultural Israeli schools define who has the capacity to govern the self and the other, who lacks such capacities, and how do such capacities become effective elements in the formation of citizens? He deploys a critical perspective to broaden civic education to encompass sociopolitical complexities in the negotiation of multiple religious and cultural identities in education. In so doing, the author problematizes how educators and student epistemologies and subjectivities play out in the quotidian practices of schools and classrooms.

In general, migration as a civic matter has been treated as "problematic," contributing to concerns with security, poverty, and job competition. Such narratives position migrants—their cultures and identities—at the center of conflict. In the new normal, mass migration equals conflict, crisis, and chaos. In education settings, young migrants encounter assaults, microaggressions, and devaluing of their ethnocultural, religious, and linguistic heritage. A poor school climate coupled with a context of resettlement in low-resourced schools that are less safe and less engaging may foster feelings of alienation, anomie, and negative attitudes toward school (see chapter by Suárez-Orozco & Marks in this volume).

However, Bekerman claims that when teachers do the hard cultural work of acknowledging the subjectivities, languages, and identities of students, students will do their part and engage. Acknowledgment and genuine recognition will be the point of departure for authentic civic education. Bekerman reviews innovative interventions including culturally relevant pedagogies that acknowledge and empower students intellectually, socially, and emotionally; deploying "funds of knowledge," teachers come to bridge, recognize, and support the skills, competencies, and sensibilities that all immigrant and minority students bring into the classroom every day.

Civic identities among immigrant and minority youth commonly are interlinked with religious, spiritual, ethnic, and culturally coded gender identities. In a move sure to be read as controversial, Bekerman argues that because the self intersects multiple identities, religious identities should not be negated in the classroom. To attempt a religious appendectomy of the self is to leave many immigrant students wounded. Furthermore, religiosity is linked to academic achievement and civic engagement. But the role of religion in public education is contested, and religiosity is generally misaligned with the secular ideologies and practices now dominant in liberal democratic nation-states. Bekerman urges teachers to examine the hegemonic formations of secular–occidental civilizational paradigms and practices in the classroom and the discursive construction of religious minorities as premodern, naive, and perpetually "Other." Educators, Bekerman argues, must focus attention on the intersection of civic and religious identities among their immigrant and minority students. The negotiation of civic, religious, and cultural identities and epistemologies plays out in complex and difficult ways in schools and in the classroom. In educational contexts where cultural, religious, and secular paradigms compete for hegemony, educators must uncover how minority youths' religious and cultural epistemologies are presented and represented in classroom facts and artifacts.

Banks (see chapter in this volume) elaborates a coherent agenda for civic education in the age of super-diversity, globalization, and growing inequality. Marginalized groups—immigrant, cultural, ethnic, racial, and linguistic groups, as well as the poor and religious minorities—must come to experience cultural recognition and civic equality within school. Policies reflecting differential exclusion—ranging from not allowing Muslim students to wear a hijab/burqua in France (while allowing some religious symbols in the same schools) to excluding immigrant students, such as the undocumented, from full social and civic participation in the United States—will undermine school engagement and disrupt the process of identification with the new society.

Academic achievement gaps and language rights remain unresolved issues in many, if not most, countries of immigration, yet they are central to citizenship education, cultural sustainability, and social cohesion. Painting a sophisticated picture of migration, Banks describes disparate settings such as China—currently experiencing massive patterns of internal migration from rural areas to urban cities—and argues that educators and scholars must conceptualize and implement effective strategies to close the wide gap between the civic ideals within a nation and actual classroom practices.

Banks claims that teachers must foster knowledge and skills necessary for employment in the global economy; incorporate multiple relevant cultures and languages in the classroom; and promote equity pedagogy and culturally relevant and responsive teaching that focuses on the resiliency and strength of students. But to achieve transformative citizenship education and to effectively engage within and across national as well as transnational super-diverse communities of the 21st century, students need to acquire democratic racial and ethnic attitudes and identities.

A 21st-century civic education must struggle against damaging stereotyping and caricatures of difference. Educators endeavoring to engage immigrant and other minority students alike would be wise to learn to engage "their stories." Indeed, telling "multiple stories" by incorporating into their teaching multicultural plays, books, films, and articles will help to stimulate thoughtful discussions of immigration, race, class, and gender and how they intersect in complex ways to structure identities, opportunities, and challenges. Civic education can thus do the work of fostering the development of knowledge, values, sensibilities, and practices required to participate effectively within multiple regional, national, and transnational communities. An authentic, organic, and sustainable allegiance to the nation-state is preordained in the structural inclusion and valuing of all citizens. Yet in an ever more interdependent and miniaturized world, more balanced regional, national, and global identifications will serve students well as they engage in citizenship practices in a variety of domains.

White and Myers (see chapter in this volume) argue that emerging models of education aiming to privilege 21st-century skills inevitably come to prioritize critical thinking and problem solving, metacognitive skills, communication and socioemotional skills, as well as intrapersonal skills such as autoregulation, responsibility, and time- and self-management skills. Concurrently, White and Myers suggest that in respect to civic education liberal democracies are striving to develop more inclusive models often animated by the spirit of cosmopolitanism, multiculturalism, and universal human rights. These are lofty yet elusive ideals. Contested histories, group identities, and alternative epistemologies are often downplayed in an attempt to build social cohesion, nourish solidarity, and minimize group differences.

Civic education is grappling to expand beyond traditional knowledge and prepare students with the skills necessary to participate in the ever more globally connected economy and society of today. But the efforts to build the architectures for more inclusive models inspired by the logic of cosmopolitanism, transnationalism, multiculturalism, and universal human rights generate anxiety and push back. White and Myers argue that some worry that such efforts and ideals are misguided and will weaken the sense of national identity, usher in political illiteracy on the nuts and bolts of democratic governance, and thwart active civic engagement (e.g., voting).

For White and Myers, valuing and nourishing multicultural richness, including languages, identities, and global consciousness, while developing strong habits of political engagement, civic savoir faire, and responsibility is very much a worthy challenge and pursuit. The authors conclude that in an ever more interconnected global world, civic education models that successfully balance multicultural sensibilities and 21st-century skills, including intercultural communication and higher-order cognitive and metacognitive skills, will lead to positive outcomes.

LANGUAGE

Mass migration is adding linguistic diversity to societies with deep and conflicted histories of multilingualism. More broadly, in both the United States and Israel, the new super-diversity in language and identity challenges modernist ideologies linking selfhood and belonging to a single national language, cultural tradition, or religious affiliation (see chapters by Banks and by Bekerman in this volume). According to the census data, there are more than 350 languages spoken in the Unites States, over half of them by immigrants (U.S. Census Bureau, 2015). Languages with more than a million speakers in 2013 were Spanish (38.4 million), Chinese (three million), Tagalog (1.6 million), Vietnamese (1.4 million), French (1.3 million), and Korean and Arabic (1.1 million each). In the New York metropolitan area, approximately half of all children and youth from immigrant-headed households spoke an estimated combined 192 different languages (U.S. Census Bureau, 2015). In Los Angeles, where 185 different languages are spoken at home, 54% of the population age five and over speak a language other than English. In the Los Angeles Unified School District, the nation's second largest, over 62% of the children and youth are English language learners (California Department of Education, 2016).

How to best develop the means to communicate in the dominant language, thereby developing advanced academic language skills required for higher-order cognitive work, and the matter of maintaining immigrant languages are fiercely debated the world over (McAndrew, 2007). Language acquisition and academic trajectories are bound together with processes of identity formation, family systems, acculturation, assimilation, and economic integration (Portes & Fernández-Kelly, 2008; Portes & Hao 1998, 2002; Portes & Zhou, 1993; Suárez-Orozco et al., 2008; M. M. Suárez-Orozco, 1989, 1991).

Two constants have defined the relationship between immigration and language. First, every wave of large-scale immigration in multiple destinations generates a fear that new immigrants will not learn the dominant language. Second, the children of immigrants from widely divergent origins inevitably gravitate toward the new language (Portes & Hao 2002; Tse, 2001) and—over time and across generations—lose their native language skills (Fillmore, 1991). Yet these mutually canceling concerns miss the defining element of mass migration in the era of globalization: Academic language learning as a cultural construct is changing what is required for this generation of immigrants to engage as citizens and productive workers. Most large-scale studies of immigrants depend on self-reported data of oral proficiency, which differs from the academic written language necessary for higher-order cognitive engagement and academic success (Cummins, 2000).

Suárez-Orozco and Marks (see chapter in this volume) argue that academic language proficiency is central to any understanding of educational trajectories of immigrant youth in high-income countries with strict accountability regimes of the high-stakes-testing variety. Scholarly research has shown a high correlation between proficiency in academic language skills and academic achievement as measured by standardized tests (Suárez-Orozco et al., 2008). First- and second-generation immigrant students are often found to score lower than their native-born peers on standardized tests in the United States as well as in European contexts (Barth, Heimer, & Pfeiffer, 2008).

A recent report of the Programme for International Student Assessment (PISA) by the Organisation for Economic Co-operation and Development (OECD), which included participation from 65 countries and economies, has shown that first- and second-generation immigrant students in the 34 OECD countries tend to lag behind their nonimmigrant counterparts in their performance in reading, mathematics, and science. In fact, the performance gap in reading reaches 43.5 average score points, in mathematics 43.7 average score points, and in science 50 average score points, which is roughly equivalent to more than one year of schooling. However, the performance gap between these students varies considerably across countries (OECD, 2012).

Although there are cross-country differences in the academic trajectories of immigrant-origin students (Christensen & Segeritz, 2008) and although, over time, some immigrant-origin youth do remarkably well (Kasinitz, Mollenkopf, Waters, & Holdaway, 2008), the general trend is worrisome, especially as the share of immigrant-origin students continues to grow in a number of countries. Suárez-Orozco and Marks (see chapter in this volume) note that underestimates of immigrant students' abilities and competencies are often a result of educational assessments that are timed, contain biased language, and fail to consider cultural knowledge or culture-of-origin content knowledge and that penalize second-language learners who process two or more languages before settling on an answer.

Research on second-language acquisition and bilingualism informs debates on educational models that promote success for immigrant youth, especially in respect to which language should be used for instruction, under what circumstances, and for how long. One recurring finding is that it takes approximately five to seven years for immigrant language learners to develop the academic language proficiency required to compete fairly with native speakers in standardized-assessment regimes at the center of education reforms the world over (Collier, 1995; Cummins, 2000; Hakuta, Butler, & Witt, 2000; National Research Council & Institute of Medicine, 1997). Another consistent finding suggests that *balanced bilinguals,* that is, youth who continuously develop their home language as they acquire a second academic language, tend to have better educational trajectories over time (Callahan & Gándara, 2014; Portes & Rumbaut, 2001).

An important consideration in this process is the fact that immigrant-origin youth often serve as *language brokers* (or translator, interpreters, advocates) for family members and others, while at the same time navigating new schools and acquiring academic language and cultural skills (see Orellana, 2009; chapter by Suárez-Orozco & Marks in this volume). Language brokering not only shapes the routine lives of immigrant youth and adults alike, but it is also linked to academic outcomes. In fact, language brokering has been found to be positively linked to standardized test scores. Consequently, researchers suggest that cultivating similar experiences at school might improve bilingual students' achievement (Dorner, Orellana, & Li-Grining, 2007). This might also mitigate some of the psychological and developmental pressures these youth face as language brokers (e.g., isolation, marginalization; see chapter by Suárez-Orozco & Marks in this volume). Thus the simplistic argument that, over time and across generations, immigrant youth lose their native language skills (Fillmore, 1991) is not true of all immigrant youth and is complicated by a myriad of factors.

Valdés (see chapter in this volume) examines the complex relationships between second-language acquisition, learner differences, and teacher knowledge for 21st-century classrooms. What does it take to create conditions needed to develop elective bilingualism in traditional classrooms? Acquiring and using more than one language is a result of language contact in the context of trade and commerce, invasion, conquest and colonization, and, of course, immigration. In the era of globalization and mass migration, research on multiculturalism has raised important questions about languages: Are they discrete and bounded entities? Are they constructs of the nation-state? Are monolingual norms anachronistic in an age of globalization? English both plays an increasingly decisive role as the lingua franca and threatens multilingualism across the world. Yet, new arrivals replenish immigrant languages the world over.

Valdés argues that bi- or multilingualism does not depend on formal instruction but instead depends on access to proficient speakers of the target language. However, in segregated settings where access and interaction is limited, formal language instruction is needed for systematic exposure to a new language, especially for immigrants. Valdés calls for both global educational reforms and changing theoretical perspectives on language. Differences in the conceptualization of language align with different perspectives on the ways in which language is acquired.

The current approaches to second-language acquisition take into account the social processes that take place in interactions between learners and speakers of the target language as opposed to focusing solely on the cognitive process at the individual level. Monolingual competence and monolingual performance has been the norm, and deviation from the norm has resulted in labels such as incomplete acquisition, fossilization, and interlanguage. Because bilinguals are specific speaker-hearers, this raises concerns about the construct of language proficiency as it has been used to measure bilingualism. Educational systems come to develop sets of standards often with little or no empirical evidence or relevant theoretical compass. As for immigrant language learners, the heavy-handed regime of standardized testing often fails to consider differences in learner characteristics (e.g., age of arrival, prior school attainment, interrupted schooling, trauma), or social variables such as segregation and exposure to destination language.

Valdés (see chapter in this volume) raises important questions about the reliability and validity of current language assessments across time and the quality of evidence about best practices and their use with children at different places in the developmental cycle. Valdés concludes that native-like proficiency in a second language can be attained by most immigrants, but it must be fostered by taking into account learner differences in the planning and designing of language-teaching programs. The research community, policymakers, and teachers alike must do more and better-coordinated work to meet the needs of immigrant language learners. Additionally, Suárez-Orozco and Marks (see chapter in this volume) remind us that programs should aim to include student as well as adult advisors who speak the same language as the "newcomer" students to help them with socioemotional, academic, and cultural transitions. Valdés also believes that programs need to do more to mitigate some of the challenges these youth face as a result of interrupted schooling and should pay more attention to academic second-language acquisition in the content areas.

INEQUALITY

Immigrants seldom originate in the poorest regions of the world. Some migrants are among the most educated people in our nation, comprising 47% of scientists with doctorates, a quarter of all physicians, and 24% of engineers. In 2013, 41% of newly arrived immigrants had at least a bachelor's degree. Yet research suggests that they are more likely than their native counterparts to encounter poverty in their new societies (Kazemipur & Halli, 2001). *Poverty,* defined as a "condition of relative deprivation within society" (Kurtz, 1973, p. 53), is created in part by unique disadvantages that are often associated with immigrant status, such as "language barriers, incompatibility of educational credentials, limited transferability of job skills, unfamiliarity with the market demands, and lack of access to job and educational networks" (Kazemipur & Halli, 2001, p. 1132; see also de Haan & Yaqub, 2009).

The children of immigrants have "greater market-income poverty rates than children in native-born families" (Hernandez, Macartney, & Blanchard, 2010, p. 425). In affluent countries worldwide, poverty among children of immigrants has increased steadily in recent years, with gaps between native-born and immigrants ranging from 7% in Australia and Germany to 12% in the United States and to 26–28% in England and France (Hernandez et al., 2010). Differences among ethnic groups are also prevalent. U.S. data on Latino children show that, in 1999, 22.8% were living in poverty compared with 7.7% of Whites (Therrien & Ramirez, 2001). In 2006, however, the poverty rate for Latino children had nearly doubled that of White native-born children, 28% and 16%, respectively (Fry & Gonzales, 2008). For immigrant Latino families, poverty rates reach higher percentages, with 35% of foreign-born Latino immigrants living in poverty compared with 27% of their second- or third-generation counterparts (Fry & Gonzales, 2008).

In the United States, children of immigrants are more likely than native-born children to come from poor and low-income backgrounds (49% vs. 35%, respectively), live in crowded housing conditions (7% vs. 2%, respectively), and experience inadequate nutrition (25% vs. 21%, respectively) (Chaudry & Fortuny, 2010). Children raised in poverty are also vulnerable to instability of residence as well as to an array of distresses including difficulties concentrating and sleeping, anxiety, and depression, as well as a heightened exposure to delinquency and violence. Poverty has long been recognized as a significant risk factor for poor educational outcomes (Luthar, 1999; Weissbourd, 1996).

Poverty coexists with a variety of other factors that augment risks, such as single parenthood, residence in violence-ridden neighborhoods, gang activity, and drug trade, as well as school environments that are segregated, overcrowded, understaffed, and poorly funded (Suárez-Orozco, Yoshikawa, & Tseng, 2015). Poverty, however, is not solely an inner-city phenomenon. In the United States since the 1990s, poverty grew in the suburbs for the first time and at a greater rate than in cities (Murphy, 2010). Poverty is also associated with high rates of housing mobility and concurrent school transitions that can be highly disruptive to educational performance (Gándara & Contreras, 2009). For instance, immigrant-origin Latino children are the most segregated students in U.S. schools, particularly in the West (Orfield & Frankenberg, 2014; Orfield & Lee, 2005). Immigrants who settle in predominantly minority neighborhoods may have little, if any, direct, continuous, and intimate contact with peers from the nonimmigrant mainstream population. A pattern of triple segregation—by race, language, and poverty—shapes the lives of many new immigrants in varied countries.

Poverty and segregation are often compounded by unauthorized status. The United Nations estimates that there are between 30 and 40 million unauthorized migrants worldwide (Papademetriou, 2005). The United States has a very large concentration of undocumented immigrants—as of 2014, approximately 11.3 million people (or 3.5% of the nation's population) were unauthorized (Krogstad & Passel, 2015), and about 775,000 were children, according to 2012 data (Passel, Cohn, Krogstad, & Gonzalez-Barrera, 2014). Research suggests that undocumented children often arrive after multiple family separations and traumatic border crossings (M. M. Suárez-Orozco, 2015). They may continue to experience fear and anxiety about being apprehended, separated again from their parents, and deported (see chapter by Suárez-Orozco & Marks in this volume; see also Chaudry et al., 2010; Suárez-Orozco et al., 2008).

A large proportion of undocumented workers are employed in low-paying professions with erratic working conditions (Capps, 2001; Gándara & Contreras, 2009; Yoshikawa, 2011). This may also be the case for migrants who have low levels of education and who gravitate to sectors of the U.S. labor market relying on "low-skilled" workers, such as agriculture, service industries, and construction. Unauthorized migrants do not access social services that could serve to mitigate the harshest conditions of their poverty (Yoshikawa, 2011). Psychological and emotional duress takes a toll on the experiences of youth raised in the shadow of the law (Cervantes, Mejía, & Mena, 2010), which has also been documented through narrative and qualitative research (Bagley & Castro-Salazar, 2010; Gonzales, 2009; M. M. Suárez-Orozco, 1989).

Protracted poverty, deep segregation, xenophobia, and unauthorized status are the ingredients for immigration dystopia and alienated belonging of the second generation in many immigrant-impacted societies. At the very least, structural factors accelerate the processes of racialization via cultural disparagement (De Vos & Suárez-Orozco, 1990) and negative "social mirroring" (Suárez-Orozco, 2004) of new immigrants of color. C. Suárez-Orozco has examined how the barrage of derogatory portraits of immigrants (such as undocumented immigrants in the United States and the children of Muslim immigrants in Europe) in the media, in schools, and community settings will shape at the individual level a number of critical developmental outcomes for these children and youth.

The arrival of large numbers of immigrants into the high-income countries of the world has resulted in isomorphic patterns of residential segregation and can be related to broader dynamics of racialization of "marked" native minorities. The idea of "race," the stepchild of 19th-century pseudoscience, included in these earlier iterations craniometrics (measuring of skulls) as a means of classifying groups of people (Mosse, 1964) into fixed hierarchical relationships of superiority and inferiority (De Vos & Wagatsuma, 1972; Gould, 1996). As Boas (1940) observed, "A stratification of society in social groups that are racial in character will always lead to racial discrimination. As in all other sharp social groupings the individual is not judged as an individual but as a member of his class" (pp. 16–17).

Racialized hierarchies often appropriate the aura of science and attach atavistic superstitions that people of "purer" origin avoid the danger of contamination by "outsiders" (Zollschan, as cited in Mosse, 2000, pp. 201–202). As applied to immigrants, "racialization" (Bashi, 1998; Omi & Winant, 1994; Shih, 2008) is an appropriate construct foregrounding the sociohistorical processes of segregation, marginalization, micro- and macroaggressions, as well as collective disenfranchisement. In countries such as the United States, large and growing numbers of poor immigrants of color and the undocumented are de facto relegated to spaces where a socially constructed phenotype (Bonilla-Silva, 2004; Gilman, 2000) aligns with entrenched patterns of segregation and marginalization of native minorities (Corni, 2002; Ogbu & Simons, 1998; Vigil, 2002). Portes and Zhou (1993) have appropriately termed this dynamic "segmented assimilation" wherein poor immigrants of color join the marginalized space of native minorities creating what they term a new "rainbow underclass" (see also, Portes, 1996).

Beyond the United States, countries the world over have witnessed the emergence of a complex interweaving of factors racializing immigrants and other minorities. These can include religion (see chapter by Agbaria in this volume; Germany and its Turkish minorities), country of origin (Japan and its Brazilian, Korean, and other minorities), and social class (Spain and its Roma minorities). Restricted mobility (Massey & Denton, 1989), concentrated disadvantage, negative social mirroring (Suárez-Orozco, 2004), and inequitable access to quality education (Orfield & Lee, 2005) among the children of immigrants are not an isolated U.S. and Israeli phenomenon, as the cases of Koreans and other minorities in Japan (Castro-Vazquez, 2009; Lee & De Vos, 1981; Moon, 2012) and Muslim minorities in Europe attest (Meer, Pala, Modood, & Simon, 2009).

Ben-Peretz and Aderet-German (see chapter in this volume) examine the case of Ethiopian immigrants in Israel. The authors rely on a semi-structured narrative interview to present findings on the experiences of nine successful young adult Ethiopian immigrants in Israel. The themes that come to the fore include experiences of racism, discrimination, and skin color; dual cultural identity; personal autonomy; and sense of purpose.

All participants reported dealing with Israeli racism based on skin color. In a pattern reminiscent of immigrants of color in the United States and elsewhere, participants revealed that it was when they arrived in Israel when they "became Black" and began to experience new forms of racial discrimination—a journey similar to that of other immigrants of color (Bailey, 2002; Zéphir, 2004). They also reported experiencing religious discrimination from the Israeli mainstream establishment. As "Black" immigrants, they faced "doubts" about the authenticity of their Jewishness. Overcoming racism, discrimination, and "doubts" seemed to be a drive to success.

Grappling with stigma and issues of belonging led to resisting imposed ideas and norms of citizenship. Some described how teachers and others provided them socioemotional support and assisted them in overcoming difficulties. These stories are somewhat parallel to the experiences of the U.S. children (i.e., "High Achievers") in that academic and social support from others was central for overcoming some of the transitional and academic challenges (see chapter by Suárez-Orozco & Marks in this volume). Additionally, some participants also found boarding school experiences positive and rewarding, despite the fact that they were away from families. Although some stayed in schools organized for young new immigrants, they were later encouraged to move to schools with few immigrants as a way to integrate into Israeli society.

Participants described in disparate ways their evolving sense of self, identities, and agency. Some talked about developing dual identities as Ethiopians and as new Israeli citizens. Dual cultural identity development was a difficult and painful experience, especially for those who felt the need to separate the two identities and forefront the Israeli identity by distancing themselves from the Ethiopian immigrant community. Over time, however, some participants came to integrate both identities, claiming that each provided them with a sense of selfhood and affinity to both the "heritage" culture and the "new" culture.

A sense of purpose guided them to career choices that eventually enabled them to serve other immigrants in the Ethiopian community. Some began volunteering and more actively engaging in the civic sphere. Volunteering seemed to be one way through which immigrants learned the host language, cultural norms, and knowledge needed to further integrate into a new society. The sense of mission can be understood as the realization of active participation as engaged and effective citizens.

Israel, like the United States, is a complex multiethnic society composed of both voluntary and involuntary minorities. The contentious and polarizing debate over the Israeli government's banning schools from teaching students a book about a romance between a Jewish woman and a Palestinian man that took place in 2015 is a dramatic example of the challenges for citizenship education in deeply divided societies. The novel was removed from the list of "required reading for Hebrew high school literature classes, prompting a stormy debate over how Israeli society deals with its cultural divides" (Kershner, 2015).

Unlike the immigrant Ethiopian minorities in Israel, the Palestinian Israelis became minorities in a pattern akin to conquest and colonialism. Agbaria (see chapter in this volume) turns to the matter of Israeli multiculturalism in regards to the 1.2 million Palestinians who remained within the boundaries of the newly created State of Israel after the war of 1948. Israeli Palestinians constitute approximately 17% of the total population of Israel.

Agbaria examines citizenship education in tandem with changes in Israeli political culture and ethnonationalistic vicissitudes. The author also reflects on Israeli Palestinian teachers' resistance pedagogies and counterhegemonic attempts to challenge the ethnonationalist agenda of the right in Israel. Agbaria defines ethnonationalism as an isomorphic variant of nationalism. This principle is akin but not identical to the practice of *jus sanguinis* (law or right of blood), the condition when citizenship is determined by parentage, versus *jus soli* (law or right of the soil) when membership in the family of the nation is given by birth on the "soil" (territory) regardless of parentage. In current Israeli practice, belonging is given not by blood as such but by religious parentage.

Agbaria argues that with the decline of the Israeli left and the concurrent rise of the right in Israeli politics, a newfound sense of ethnonationalism has come to permeate the education system. Although Jewish and Arab schoolchildren, as well as secular and religious Jews, attend different schools, a common feature of the Israeli education system is to uphold the Jewishness of the state and its national ethos, overlooking and silencing the Palestinian narrative (history and culture, *inter alia*) in textbooks or in school curricula. Even a teary-eyed love story between a Palestinian and Israeli youth in New York is grist for the ethnonationalistic mill and the erasure of Palestinian perspectives.

According to Agbaria, the Israeli education system, in its current practices may stigmatize Israeli Palestinians, instilling feelings of inferiority, silencing, and denationalizing their identities while glorifying the history, culture, and achievements of the Jewish majority. Palestinian teachers counter the "official story" by providing alternative narratives. Teachers introduce "Other" accounts and interpretations of the historical trajectory of the Palestinian minority in Israel. Some teachers contextualize narratives of discrimination and racism in violence, poverty, unemployment, and poor infrastructure in the Arab communities qua the specifics of Israeli society and political economy.

In a move revealing an inherent paradox concerning immigration and super-diversity in all liberal democracies, teachers are encouraging students to know in depth the democratic characteristics of the Israeli political system and the possibilities that its democratic core affords for their own empowerment. Israel is a liberal democracy, rules-bound and largely fair in protecting individual rights. The teachers thus telecast the lesson that they too are citizens who must learn the law and thus avail themselves of its democratic protections. Citizenship education offers tools for Arab students to become aware of the rights that protect them against discrimination—rights they can put to work as they navigate career paths moving forward.

Teachers encourage students to learn the history of their communities and to question the failures of both Israeli and Arab leadership resulting in conditions of poverty, unemployment, and lack of opportunity. Teachers outline a citizenship practice that is eclectic and hybrid, positioning the local community as the main sphere for belonging and civic action. Local citizenship is advocated as a viable alternative to state-centered citizenship to resist the state's erasure, to create agency, and to assume responsibility for social change.

In Chapter 8 of this volume, Nieto offers a series of reflections on the changing roles of teachers in our globalizing world and makes thoughtful suggestions for civic education and civic inclusion focusing on ethnic studies and youth participatory research. Nieto's fundamental premise is that young people's identities and basic human rights must be recognized and affirmed in schools. However, immigrants and minorities, especially those from impoverished backgrounds, are often seen as "problems" by public commentators. Immigrants are blamed for the low quality of schools in the communities in which they settle. Immigrant and other minority students are marginalized. Too often, they are invisible—*los desaparecidos* (the disappeared). In other contexts, histories, languages, identities, and cultures are misappropriated and misrepresented with crass or obtuse insensitivity. When immigrants and minority students are excluded from the narrative of a nation, their sense of belonging is malformed or deformed. The loss of power and control by the (shrinking) majority might be driving the fierce hegemony momentum reflected in recent policies, curriculum and pedagogy, and new patterns of segregation. The concurrent lack of authentic outreach further marginalizes poor students of color, as well as their families and communities.

For Nieto the status quo will not do. To engage the most diverse cohort of students ever enrolled in U.S. schools (but also in Israel and elsewhere), schools need explicit inclusion of the history, language, and perspectives of people other than the majority. Nieto joins Banks, White and Myers, and others in this volume in suggesting ways in which smart and humane multicultural education, bilingual education, culturally responsive pedagogy, and social justice education can be put to the service of cognitive, relational, and behavioral engagement (see also Suárez-Orozco et al., 2008). Nieto calls for a civic education that allows multiple voices to enter the dialogue, mimicking a democracy that actually includes all. Inclusion and support systems are necessary to spur resiliency and positive psychosocial and academic adjustment (see also chapter by Suárez-Orozco & Marks in this volume). For Nieto, Youth Participatory Action Research is another way to possibly engage student civic involvement.

Nieto concludes by raising important questions, some of which are echoed in various chapters: Should schools respond to the new global realities of the 21st century by building efforts to nourish in all students a broader consciousness, multiple languages, identities, and belonging as world citizens? Or, should the response be to redouble functionalist efforts to prepare youth for the new, more fiercely competitive workplace of today? How can classrooms and teachers change to better promote relevant and authentic civic engagement?

FINAL THOUGHTS

Mass migration and demographic change is, under the best of circumstances, destabilizing and generates disequilibrium in societies like Israel and the United States, where immigrants and other minorities are increasing rapidly. Deep segregation, concentrated poverty, and psychosocial disparagement stimulate malassimilation and subvert the human struggle to balance multiple identities and differences. In dystopic assimilation, the immigrant and minority family is assaulted and undermined in its legislative, social, and symbolic forms (Lacan, 2006). State policies and growing inequality de facto and de jure dismember millions of immigrant and minority families. Millions of families are segregated, millions are separated (Suárez-Orozco & Suárez-Orozco, 2001), millions are deported, millions are incarcerated, and millions more inhabit a subterranean world of illegality and alienated belonging. To echo Tolstoy, all immigrant and minority families are unhappy in the same way.

Global transnational displacements bring race, language, religion, and identities to the forefront, interrupting the taken-for-granted cultural schemas and social practices that structure belonging to, and membership in, advanced liberal democracies. The institutions of state-making in the modernist era, above all schools in their civic function, are geared toward producing loyal citizens, workers, and consumers of a nation-state rather than individuals with multiple identities, languages, and global sensibilities. Reimagining the narrative of belonging and recalibrating the institutions of the nation-state, above all schools, are a sine qua non to move beyond the current global immigration dystopia worldwide.

NOTE

1. "An imaginary place where people lead dehumanized and often fearful lives." Source Merriam-Webster Dictionary: http://www.merriam-webster.com/dictionary/dystopia

REFERENCES

Abel, G. J., & Sander, N. (2014). Quantifying global international migration flows. *Science, 343*(6178), 1520–1522. Retrieved from www.sciencemag.org/content/343/6178/1520.short

Bagley, C., & Castro-Salazar, R. (2010). Envisioning undocumented historias: Evoking a critical performance ethnography. *New Frontiers in Ethnography: Studies in Qualitative Methodology, 11*, 141–60.

Bailey, B. (2002). *Language, race, and negotiation of identity: A study of Dominican Americans*. New York, NY: LFB Scholarly Publishing.

Barth, H., Heimer, A., & Pfeiffer, I. (2008). Integration through education: Promising practices, strategies, and initiatives in ten countries. In C. Morehouse (Ed.), *Immigrant stu-*

dents can succeed: Lessons from around the globe (pp. 119–188). Gütersloh, Germany: Verlag Bertelsmann Stiftung.

Bashi, V. (1998). Racial categories matter because racial hierarchies matter: A commentary. *Ethnic and Racial Studies, 21*(5), 959–968.

Boas, F. (1940). *Race, language and culture.* London, United Kingdom: Collier-Macmillan.

Bonilla-Silva, E. (2004). From bi-racial to tri-racial: Towards a new system of racial stratification in the USA. *Ethnic and Racial Studies, 27*(6), 931–950.

California Department of Education, Educational Demographics Office. (2016, January 12). *Los Angeles Unified District Language Group Data: Districtwide for 2013–14.* Retrieved from dq.cde.ca.gov/dataquest/lc/DistrictLC.aspx?cYear=2013-14&cSelect=1964733--LOS+ANGELES+UNIFIED

Callahan, R. M., & Gándara, P. C. (Eds.). (2014). *The bilingual advantage: Language, literacy, and the US labor market.* Bristol, United Kingdom: Multilingual Matters.

Capps, R. (2001, February). Hardship among children of immigrants: Findings from the 1999 National Survey of American Families, *New Federalism: An Urban Institute Program to Assess Changing Social Policies, Series B* (No. B-29). Retrieved from www.urban.org/sites/default/files/alfresco/publication-pdfs/310096-Hardship-Among-Children-of-Immigrants.PDF

Castro-Vázquez, G. (2009). Immigrant children from Latin America at Japanese schools: Homogeneity, ethnicity, gender, and language in education. *Journal of Research in International Education, 8*(1), 57–80.

Cervantes, J. M., Mejía, O. L., & Mena, A. G. (2010). Serial migration and the assessment of extreme and unusual psychological hardship with undocumented Latina/o families. *Hispanic Journal of Behavioral Sciences, 32*(2), 275–291.

Chaudry, A., Capps, R., Pedroza, J., Castaneda, R. M., Santos, R., & Scott, M. M. (2010). *Facing our future: Children in the aftermath of immigration enforcement.* Washington, DC: The Urban Institute. Retrieved from www.urban.org/research/publication/facing-our-future

Chaudry, A., & Fortuny, K. (2010). *Children of immigrants: Economic well-being* (Brief No. 4). Washington, DC: The Urban Institute. Retrieved from fcd-us.org/sites/default/files/TUI%20Children%20of%20Immigrants%20Economic%20Well-Being.pdf

Christensen, G., & Segeritz, M. (2008). An international perspective on student achievement. In Bertelsmann Stiftung (Ed.), *Immigrant students can succeed: Lessons from around the globe, Carl Bertelsmann Prize 2008* (pp. 11–33). Gütersloh, Germany: Verlag Bertelsmann Stiftung

Coatsworth, J. H. (2004). Globalization, growth, and welfare in history. In M. M. Suárez-Orozco & D. B. Qin-Hilliard (Eds.), *Globalization: Culture and education in the new millennium* (pp. 38–55). Berkeley, CA: University of California Press.

Collier, V. P. (1995). Acquiring a second language for school. *Directions in Language and Education, 1*(4): 1–14.. Retrieved from http://www.usc.edu/dept/education/CMMR/CollierThomas_Acquiring_L2_for_School

Corni, G. (2002). *Hitler's ghettos: Voices from a beleaguered society 1939-1944.* London, United Kingdom: Arnold.

Cummins, J. (2000). *Language, power, and pedagogy: Bilingual children in the crossfire.* Clevedon, United Kingdom: Multilingual Matters.

de Haan, A., & Yaqub, S. (2009). *Migration and poverty: Linkages, knowledge gaps and policy implications.* Geneva: United Nations Research Institute for Social Development

(UNRISD). Retrieved from www.unrisd.org/80256B3C005BCCF9/%28httpPublications%29/82DCDCF510459B36C12575F400474040?OpenDocument

De Vos, G., & Suárez-Orozco, M. (1990). *Status inequality: The self in culture.* Newbury Park, CA: Sage.

De Vos, G., & Wagatsuma, H. (1972). *Japan's invisible race: Caste in culture and personality.* Berkeley, CA: University of California Press.

Dorner, L. M., Orellana, M. F., & Li-Grining, C. P. (2007). "I helped my mom," and it helped me: Translating the skills of language brokers into improved standardized test scores. *American Journal of Education, 113*(3), 451–478.

Fillmore, L. W. (1991). When learning a second language means losing the first. *Early Childhood Research Quarterly, 6*(3), 323–346.

Fine, M., & Jaffe-Walter, R. (2007). Swimming: On oxygen, resistance, and possibility for immigrant youth under siege. *Anthropology and Education Quarterly, 38*(1), 76–96.

Fry, R., & Gonzales, F. (2008, August 26). One-in-five and growing fast: A profile of Hispanic public school students. In *Pew Research Center, Hispanic Trends.* Retrieved from www.pewhispanic.org/2008/08/26/one-in-five-and-growing-fast-a-profile-of-hispanic-public-school-students/

Gándara, P., & Contreras, F. (2009). *The Latino education crisis: The consequences of failed social policies.* Cambridge, MA: Harvard University Press.

Gilman, S. L. (2000). Are Jews white? Or the history of the nose job. In L. Back & J. Solomos (Eds.), *Theories of racism* (pp. 229–237). London, United Kingdom: Routledge.

Gindling, T. H., & Poggio, S. (2009). *Family separation and the educational success of immigrant children* (UMBC Policy Brief No. 7). Baltimore, MD: Department of Public Policy, University of Maryland–Baltimore County. Retrieved from www.umbc.edu/blogs/pubpol/Immigrationbrief.pdf

Gonzales, R. G. (2009). *Young lives on hold: The college dreams of undocumented immigrants.* New York, NY: College Board. Retrieved from secure-media.collegeboard.org/digital-Services/pdf/professionals/young-lives-on-hold-undocumented-students.pdf

Gould, S. (1996). *The mismeasure of man.* New York, NY: Norton.

Hakuta, K., Butler, Y. G., & Witt, D. (2000). *How long does it take English learners to attain proficiency?* (Policy Report 2000-1). University of California Linguistic Minority Research Institute. Retrieved from escholarship.org/uc/item/13w7m06g#page-2

Hernandez, D. J., Macartney, S., & Blanchard, V. L. (2010). Children of immigrants: Family and socioeconomic indicators for affluent countries. *Child Indicators Research, 3*(4), 413–437.

International Organization for Migration (IOM). (2010). *World Migration Report: The future of migration: Building capacities for change* (Executive summary). Geneva, Switzerland: Author. Retrieved from publications.iom.int/system/files/pdf/wmr2010_summary.pdf

Jacobo-Suárez, M., & Espinosa-Cárdenas, F. (2016). Retos al pleno derecho a la educación de la niñez transnacional en contexto de migración en México: El caso de la dispensa de la apostilla del Acta de Nacimiento extranjera. [Challenges to the full educational rights of transnational children in the context of migration: The case of the exception to the act of the foreign born]. Unpublished manuscript, Colegio de la Frontera Norte, Tijuana, Baja California, Mexico.

Kasinitz, P., Mollenkopf, J. H., Waters, M. C., & Holdaway, J. (2008). *Inheriting the city: The children of immigrants come of age.* New York, NY: Russell Sage Foundation.

Kazemipur, A., & Halli, S. S. (2001). Immigrants and "new poverty": The case of Canada. *International Migration Review, 35*(4), 1129–1156.

Kershner, I. (2015, December 31). Jewish-Arab love story excluded from Israeli classrooms. *The New York Times,* p A6. Retrieved from www.nytimes.com/2016/01/01/world/middleeast/borderlife-dorit-rabinyan-israel-ministry-education.html?_r=0

Krogstad, J. M., & Passel, J. S. (2015, November 19). 5 facts about illegal immigration in the U.S. In *Pew Research Center, ThinkTank.* Retrieved from www.pewresearch.org/fact-tank/2015/11/19/5-facts-about-illegal-immigration-in-the-u-s/

Kurtz, D. (1973). The rotating credit association: An adaptation to poverty. *Human Organization, 32*(1), 49–58.

Kwong, K., Chung, H., Sun, L., Chou, J. C., & Taylor-Shih, A. (2009). Factors associated with reverse-migration separation among a cohort of low-income Chinese immigrant families in New York City. *Social Work in Health Care, 48*(3), 348–359.

Lacan, J. (2006). *Écrits: The first complete edition in English* (B. Fink, Trans.). New York, NY: W.W. Norton.

Lee, C., & De Vos, G. (1981). *Koreans in Japan: Ethnic conflict and accommodation.* Berkeley: University of California Press.

Luthar, S. S. (1999). *Poverty and children's adjustment.* Thousand Oaks, CA: Sage.

Massey, D. S., & Denton, N. A. (1989). Hypersegregation in US metropolitan areas: Black and Hispanic segregation along five dimensions. *Demography, 26*(3), 373–391.

McAndrew, M. (2007). The education of immigrant students in a globalized world: Policy debates in a comparative perspective. In M. Suárez-Orozco (Ed.), *Learning in the global era: International perspectives on globalization and education* (pp. 255–277). Berkeley, CA: University of California Press.

Meer, N., Pala, V. S., Modood, T., & Simon, P. (2009). Cultural diversity, Muslims, and education in France and England: Two contrasting models in Western Europe. In J. A. Banks (Ed.), *The Routledge international companion to multicultural education* (pp. 413–424). New York, NY: Routledge.

Migration Policy Institute. (2016). *Migration data hub.* Retrieved from: www.migrationinformation.org/datahub/gcmm.cfm#map1list

Moon, S. (2012). Korea, multicultural education in. In J. A. Banks (Ed.), *Encyclopedia of diversity in education* (Vol. 3, pp. 1307–1312). Thousand Oaks, CA: Sage.

Mosse, G. L. (1964). *The crisis of German ideology: Intellectual origins of the Third Reich.* New York, NY: Grosset & Dunlap.

Mosse, G. L. (2000). The Jews: Myth and counter-myth. In L. Back & J. Solomos (Eds.), *Theories of racism: A reader* (pp. 195–205). London, United Kingdom: Routledge.

Murphy, A. K. (2010). The symbolic dilemmas of suburban poverty: Challenges and opportunities posed by variations in the contours of suburban poverty. *Sociological Forum 25*(3), 541–569.

National Research Council & Institute of Medicine. (1997). Improving schooling for language-minority children: A research agenda. In D. August & K. Hakuta (Eds.), *Committee on developing a research agenda on the education of limited-English-proficient and bilingual students.* Washington, DC: National Academies Press.

OECD. (2012). *Untapped skills: Realising the potential of immigrant students* (Preliminary version). Retrieved from www.oecd.org/edu/Untapped%20Skills.pdf

Ogbu, J. U., & Simons, H. D. (1998). Voluntary and involuntary minorities: A cultural-ecological theory of school performance with some implications for education. *Anthropology & Education Quarterly, 29*(2), 155–188.

Omi, M., & Winant, H. (1994). *Racial formation in the United States*. New York, NY: Routledge.

Orellana, M. F. (2009). *Translating childhoods: Immigrant youth, language, and culture*. New Brunswick, NJ: Rutgers University Press.

Orfield, G., & Frankenberg, E. (with Ee, J., & Kuscera, J.). (2014). *Brown at 60: Great progress, a long retreat and an uncertain future*. Los Angeles, CA: Civil Rights Project/Proyecto Derechos Civiles. Retrieved from civilrightsproject.ucla.edu/research/k-12-education/integration-and-diversity/brown-at-60-great-progress-a-long-retreat-and-an-uncertain-future/Brown-at-60-051814.pdf

Orfield, G., & Lee, C. (2005). *Why segregation matters: Poverty and education inequality*. Cambridge, MA: Harvard University Press.

Papademetriou, D. G. (2005, September 1). The global struggle with illegal migration: No end in sight. *Migration Information Source*. Retrieved from www.migrationpolicy.org/article/global-struggle-illegal-migration-no-end-sight

Passel, J. S., Cohn, D., Krogstad, J. M., & Gonzalez-Barrera, A. (2014, September 3). As growth stalls, unauthorized immigrant population becomes more settled. In Pew Research Center, Hispanic Trends. Retrieved from www.pewhispanic.org/2014/09/03/as-growth-stalls-unauthorized-immigrant-population-becomes-more-settled/#parents-of-u-s-born-children

Pew Research Center, Hispanic Trends.. (2015a, September 28). Modern immigration wave brings 59 million to U.S., driving population growth and change through 2065: Views of immigration's impact on U.S. society mixed. Retrieved from www.pewhispanic.org/2015/09/28/modern-immigration-wave-brings-59-million-to-u-s-driving-population-growth-and-change-through-2065/

Pew Research Center, Hispanic Trends (2015b, September 28). The changing characteristics of recent immigrant arrivals since 1970. Chapter 3 of Modern immigration wave brings 59 million to U.S., driving population growth and change through 2065: Views of immigration's impact on U.S. society mixed. Retrieved from www.pewhispanic.org/2015/09/28/chapter-3-the-changing-characteristics-of-recent-immigrant-arrivals-since-1970/

Pew Research Center, Hispanic Trends (2015c, January 15). Unauthorized immigrants: Who they are and what the public thinks. Retrieved from www.pewresearch.org/key-data-points/immigration/

Piketty, T. (2014). *Capital in the 21st century*. Cambridge, MA: Harvard University Press.

Portes, A. (1996). Children of immigrants: Segmented assimilation and its determinants. In A. Portes (Ed.), *The economic sociology of immigration: Essays on networks, ethnicity, and entrepreneurship* (pp. 248–280). New York, NY: Russell Sage Foundation.

Portes, A., & Fernández-Kelly, P. (2008). No margin for error: Educational and occupational achievement among disadvantaged children of immigrants. *Annals of the American Academy of Political and Social Science, 620*(1), 12–36.

Portes, A., & Hao, L. (1998). E pluribus unum: Bilingualism and loss of language in the second generation. *Sociology of Education, 71*(4), 269–294.

Portes, A., & Hao, L. (2002). The price of uniformity: Language, family and personality adjustment in the immigrant second generation. *Ethnic and Racial Studies, 25*(6), 889–912.

Portes, A., & Rumbaut, R. G. (2001). *Legacies: The story of the immigrant second generation*. Berkeley: University of California Press.

Portes, A., & Zhou, M. (1993). The new second generation: Segmented assimilation and its variants. *Annals of the American Academy of Political and Social Science, 530*(1), 74–96.

Rousseau, C., Hassan, G., Measham, T., Moreau, N., Lashley, M., Castro, . . . McKenzie, G. (2009). From the family universe to the outside world: Family relations, school attitude, and perception of racism in Caribbean and Filipino adolescents. *Health and Place, 15*(3), 751–760.

Shih, S. M. (2008). Comparative racialization: An introduction. *Modern Language Association, 123*(5), 1347–1362.

Suárez-Orozco, C. (2004). Formulating identity in a globalized world. In M. M. Suárez-Orozco & D. Qin-Hilliard (Eds.), *Globalization: Culture and education in the new millennium* (pp. 173–202). Berkeley: University of California Press.

Suárez-Orozco, C., Gaytán, F. X., Bang, H. J., Pakes, J., O'Connor, E., & Rhodes, J. (2010). Academic trajectories of newcomer immigrant youth. *Developmental Psychology, 46*(3), 602–618.

Suárez-Orozco, C., & Suárez-Orozco, M. M. (2001). *Children of immigration.* Cambridge, MA: Harvard University Press.

Suárez-Orozco, C., & Suárez-Orozco, M. M. (2013). Transnationalism of the heart: Familyhood across borders. In D. Cere & L. McClain (Eds.), *What is parenthood?* (pp. 279–298). New York, NY: NYU Press.

Suárez-Orozco, C., Suárez-Orozco, M. M., & Todorova, I. (2008). *Learning a new land: Immigrant students in American society.* Cambridge, MA: Harvard University Press.

Suárez-Orozco, C., Yoshikawa, H., Teranishi, R., & Suárez-Orozco, M. M. (2011). Growing up in the shadows: The developmental implications of unauthorized status. *Harvard Educational Review, 81*(3), 438–473.

Suárez-Orozco, C., Yoshikawa, H., & Tseng, V. (2015). *Intersecting inequalities: Research to reduce inequality for immigrant-origin children and youth,* New York, NY: William T. Grant Foundation. Retrieved from www.immigrationresearch-info.org/system/files/Intersecting_Inequalities_final.pdf

Suárez-Orozco, M. M. (1989). *Central American refugees and US high schools: A psychosocial study of motivation and achievement.* Stanford, CA: Stanford University Press.

Suárez-Orozco, M. M. (1991). Immigrant adaptation to schooling: A Hispanic case. In M. A. Gibson & J. U. Ogbu (Eds.), *Minority status and schooling: A comparative study of immigrant and involuntary minorities* (pp. 37–61). New York, NY: Garland

Suárez-Orozco, M. M. (2015). Las tres caras de Herodes: Éxodo de criaturas, migraciones catastróficas y vida en sombras [The three faces of Herodes: Children's exodus, catastrophic migrations & shadowed lives]. *Multidisciplinary Journal of Educational Research, 5*(1), 1–27.

Suro, R., Suárez-Orozco, M., & Canizales, S. L. (2015). *Removing insecurity: How American children will benefit from President Obama's executive action on immigration.* Los Angeles, CA: Tomás Rivera Policy Institute at USC & Institute for Immigration, Globalization, and Education at UCLA. Retrieved from trpi.org/pdfs/research_report.pdf

Therrien, M., & Ramirez, R. R. (2001, March). *The Hispanic population in the United States: March 2000* (Current Population Reports, P20-535). Washington, DC: U.S. Census Bureau. Retrieved from www.census.gov/prod/2001pubs/p20-535.pdf

Tse, L. (2001). *Why don't they learn English? Separating fact from fallacy in the U.S. language debate.* New York, NY: Teachers College Press.

U.S. Census Bureau. (2015, November 30). *Census bureau reports at least 350 languages spoken in U.S. homes* [Press release]. Retrieved from www.census.gov/newsroom/press-releases/2015/cb15-185.html

United Nations High Commissioner for Refugees. (2016, August 2). Figures at a glance. Retrieved from www.unhcr.org/en-us/figures-at-a-glance.html

United Nations, Department of Economic and Social Affairs, Population Division. (2016). *International migration 2015* (ST/ESA/SER.A/376). Retrieved from www.un.org/en/development/desa/population/migration/publications/wallchart/docs/MigrationWallChart2015.pdf

United Nations, Economic and Social Commission for Asia and the Pacific (ESCAP). (n.d.). *International migration.* Retrieved from www.unescap.org/our-work/social-development/international-migration/about

Vigil, J. D. (2002). *A rainbow of gangs: Street cultures in the mega-city.* Austin, TX: University of Texas Press.

Weissbourd, R. (1996). *The vulnerable child.* Reading, MA: Perseus Books.

World Bank. (n.d.). *Migration, remittances, diaspora and development.* Retrieved January 10, 2016, from www.worldbank.org/en/topic/migrationremittancesdiasporaissues

Yoshikawa, H. (2011). *Immigrants raising citizens: Undocumented parents and their children.* New York, NY: Russell Sage Foundation.

Zéphir, F. (2004). *The Haitian Americans.* Westport, CT: Greenwood Press.

Part I

GLOBAL MIGRATION AND EDUCATION: CONCEPTS AND ISSUES

CHAPTER 1

Civic Education in the Age of Global Migration

James A. Banks

The goal of the workshop from which this book originated was to clarify the relationship between *immigration, cultural sustainability,* and *social cohesion* and to identify the educational implications of these concepts. The précis for the workshop states, "Modern education systems were established in order to build social cohesion through homogenization and maintain social control." The assimilationist ideology was used in nations around the world to "maintain social control" and to attain "social cohesion." This was the situation in nations with different types of governments—including democratic republics such as the United States and South Korea; federal republics such as Germany and Brazil; Communist nations such as China and Cuba; Islamic republics such as Iran and Pakistan; and monarchies such as Saudi Arabia and the United Arab Emirates. The kind of social cohesion that was acquired through punitive assimilationist policies was problematic in nations with different types of governments because factors such as social-class inequality and institutionalized xenophobia and discrimination prevented these policies from being implemented in ways that enabled marginalized groups to experience civic equality and structural inclusion.

THE NEED TO RECONCEPTUALIZE SOCIAL COHESION AND CITIZENSHIP EDUCATION

The global migration that has occurred since the ethnic revitalization movements of the 1960s and 1970s has made harsh and severe assimilationist policies even less effective than they were in the past because racial, ethnic, cultural, linguistic, and religious groups are insisting that they have the right to maintain their home and community cultures as well as participate as full citizens in their nation-states (Kymlicka, 1995; Young, 1989). Consequently, the push by structurally excluded groups for cultural sustainability is challenging traditional and institutionalized notions of social cohesion. Social cohesion needs to be reimagined and reconceputalized in this age of global migration because it has been appropriated by conservative groups in nations such as Canada (Joshee, 2009) and the United Kingdom (Gillborn, 2008), and is frequently used to justify denying marginalized groups cultural sustainability, self-determination, and equality.

Global migration and the desire by diverse groups for cultural sustainability require educators to conceptualize social cohesion in ways that will enable marginalized groups to experience cultural recognition, civic equality (Gutmann, 2004), self-determination, and structural inclusion. Social cohesion that is sustainable and equitable cannot be attained by forced assimilation and the disempowerment of diverse groups—strategies that were used in the past that failed to attain a form of social cohesion that was viable and sustainable. To protect the rights of diverse groups and to construct and sustain a cohesive polity, a nation-state must have coherent values, ideals, and an ethos around which it is organized, such as the American creed values that Myrdal (1944) explicated or ideals related to Confucianism within a Marxist political and economic context that Chinese scholars have identified (Leibold & Yangbin, 2014). Because the ideals within different types of political systems can be interpreted in myriad ways, diverse groups must be provided the opportunity to participate in deliberations and decisions that determine how the national ideals of a nation are interpreted and implemented in institutions (Young, 2000). The participation of diverse groups in the interpretation and implementation of a nation's ideals will result in a "strong" implementation of these national ideals. I am adapting Harding's (1991) concept of "strong objectivity," which results when diverse groups participate in the formulation of objectivity.

A transformative conception of citizenship education—which I contend is essential in this age of global mass migration—should help students understand not only how migrant groups are changed by the host society and nation, but also how the host society and nation are changed in significant ways by the cultures of migrant and marginalized groups. A process that I call *multiple acculturation* (Banks, 2016) takes place when migrant groups interact with Indigenous groups and other migrant groups. In an interview, Eric Liu (NPR Staff, 2014) discussed the significant ways in which Chinese immigrants have influenced American culture: "There are four million-plus Chinese Americans today. Chinese Americans have been shaping and changing . . . [American] culture from minute one." Liu also stated that Chinese Americans have changed the picture of who Americans are. Another powerful example of the ways in which diverse groups have changed and are changing American culture is the deep influence of African American culture on American culture, which includes contributions to American music (such as jazz, rock and roll, spirituals, and hip-hop), sports, and U.S. language. African American hip-hop music and popular culture have also been influential in nations around the world. Latino immigrants in the United States have enriched it with their language and values, including giving a high priority to strong family connections.

GLOBAL MIGRATION AND EDUCATION

Migration within and across nation-states is a worldwide phenomenon. The movement of peoples across national boundaries is as old as the nation-state itself. However, never before in the history of the world has the movement of diverse racial, cultural, ethnic, religious, and linguistic groups within and across nations been as extensive or raised as many complex and intractable questions about citizenship, cultural sustainability, social cohesion, and education (Castles, 2004; Suárez-Orozco, 2007; Suárez-Orozco & Qin-Hillard, 2004). There were approximately 244 million international migrants in the world in 2015 (United Nations, 2016). Many of these migrants have ambiguous citizenship status and are victims of structural exclusion, racial microaggressions, cultural erasure, deculturalization (Spring, 2010)—and sometimes violence.

Many worldwide trends and developments are challenging traditional civic education programs whose major aim is to help students develop unquestioning allegiance to their nation of residence and fail to help them acquire cross-cultural competency and global consciousness (Osler, 2009; Westheimer & Kahne, 2004). These trends include the ways in which people are moving back and forth across national borders, the rights of movement permitted and sanctioned by supranational organizations such as the European Union and the Council of Europe, the rights codified in the Universal Declaration of Human Rights, and the weakening of national boundaries because of the powerful forces of globalization (Appadurai, 1996).

This chapter describes ways in which educators can work toward a sustainable version of social cohesion by providing diverse racial, ethnic, cultural, linguistic, and religious groups with an education that advances civic equality, recognition, and structural inclusion. It reveals how global migration is challenging national conceptions of citizenship and citizenship education, and how selected nations are reconceptualizing citizenship and citizenship education to respond to global migration. It also examines the educational problems and promises caused by the diversity that is a consequence of global migration and reviews theory and research that provide guidelines for helping students acquire the knowledge, skills, and values required to become effective citizens of their communities, nation, and world in this age of global migration.

ASSIMILATION, DIVERSITY, AND GLOBAL MIGRATION

Prior to the ethnic revitalization movements of the 1960s and 1970s, the aim of schools in most nation-states was to develop citizens who internalized national values, venerated national heroes, and accepted glorified versions of national histories (Osler, 2009; Westheimer, 2007). These goals of citizenship education are dysfunctional in the age of globalization and massive migration because many individuals have identities and commitments to their original homelands as well as to their countries of residence (Castles, 2004, 2009; Maira, 2004; Nguyen, 2012). Other individuals live in more than one nation-state (Castles, 2009). However, the development of citizens who have global and cosmopolitan identities and commitments is contested in the United States (Glazer, 2002; Huntington, 2004), as well as in many other nations because nationalism remains strong (Osler, 2009; Osler & Starkey, 2005). Nationalism and globalization coexist in tension in nations around the world. The number of recognized nation-states increased from 43 in 1900 to approximately 195 in 2012 (U.S. Department of State, 2012). The number of international migrants living abroad grew from 154 million in 1990 to 232 million in 2013, which was 3.2 percent of the world's population of 7 billion (United Nations, 2013).

Nations with the different kinds of political systems described earlier in this chapter must deal with complex educational and citizenship issues when trying to respond to the problems caused by global migration in ways consistent with their ideologies, fundamental principles, and declarations—and in ways that advance cultural sustainability, the structural inclusion of diverse groups, and the construction of a nation-state to which diverse groups will have identity and allegiance (Banks, 2015; Ladson-Billings, 2004). Researchers have amply documented the wide gap between ideals related to citizenship and citizenship education and the school experiences of minority groups in nations around the world (Banks, 2009). Students such as the Maori in New Zealand (Bishop, 2012), Muslims in France (Lemaire, 2009), Mexican Americans in the United States (Hernandez, 2012), and Hui students in China (Leibold & Yangbin, 2014) experience discrimination in school because of their cultural, ethnic, racial, religious, and linguistic differences, despite the political ideologies and ideals declared by the nations in which these students live.

When they are marginalized within school and treated as the "Other," ethnic and religious minority students, such as Turkish students in Germany (Luchtenberg, 2009) and Muslim students in England (Tomlinson, 2009) and China (Postliglione, 2014), tend to emphasize their ethnic or religious identity and have weaker attachments to their nation-state than mainstream students who feel structurally included and recognized within their schools and nations (Banks, 2015; Bhatia, 2010; Nguyen, 2012). Consequently, in order to develop a society that is culturally sustainable and has social cohesion that results from structural inclusion and not from a policy of forced assimilation and deculturalization (Spring, 2010), marginalized ethnic, cultural, linguistic, and religious groups must experience cultural recognition and civic equality within schools, colleges, and universities and within society writ large (Banks, 2015; Gutmann, 2004).

Nations with different types of political systems and their educational institutions must grapple with a number of salient issues, paradigms, and ideologies related to citizenship and citizenship education as their populations become more culturally, racially, ethnically, linguistically, and religiously diverse. Most of the ethnic groups in China are indigenous; consequently, it must grapple with these issues as ethnic groups demand more recognition and rights and as large numbers of rural residents migrate to major cities (Wang, 2015; National Bureau of Statistics of China, 2013). The extent to which nation-states make multicultural citizenship possible, the achievement gap between minority and majority groups, and the language rights of immigrant and minority groups are among the unresolved and contentious issues related to citizenship education, cultural sustainability, and social cohesion with which diverse nations and schools must deal in this age of globalization and mass migration.

National Responses to Global Migration

Nations throughout the world are trying to determine whether they will perceive themselves as multicultural and allow immigrants to experience *multicultural citizenship* as conceptualized by Kymlicka (1995), the Canadian political theorist, or continue to embrace an *assimilationist* ideology, as described by Gordon (1964), the American sociologist. In nation-states that embrace Kymlicka's idea of multicultural citizenship, immigrant and minority groups can retain important aspects of their languages and cultures as well as exercise full citizenship rights in the mainstream political, economic, and cultural systems. The assimilationist ideology requires ethnic, cultural, linguistic, and religious groups to surrender their community and cultural characteristics in order to become full participants in mainstream civic society. Spring (2010) calls this process "deculturalization." Valenzuela (1999) refers to it as "subtractive schooling."

According to the philosophical and conceptual work advanced by citizenship theorists such as Kymlicka (1995), Gutmann (2004), and Young (1989), cultural sustainability and workable and legitimate social cohesion require that nation-states provide citizens and noncitizens with cultural options and alternatives. Strong assimilation theories and policies that deny individuals and groups cultural and linguistic options result in the eradication of diversity and in a manifestation of social cohesion that is not sustainable because it is coerced and is not viewed as legitimate by marginalized groups.

Nations in various parts of the world have responded to the citizenship and cultural rights of immigrant and minority groups in different ways. Since the ethnic revitalization movements of the 1960s and 1970s, many of the national leaders and citizens in the United States, Canada, and Australia have viewed their nations as multicultural democracies (Banks, 2009; Banks & Lynch, 1986). An ideal exists within these nations that minority and immigrant groups can retain important elements of their community cultures and participate fully in the national civic community. However, there is a wide gap between the ideals within these nations and the experiences of ethnic groups. Ethnic, cultural, linguistic, and religious minority groups in the United States (Nieto, 2009), Canada (Joshee, 2009), and Australia (Inglis, 2009) experience discrimination in both the schools and the wider society.

Other nations, such as Japan (Hirasawa, 2009), Korea (Moon, 2012), and Germany (Luchtenberg, 2009), have not historically viewed themselves as multicultural. Citizenship in these nations has been closely linked to biological heritage and characteristics, or what Luchtenberg (2004) describes as *"jus sanguinis* (right of blood, i.e., nationality by descent) as distinct from *jus soli* (right of soil, i.e., nationality or birthplace" (p. 247). Although the biological conception of citizenship in Japan, Korea, and Germany has eroded within the last decade, it has left a tenacious legacy in these nations. Castles (2004) refers to Germany's response to immigrants as "differential exclusion," which is "partial and temporary integration of immigrant workers into society—that is, they are included in those subsystems of society necessary for their economic role: the labor market, basic accommodation, work-related health care, and welfare" (p. 32). However, immigrants are excluded from full social, economic, and civic participation in Germany.

Since the 1960s and 1970s the French have dealt with immigrant groups in ways distinct from the United States, Canada, and Australia. *La laïcité* is a powerful and enduring concept in France, the aim of which is to keep church and state separate (Lemaire, 2009). *La laïcité* emerged in response to the hegemony the Catholic Church exercised in France over the schools and other institutions for several centuries. A major goal of state schools in France is to assure that youth obtain a secular education. Muslim students in French state schools, for example, are prevented from wearing the hijab (veil) and other religious symbols (Bowen, 2007; Scott, 2007). In France the explicit goal is assimilation (called *integration*) and inclusion (Castles, 2004). Immigrant groups in France are expected to surrender their languages and cultures in order to become full citizens. In 2010 the French Senate banned the wearing of the burqa or any veils that cover the face in public spaces, which was a significant and highly visible and symbolic victory for the assimilationist forces in France.

Internal Migration and the Education of Ethnic Groups in China

China is now experiencing massive waves of internal migration from rural to urban areas and has one of the world's largest internal migrations, which consisted of 236 million people in 2013. Rural inhabitants are settling in large waves in cities such as Beijing, Shanghai, Guangzhou, and Shenzhen (National Bureau of Statistics of China, 2013). China has been ethnically, linguistically, and religiously diverse throughout its history. Although the Han Chinese make up about 92% of the national population, China has 55 officially designated ethnic minority groups (Postiglione, 2009). After the establishment of the People's Republic of China (PRC) in 1949, the Communist Party of China (CPC) developed an official state policy that proclaims that ethnic groups have a right to be educated in their native languages, permits the recognition of ethnic and community cultures in state schools, and makes special provisions for ethnic groups to attain educational equality (Wan, 2004). Although minority cultures and languages can be recognized in state schools, the central government "emphasize[s] national unity and identification with the socialist system" (Wan, 2004, pp. 360–361).

Researchers have described the ways in which state policy and rhetoric about recognition and educational equality for ethnic groups are contradicted and violated by teachers and other educational practitioners in China (Leibold & Yangbin, 2014; Postiglione, 2014), as they are in Western nations such as Canada, the United States, and Canada. He Baogang's (He, 2014) discussion of "linguistic imperialism" is a compelling example of the gap between national ideals and practices in China. Another example is the ways in which ethnic minority groups are marginalized in textbooks (Chu, 2015). An enormous challenge for educators and scholars in China—like those in the Western nations—is to conceptualize and implement effective ways to close the wide gap between national ideals and classroom practices, which Banks (2004a) calls "the citizenship education dilemma" (p. 9): the discrepancy between the ideals within a nation and the actual practices in classrooms and schools.

REFORMING SCHOOLS TO ACTUALIZE TRANSFORMATIVE CITIZENSHIP EDUCATION

To become effective citizens, students are required to attain the knowledge, values, and skills needed to participate in their home and community cultures, within other cultures within their nation, within the national civic culture, and in the global community (Banks, 2004a). Consequently, the low academic achievement of most minority and immigrant students in nations around the world makes it difficult for them to become knowledgeable and engaged citizens (Banks, 2009, 2012). Students need knowledge and skills in reading, writing, and math, as well as political literacy, to become effective citizens. However, one unfortunate outcome of the emphasis on achievement in the basic skills and on standardized testing is that schools in the United States today are devoting little attention to citizenship education, which has historically been an important aim of its public schools. Write Malin, Ballard, Attai, et al.:

> Despite the urgency of this mission, civic education as practiced in schools throughout the United States is not preparing students for effective participation in civic life. Few young people are sufficiently motivated to become engaged in civic and political activity. Students are not finding inspiration in civic values as taught in schools today, nor are they gaining a sense that they are able to engage effectively in civic and political domains. (Malin, Ballard, Attai, Colby, & Damon, 2014, p. 7)

To create democratic classrooms and to implement what I have conceptualized as *transformative citizenship education* (Banks, 2008), teachers are required to help students develop the knowledge, values, and skills needed to participate effectively within their cultural, national, regional, and world communities. Students also need to acquire democratic racial and ethnic attitudes in order to participate effectively within and across communities and within the national civic culture. I will provide brief summaries of empirical studies from which educators can derive guidelines for reforming schools and classrooms in order to enable minority and immigrant students to increase their levels of academic achievement and to attain the knowledge, skills, and values needed to become reflective and active citizens in multicultural nations and societies in a world characterized by massive global migration.

Increasing Academic Achievement by Using Culturally Responsive Teaching

To implement transformative citizenship education, schools are required to help all students—including ethnic, linguistic, and religious minority students—to acquire the attitudes, knowledge, and skills needed for productive employment in a highly technological and interconnected global society, participate effectively in the political system, and take action to increase equity in society. Schools in the U.S. need to work to close the wide achievement gap that exists between middle-class White students, some groups of Asian American students, and students such as African Americans, Mexican Americans, and American Indians. Some of the research and theory that is grounded in the cultural difference paradigm and *culturally responsive* (also called *culturally relevant*) teaching indicates that if teachers incorporate the cultures and languages of diverse groups into instruction, the academic achievement of these students will increase.

Unlike the cultural deprivation paradigm, the cultural difference paradigm rejects the idea that students of color have cultural deficits (Valencia, 2010). Cultural difference theorists believe that groups such as African Americans, Mexican Americans, and American Indians have strong, rich, and diverse cultures (Delpit, 1995; González, Moll, & Amanti, 2005; Ladson-Billings, 2009). These cultures, they contend, consist of languages, values, behavioral styles, and perspectives that can enrich the lives of all students. Schools frequently fail to help ethnic minority, immigrant, and low-income students achieve because they ignore or try to alienate these students from their home and community cultures and languages (Wong Fillmore, 2005). Proponents of cultural difference are critical of the value assumptions underlying deficit thinking and argue that understanding cultural conflicts rather than deficits is the key to explaining underachievement (Banks & Banks, 2004; Delpit, 1995; Gay, 2010; Irvine, 2003; Ladson-Billings, 2009; Valencia, 2010).

Cultural difference researchers theorize that to increase the academic achievement of students from immigrant and diverse groups the school must change in ways that will enable it to respect and reflect the rich cultural strengths of students from diverse groups and use teaching strategies that are consistent with their cultural characteristics. Banks has called this approach to teaching "equity pedagogy" (Banks, 2004b, pp. 5–6). It is also known in the literature as "culturally relevant" (Ladson-Billings, 2009) and "culturally responsive" teaching (Gay, 2010).

Cultural difference theorists cite research that shows how the cultures of the school and of ethnic minority and low-income youth differ in values, behaviors (Gay, 2010), languages (Heath, 2012; Lee, 2007; Valdés, 2001), dialects (Smitherman, 2000), and cultures (González et al., 2005). Studies by John (1972) and Heath (2012) are examples of these types of studies. John describes the ways in which verbal interactions differ in the school and in the homes of Navajo students. Heath explains how language use differs among White middle-class teachers, the White working-class, and the African American working-class.

Some studies provide empirical support for the premise that when teachers use culturally responsive pedagogy the academic achievement of minority students increases. Au (1980) found that if teachers used participation structures in lessons that were similar to the Hawaiian speech event "talk story," the reading achievement of Native Hawaiian students increased significantly. Lee's (2007) research indicates that the achievement of African American students increases when they are taught literary interpretation with lessons that use the African American practice of signifying. González, Moll, and Amanti (2005) found that when teachers gain an understanding of the "funds of knowledge" of Mexican American households and community networks—and incorporate this knowledge into their teaching—Mexican American students become more active and engaged learners. Research by Ladson-Billings (2009) indicates that the ability to scaffold student learning by bridging home and community cultures is one of the important characteristics of effective teachers of African American students.

An increasing body of research provides empirical support for the cultural difference paradigm (Banks & Banks, 2004; Banks & Park, 2010). An important challenge to this body of work is to accurately describe the enormous diversity within different ethnic, racial, and linguistic groups and avoid essentializing these groups or their experiences. Some of the earliest work within the cultural difference paradigm essentialized racial and ethnic groups by claiming that ethnic groups had specific and static learning and motivational styles (for a review and critique of this research, see Irvine & York, 2001). The Nigerian novelist Chimamanda Ngozi Adichie (2009) cautions about "the danger of a single story," which results in misleading and oversimplified categorizations of individuals, groups, and nations. She warns, "If we only hear a single story about another person or country, we risk a critical misunderstanding."

Some research and theory on learning styles, if interpreted as "a single story," or generalized to an entire group, can contribute to the stereotyping of group differences and the acceptance of racialized categorizations. Lee (2007) has pointed out that a common problem in discussions of cultural difference is that culture is conceptualized as a fixed trait or characteristic. Gutiérrez and Rogoff (2003) have warned against a simple "matching strategy" of overlaying or mapping culture onto racial groups, or using a "one style per person" mode of thinking, assuming that an individual student's membership in a group automatically tells teachers about his or her preferred ways of learning (p. 19). These authors argue that this overgeneralization can lead to a kind of cultural tracking, where students receive instruction based on group categorization. Unfortunately, this strategy does not help educators develop a nuanced understanding of the history of the individual student's participation in his or her cultural community, nor does it account for within-group variation or change.

Multicultural education—whose major goal is to reform schools so that students from diverse racial, ethnic, linguistic, social-class, and religious groups will experience educational equality—is highly consistent with the cultural difference paradigm (Banks, 2016; Banks & Banks, 2016; Banks & Park, 2010). This paradigm is a critical response to cultural deficit thinking: the notion that ethnic minority students and low-income students "lack" culture, and that the solution is to expose these students to the mainstream national culture in order for them to thrive in school and in society (Riessman, 1962).

Research on Curriculum Materials and Interventions

In addition to acquiring basic skills in reading, writing, and math, students also need to develop democratic attitudes and values in order to become effective citizens who can function in their own cultural communities, within and across other cultural communities, within the national civic community, and in the global community. Research and theory indicate that curriculum interventions can help students to develop democratic values and beliefs that are required to become effective citizens in a global age.

Research on intergroup contact provides important guidelines for school interventions that will help students attain democratic attitudes and values and the skills to function effectively within and across diverse groups. Allport (1954/1979) theorized that contact between different groups would improve intergroup relations if the contact between these groups has these characteristics: (1) Individuals experience equal status; (2) individuals share common goals; (3) intergroup cooperation exists; and (4) the contact is sanctioned by authorities such as teachers and administrators, or by law or custom (Allport 1954/1979; Pettigrew 2004). One of the ways to increase equal status within classrooms is to use textbooks and other materials that describe the histories, cultures, and experiences of diverse groups (Hughes, Bigler, & Levy, 2007; Stephan, 1999). Multicultural textbooks and other materials give voice to the histories and experiences of all the students in a class and do not make any of them feel excluded, marginalized, or silenced. These classroom materials provide marginalized students civic equality and recognition (Gutmann, 2004) and also create "identity safe classrooms" for them (Steele & Cohn-Vargas, 2013).

Curriculum interventions studies have been conducted to determine the effects of teaching units and lessons, multicultural textbooks and materials, role-playing, and other kinds of simulated experiences on the racial attitudes and perceptions of students. This research indicates that the use of multicultural textbooks, other teaching materials, and cooperative teaching strategies that enable students from different racial and ethnic groups to interact positively can help students to develop positive racial attitudes. These kinds of materials and teaching strategies can also result in students choosing more friends from outside racial, ethnic, and cultural groups (Slavin, 2001).

These studies provide guidelines that can help teachers improve intergroup relations in their classrooms and schools. Trager and Yarrow (1952) conducted one of the earliest curriculum studies that examined the effects of a democratic multicultural curriculum on the racial attitudes of children in the 1st and 2nd grades. The curriculum had a positive effect on the attitudes of both students and teachers. The authors titled their study *They Learn What They Live* to highlight its major finding—if students experience democracy, they will internalize it.

Research indicates that curriculum interventions such as multiethnic readers (Litcher & Johnson, 1969); multicultural television programs (Bogatz & Ball, 1971); simulations (Weiner & Wright, 1973); multicultural social studies materials (Yawkey & Blackwell, 1974); folk dances, music, crafts and role-playing (Ijaz & Ijaz, 1981); plays (Gimmestad & DeChiara, 1982); discussions about race (Aboud & Doyle, 1996); and discussions combined with antiracist teaching (McGregor, 1993) can have positive effects on the racial attitudes of students. An intervention that induced empathy helped students develop positive racial attitudes in a study conducted by Finlay and Stephan (2006). Long-term interracial contact had a positive influence on the racial attitudes of adults in a study conducted by Wood and Sonleitner (1996).

Research on Cooperative Learning and Interracial Contact

Most researchers who have conducted studies in schools of the effects of cooperative learning and interracial contact have used Allport's (1954/1979) contact theory to conceptualize their studies. Since 1970 a group of investigators, guided by Allport's theory, have produced a rich body of cumulative research on the effects of cooperative learning groups and activities on students' racial attitudes, friendship choices, and achievement. Much of this research has been conducted as well as reviewed by investigators such as Aronson and his colleagues (Aronson & Bridgeman, 1979; Aronson & González, 1988), Cohen and her colleagues (Cohen, 1972, 1984; Cohen & Lotan, 1995; Cohen & Roper, 1972), Johnson and Johnson (1981), Slavin (1979, 1983, 1985), and Slavin and Madden (1979). Schofield (2004) has written a comprehensive and informative review of this research. Most of it has been conducted using elementary and high school students (Slavin, 1983, 1985).

This research strongly supports the notion that cooperative interracial contact situations in schools—if the conditions stated by Allport are present in the contact situations—have positive effects on both student interracial behavior and student academic achievement (Aronson & González, 1988; Slavin, 1979, 1983). In his review of 19 studies of the effects of cooperative-learning methods, Slavin (1985) found that

16 had positive effects on interracial friendships. In another review Slavin (2001) also describes the positive effects of cooperative groups on cross-racial friendships, racial attitudes, and behavior. Investigators have also found that cooperative learning activities have increased student motivation and self-esteem (Slavin, 1985), and have helped students to develop empathy (Aronson & Bridgeman, 1979).

The research by Cohen and Roper (1972) indicates that equal status between groups in interracial situations has to be deliberately structured by teachers or it will not exist. If students from different racial, ethnic, and linguistic groups are mixed in contact situations without structured interventions that create equal-status conditions, racial and ethnic conflict and stereotyping are likely to increase. Students from both privileged and marginalized groups are likely to respond in ways that will reinforce the status of the higher-status group. In a series of perceptive and carefully designed studies, Cohen and her colleagues consistently found that contact among different groups without deliberate interventions to increase equal-status and positive interactions among them will increase rather than reduce intergroup tensions (Cohen, 1984; Cohen & Lotan, 1995; Cohen & Roper, 1972).

Creating Crosscutting Superordinate Groups

Whenever ingroups and outgroups are constructed, stereotypes, prejudice, and discrimination develop. Consequently, it becomes necessary for educators to design and implement strategies to improve intergroup relations. Social psychological theory and research known as the *minimal group paradigm* indicates that when mere categorization develops, individuals favor the ingroup over the outgroup and discriminate against the outgroup (Rothbart & John, 1993; Smith & Mackie, 1995). This can occur in situations without prior historical conflict and animosity, competition, physical differences, or any kind of important difference. According to Tajfel (1970), "Whenever we are confronted with a situation to which some form of intergroup categorization appears directly relevant, we are likely to act in a manner that discriminates against the outgroup and favors the ingroup" (pp. 98–99).

In a series of studies Tajfel and his colleagues (Tajfel, 1970; Billig & Tajfel, 1973) produced considerable evidence to support the postulate that individuals are likely to evaluate the ingroup more favorably than the outgroup and to treat the ingroup more favorably even when the differences between the groups are minimal, contrived, and insignificant. This series of studies indicate the power of categorization. In one group of experiments Tajfel (1970) told a group of public school boys in Bristol (United Kingdom) that he had divided them into two groups based on whether they had under- or overestimated the number of dots projected on a screen. The subjects were then given a series of tasks in which they could provide rewards to two anonymous students. When the students gave rewards to ingroup members, they divided them equally. However, they favored the ingroup when one student was an outgroup member and the other an ingroup member. The experimenter contrived the groups. The assignment of the groups was random and was not based on the estimation of the dots by the subjects.

The minimal group paradigm, also known as *social identity theory*, is in some ways more helpful in explaining the development of ingroup–outgroup boundaries than in suggesting practices to reduce them. One implication of social identity theory is that to increase positive intergroup contact the salience of group characteristics should be minimized and a superordinate group created—such as a music club or a soccer team—with which students from different cultural and language groups can become identified. In a classroom characterized by language diversity, group salience is likely to be reduced to the extent that all students become competent in the same languages. For example, in a classroom with both Anglos and Mexican Americans, group salience is increased if only the Mexican American students speak Spanish. However, if both Mexican and Anglo-American students become competent in both English and Spanish, bilingual competency can be the basis for the formation of a superordinate group to which all of the students belong (Lambert & Cazabon, 1994).

Research indicates that creating or making salient superordinate and crosscutting group memberships improve intergroup relations (Banks et al., 2001; Stephan, 1999). According to Banks et al. (2001), "When membership in superordinate groups is salient, other group differences become less important. Creating superordinate groups stimulates cohesion, which can mitigate pre-existing animosities" (p. 9). Sports teams, Future Farmers of America, Girl Scouts, and Camp Fire are examples of crosscutting or superordinate groups. Research and theory indicate that when students from diverse cultural, racial, and language groups share a superordinate identity such as the computer club, cultural boundaries weaken. Students are consequently able to form friendships and have positive interactions and relationships with students from different racial, cultural, linguistic, and religious groups. Extra- and cocurricular activities—such as the drama club, the debating club, the basketball team, and the school chorus—create rich opportunities for structuring superordinate groups and crosscutting group memberships (Stephan, 1999; Stephan & Stephan, 2004).

When teachers create crosscutting or superordinate groups, they should make sure that the integrity of different cultures represented in the classroom is respected and given legitimacy within the framework of the superordinate group that is created. Superordinate groups that reflect only the norms and values of dominant and powerful groups within the school are not likely to improve intergroup relations among different groups in the school. If they are not carefully structured and monitored, crosscutting groups can reproduce the dominant power relationships that exist within the classroom, the school, and the larger society.

The Complicated Characteristics of Student Identifications

Historically, schools in Western democratic nations, such as the United States, Canada, and Australia—as well as schools in other nations—have focused on helping students develop national loyalty, commitments, and allegiance to the nation-state and have given little attention to their need to maintain commitments to their local communities and cultures or to their original homelands. Schools assumed that assimilation into the mainstream culture was required for citizenship and national belonging and that students could and should surrender commitments to other communities, cultures, and nations. Greenbaum (1974) states that U.S. schools taught European immigrant groups from southern, central, and eastern Europe *hope* and *shame*. They were made to feel ashamed of their home and community cultures but were given hope that once they culturally assimilated they could join the U.S. mainstream culture. Cultural assimilation worked well for most White ethnic groups (Alba & Nee, 2003), but not for groups of color, which continued to experience structural exclusion after they become culturally assimilated.

Ethnographic research studies indicate that the narrow conception of citizenship education that has been embraced historically by American schools is not consistent with the racial, ethnic, and cultural realities of U.S. society because of the complicated, contextual, and overlapping identities of immigrant students. Research by scholars studying immigrant high school students indicates that these youth have complex and contradictory *transnational* identifications. This finding is consistent across studies of high school immigrant students in the United States by Abu El-Haj (2007) of Palestinian youth, Nguyen (2012) of Vietnamese youth, and Maira (2004) of working-class Indian, Pakistani, and Bangladeshi youth. These researchers describe the nuanced and intricate identifications that immigrant youth have with the United States, their countries of origin, and their local communities. This research also indicates that the cultural and national identities of immigrant youth are complex, contextual, evolving, and continually reconstructed.

Abu El-Haj (2007), Nguyen (2012), and Maira (2004) found that the immigrant youth in their studies did not define their national identity in terms of their place of residence, but felt that they belonged to national communities that transcended the boundaries of the United States. They defined their national identities as Palestinian, Vietnamese, Indian, Pakistani, and Bangladeshi. They believed that an individual could be Palestinian or Vietnamese and live in many different nation-states. The youth in these studies distinguished *national identity* and *citizenship*. They viewed themselves as Palestinian, Vietnamese, or Pakistani but recognized and acknowledged their U.S. citizenship, which they valued for the privileged legal status and other opportunities it gave them.

Although the immigrant youth in Nguyen's (2012) study viewed themselves as citizens of the United States, they did not view themselves as Americans. One of the Vietnamese students in Nguyen's (2012) study said, "I know that you can become an American citizen. But Vietnamese and other immigrants cannot become Americans like the real Americans." (p. 120). They felt that they were not Americans because to be American required an individual to be White and mainstream. Their construction of the criteria for becoming American was a consequence of the racism, discrimination, and exclusion they were experiencing within their school and community. Both Abu El-Haj (2007) and Nguyen (2012) describe how the marginalization that immigrant students experience in schools and in the larger U.S. society reinforce their national identity with distant nations in which they imagine they can experience equality and structural inclusion (Anderson, 1983).

Maira (2004) used "cultural citizenship" to describe the transnational aspects of the citizenship identity held by the South Asian students in her study. These youth maintained contacts and connections with their homeland cultures through popular culture venues, such as websites, films, music, TV serials, cable TV, and DVDs from their homelands. Appadurai (1996) calls the global networks in which these students participate "diasporic public spheres" (p. 22).

Mainstream and Transformative Citizenship Education

It is essential to reimagine and transform citizenship education in order to prepare students to participate effectively in a globalized world that brings them into contact with peoples and cultures from many different nations (Suárez-Orozco, 2007). A transformed citizenship education program will help students to acquire the intercultural knowledge and skills required to function within and across diverse cultures and communities. To reform citizenship education, the knowledge that underlies its construction needs to shift from *mainstream* to *transformative* academic knowledge (Banks, 1993). Mainstream knowledge reinforces traditional and established knowledge in the social and behavioral sciences as well as the knowledge that is institutionalized within the popular culture and within the schools, colleges, and universities within a nation. Transformative academic knowledge consists of paradigms and explanations that challenge some of the key epistemological assumptions of mainstream knowledge. An important purpose of transformative knowledge is to interrogate the social, political, and economic structures within society that perpetuate inequality and contribute to the marginalization of excluded groups. Feminist scholars and scholars of color have been among the leading constructors of transformative academic knowledge in the United States (Harding, 1991; Takaki, 1993).

Mainstream citizenship education is grounded in mainstream knowledge and assumptions and reinforces the status quo and the dominant power relationships in society. It is practiced in most social studies classrooms in schools around the world (Hahn, 1998) and does not challenge or disrupt the class, racial, and gender discrimination within schools and society (Westheimer & Kahne, 2004). It does not help students understand their multiple and complex identities nor the ways in which their lives are influenced by globalization, or what their role should be in a global world. The emphasis is on memorizing facts about constitutions and other legal documents, learning about various branches of government, and developing patriotism to the nation-state (Malin et al., 2014; Osler, 2009). Critical thinking skills, decision-making, and action are not important components of mainstream citizenship education.

Transformative citizenship education needs to be implemented within the schools in order for students to attain clarified and reflective cultural, national, regional, and global identifications, and to understand how these identities are interrelated and constructed (Banks, 2007). Transformative citizenship education also recognizes and validates the cultural identities of students and provides them civic equality and recognition in the classroom and school (Gutmann, 2004). It is rooted in transformative academic knowledge and enables students to acquire the information, skills, and values needed to challenge inequality within their communities, their nations, and the world; to develop cosmopolitan values and perspectives; and to take actions to create just and democratic multicultural communities and societies. Transformative citizenship education helps students develop decision-making and social-action skills that are needed to identify problems within society, acquire knowledge related to their home and community cultures and languages, identify and clarify their values, and take thoughtful individual or collective civic action that will improve their local communities, nation-states, and the world.

THE DEVELOPMENT OF CULTURAL, NATIONAL, REGIONAL, AND GLOBAL IDENTIFICATIONS

Assimilationist notions of citizenship are ineffective today because of the deepening diversity throughout the world and the quests by marginalized groups for cultural recognition and rights. *Multicultural citizenship* and *cultural democracy* are essential in today's global age (Kymlicka, 1995). These concepts recognize and legitimize the right and need of citizens to maintain commitments both to their cultural communities and to the national civic culture. Research and theory indicate that citizens must be structurally included within their nation in order to develop a strong allegiance and a reflective commitment to it (Deaux, 2006; Nguyen, 2012).

Students need to develop a delicate balance of *cultural, national, regional*, and *global* identifications and allegiances in order to be effective citizens in a world characterized by globalization and global migration (see Figure 1.1). These four identifications are highly interrelated, complex, contextual, and dynamic. Citizenship education should help students develop thoughtful and clarified identifications with their cultural communities and their nation-states (Banks, 2004a; Banks, 2008). It should also help them develop clarified global identifications and deep understandings of their roles in the world community. Students need to understand how life in their cultural communities and nations influences other nations and the cogent influence that international events have on their daily lives. Global education should have as major goals helping students develop understandings of the interdependence among nations in the world today, clarified attitudes toward other nations, and reflective identifications with the world community. I conceptualize global identification similar to the way in which Nussbaum (1994/2002) defines *cosmopolitanism.*

Figure 1.1. Cultural, National, Regional, and Global Identifications

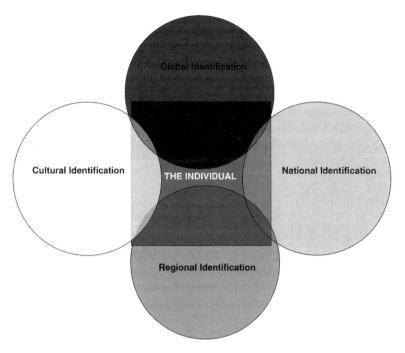

Nonreflective and unexamined cultural attachments may prevent the development of a cohesive nation with clearly defined national goals and policies. Although educators need to help students develop reflective and clarified cultural identifications, they also need to be helped to clarify their identifications with their nation-states. However, blind nationalism may prevent students from developing reflective and positive global identifications (Westheimer, 2007; Westheimer & Kahne, 2004). Nationalism and national attachments in most nations are strong and tenacious. An important aim of transformative citizenship education should be to help students develop global identifications and global consciousness. They also need to develop a deep understanding of the need to take action as citizens of the global community to help solve the world's difficult global problems. Transformative citizenship education helps students develop cultural, national, regional, and global identifications that are balanced, interactive, contextual, and fluid, and the knowledge, values, and skills required to be effective citizens in an age of global migration.

REFERENCES

Aboud, F. E., & Doyle, A. B. (1996). Does talk foster prejudice or tolerance in children? *Canadian Journal of Behavioural Science, 28*(3), 161–171.

Abu El-Haj, T. R. (2007). "I was born here, but my home, it's not here": Educating for democratic citizenship in an era of transnational migration and global conflict. *Harvard Educational Review, 77*(3), 285–316.

Adichie, C. N. (2009). *The danger of a single story.* Retrieved from www.ted.com/talks/chimamanda_adichie_the_danger_of_a_single_story.html

Alba, R., & Nee, V. (2003). *Remaking the American mainstream: Assimilation and contemporary immigration.* Cambridge, MA: Harvard University Press.

Allport, G. W. (1979). *The nature of prejudice* (25th anniversary ed.). Reading, MA: Addison-Wesley. (Original work published 1954)

Anderson, B. (1983). *Imagined communities: Reflections on the origin and spread of nationalism.* New York, NY: Verso.

Appadurai, A. (1996). *Modernity at large: Cultural dimensions of globalization.* Minneapolis, MN: University of Minnesota Press.

Aronson, E., & Bridgeman, D. (1979). Jigsaw groups and the desegregated classroom: In pursuit of common goals. *Personality and Social Psychology Bulletin, 5,* 438–446.

Aronson, E., & González, A. (1988). Desegregation, jigsaw, and the Mexican–American experience. In P. A. Katz & D. A. Taylor (Eds.), *Eliminating racism: Profiles in controversy* (pp. 301–314). New York, NY: Plenum Press.

Au, K. H. (1980). Participation structures in a reading lesson with Hawaiian children: Analysis of a culturally appropriate teaching event. *Anthropology and Education Quarterly, 11,* 91–115.

Banks, J. A. (1993). The canon debate, knowledge construction, and multicultural education. *Educational Researcher, 22*(5), 4–14.

Banks, J. A. (2004a). Introduction: Democratic citizenship education in multicultural societies. In J. A. Banks (Ed.), *Diversity and citizenship education: Global perspectives* (pp. 3–15). San Francisco, CA: Jossey-Bass.

Banks, J. A. (2004b). Multicultural education: Historical development, dimensions, and practice. In J. A. Banks & C. A. M. Banks (Eds.), *Handbook of research on multicultural education* (pp. 3–29). San Francisco, CA: Jossey-Bass.

Banks, J. A. (2007). *Educating citizens in a multicultural society* (2nd ed.). New York, NY: Teachers College Press.

Banks, J. A. (2008). Diversity, group identity, and citizenship education in a global age. *Educational Researcher, 37*(3), 129–139.

Banks, J. A. (Ed.). (2009). *The Routledge international companion to multicultural education.* New York, NY, & London, United Kingdom: Routledge.

Banks, J. A. (2012). Introduction. In J. A. Banks (Ed.), *Encyclopedia of diversity in education* (Vol. 1, pp. xlvii–liii). Thousand Oaks, CA: Sage.

Banks, J. A. (2015). Failed citizenship, civic engagement, and education. *Kappa Delta Pi Record, 51*(4), 151–154.

Banks, J. A. (2016). *Cultural diversity and education: Foundations, curriculum, and teaching* (6th ed.). New York, NY, & London, United Kingdom: Routledge.

Banks, J. A., & Banks, C. A. M. (Eds.). (2004). *Handbook of research on multicultural education* (2nd ed.). San Francisco, CA: Jossey-Bass.

Banks, J. A., & Banks, C.A.M. (Eds.). (2016). *Multicultural education: Issues and perspectives* (9th ed.). Hoboken, NJ: Wiley.

Banks, J. A., & Lynch, J. (Eds.). (1986). *Multicultural education in Western societies.* New York, NY & London, United Kingdom: Holt.

Banks, J. A., Cookson, P., Gay, G., Hawley, W. D., Irvine, J. J., Nieto, S., Schofield, J. W., & Stephan, W. G. (2001). *Diversity within unity: Essential principles for teaching and learning in a multicultural society.* Seattle, WA: University of Washington, Center for Multicultural Education.

Banks, J. A., & Park, C. (2010). Race, ethnicity, and education: The search for explanations. In P. H. Collins & J. Solomos (Eds.), *The Sage handbook of race and ethnic studies* (pp. 383–413). London, United Kingdom: Sage.

Bhatia, S. (2010). Interpreting the meanings of schooling, hybridity, and multicultural citizenship in diaspora communities. *Yearbook of the National Society for the Study of Education, 109,* 66–81.

Billig, M. G., & Tajfel, H. (1973). Social categorization and similarity in intergroup behaviour. *European Journal of Social Psychology, 3,* 27–52.

Bishop, R. (2012). Maori, education of. In J. A. Banks (Ed.), *Encyclopedia of diversity in education* (Vol. 3, pp. 1435–1440). Thousand Oaks, CA: Sage.

Bogatz, G. A., & Ball, S. (1971). *The second year of Sesame Street: A continuing evaluation.* Princeton, NJ: Educational Testing Service.

Bowen, J. R. (2007). *Why the French don't like headscarves: Islam, the state, and public space.* Princeton, NJ: Princeton University Press.

Castles, S. (2004). Migration, citizenship, and education. In J. A. Banks (Ed.), *Diversity and citizenship education: Global perspectives* (pp. 17–48). San Francisco, CA: Jossey-Bass.

Castles, S. (2009). World population movements, diversity, and education. In J. A. Banks (Ed.), *The Routledge international companion to multicultural education* (pp. 49–61). New York, NY, & London, United Kingdom: Routledge.

Chu, Y. (2015). The power of knowledge: A critical analysis of the depiction of ethnic minorities in China's elementary textbooks. *Race Ethnicity and Education, 18*(4), 469–487.

Cohen, E. G. (1972). Interracial interaction disability. *Human Relations, 25,* 9–24.

Cohen. E. G. (1984). Talking and working together: Status, interaction, and learning. In P. Peterson, L. C. Wilkinson, & M. Hallinan (Eds.), *The social context of instruction* (pp. 171–186). New York, NY: Academic Press.

Cohen, E. G., & Lotan, R. A. (1995). Producing equal-status interaction in the heterogeneous classroom. *American Educational Research Journal, 32,* 99–120.

Cohen, E. G., & Roper, S. S. (1972). Modification of interracial interaction disability: An application of status characteristic theory. *American Sociological Review, 37,* 643–657.

Deaux, K. (2006). *To be an immigrant.* New York, NY: Russell Sage Foundation.

Delpit, L. (1995). *Other people's children: Cultural conflict in the classroom.* New York, NY: New Press.

Finlay, K., & Stephan, W. (2006). Improving intergroup relations: The effects of empathy on racial attitudes. *Journal of Applied Social Psychology, 30*(8), 1720–1737.

Gay, G. (2010). *Culturally responsive teaching: Theory, research, and practice* (2nd ed.). New York, NY: Teachers College Press.

Gillborn, D. (2008). *Racism and education: Coincidence or conspiracy?* London, United Kingdom, & New York, NY: Routledge.

Gimmestad, B. J., & DeChiara, E. (1982). Dramatic plays: A vehicle for prejudice reduction in the elementary school. *Journal of Educational Research, 76*(1), 45–49.

Glazer, N. (2002). Limits of loyalty. In M. C. Nussbaum with J. Cohen (Ed.), *For love of country?* (pp. 61–65). Boston, MA: Beacon Press.

González, N., Moll, L. C., & Amanti, C. (2005). *Funds of knowledge: Theorizing practices in households, communities, and classrooms.* Mahwah, NJ: Lawrence Earlbaum.

Gordon, M. M. (1964). *Assimilation in American life: The role of race, religion, and national origins.* New York, NY: Oxford University Press.

Greenbaum, W. (1974). America in search of a new ideal: An essay on the rise of pluralism. *Harvard Educational Review, 44*(3), 411–440.

Gutiérrez, K. D., & Rogoff, B. (2003). Cultural ways of learning: Individual traits or repertoires of practice. *Educational Researcher, 32*(5), 19–25.

Gutmann, A. (2004). Unity and diversity in multicultural education: Creative and destructive tensions. In J. A. Banks (Ed.), *Diversity and citizenship education: Global perspectives* (pp. 71–96). San Francisco, CA: Jossey-Bass.

Hahn, C. L. (1998). *Becoming political: Comparative perspectives on citizenship education.* Albany, NY: State University of New York Press.

Harding, S. (1991). *Whose knowledge? Whose science? Thinking from women's lives.* Ithaca, NY: Cornell University Press.

He, B. (2014). The power of Chinese linguistic imperialism and its challenges to multicultural education. In J. Leibold & C. Yangbin (Eds.), *Minority education in China: Balancing unity and diversity in an era of critical pluralism* (pp. 45–64). Hong Kong, China: Hong Kong University Press.

Heath, S. B. (2012). *Words at work and play: Three decades in family and community.* New York, NY: Oxford University Press.

Hernandez, H. (2012). Mexican Americans, education of. In J. A. Banks (Ed.), *Encyclopedia of diversity in education* (Vol. 3, pp. 1475–1479). Thousand Oaks, CA: Sage.

Hirasawa, Y. (2009). Multicultural education in Japan. In J. A. Banks (Ed.), *The Routledge international companion to multicultural education* (pp. 159–169). New York, NY, & London, United Kingdom: Routledge.

Hughes, J., Bigler, R., & Levy, S. (2007). Consequences of learning about historical racism among European American and African American children. *Child Development, 78*(6), 1689–1705.

Huntington, S. P. (2004). *Who are we? The challenge to America's national identity.* New York, NY: Simon & Schuster.

Ijaz, M. A., & Ijaz, I. H. (1981). A cultural program for changing racial attitudes. *History and Social Science Teacher, 17*(1), 17–20.

Inglis, C. (2009). Multicultural education in Australia: Two generations of evolution. In J. A. Banks (Ed.), *The Routledge international companion to multicultural education* (pp. 109–120). New York, NY, & London, United Kingdom: Routledge.

Irvine, J. J. (2003). *Educating teachers for diversity: Seeing with a cultural eye.* New York, NY: Teachers College Press.

Irvine, J. J., & York, D. E. (2001). Learning styles and culturally diverse students: A literature review. In J. A. Banks & C. A. M. Banks (Eds.), *Handbook of research on multicultural education* (pp. 484–497). San Francisco, CA: Jossey-Bass.

John, V. P. (1972). Styles of learning—styles of teaching: Reflections on the education of Navajo children. In C. B. Cazden, V. P. John, & D. Hymes (Eds.), *Functions of language in the classroom* (pp. 331–343). New York, NY: Teachers College Press.

Johnson, D. W., & Johnson, R. T. (1981). Effects of cooperative and individualistic learning experiences on interethnic interaction. *Journal of Educational Psychology, 73*, 444–449.

Joshee, R. (2009). Multicultural policy in Canada: Competing ideologies, interconnected discourses. In J. A. Banks (Ed.), *The Routledge international companion to multicultural education* (pp. 96–108). New York, NY: Routledge.

Kymlicka, W. (1995). *Multicultural citizenship: A liberal theory of minority rights.* Oxford, United Kingdom: Oxford University Press.

Ladson-Billings, G. (2004). Culture versus citizenship: The challenge of racialized citizenship in the United States. In J. A. Banks (Ed.), *Diversity and citizenship education: Global perspectives* (pp. 99–126). San Francisco, CA: Jossey-Bass.

Ladson-Billings, G. (2009). *The dreamkeepers: Successful teachers of African American children* (2nd ed.). San Francisco, CA: Jossey-Bass.

Lambert, W. E., & Cazabon, M. (1994). *Students' views of the Amigos program.* Santa Cruz: University of California, National Center for Research on Cultural Diversity and Second Language Learning.

Lee, C. D. (2007). *Culture, literacy, and learning: Taking bloom in the midst of the whirlwind.* New York, NY: Teachers College Press.

Leibold, J., & Yangbin, C. (Eds.). (2014). *Minority education in China: Balancing unity and diversity in an era of critical pluralism.* Hong Kong, China: Hong Kong University Press.

Lemaire, E. (2009). Education, integration, and citizenship in France. In J. A. Banks (Ed.), *The Routledge international companion to multicultural education* (pp. 323–333). New York, NY, & London, United Kingdom: Routledge.

Litcher, J. H., & Johnson, D. W. (1969). Changes in attitudes toward Negroes of White elementary school students after use of multiethnic readers. *Journal of Educational Psychology, 60,* 148–152.

Luchtenberg, S. (2004). Ethnic diversity and citizenship education in Germany. In J. A. Banks (Ed.), *Diversity and citizenship education: Global perspectives* (pp. 245–271). San Francisco, CA: Jossey-Bass.

Luchtenberg, S. (2009). Migrant minority groups in Germany: Success and failure in education. In J. A. Banks (Ed.), *The Routledge international companion to multicultural education* (pp. 463–473). New York, NY, & London, United Kingdom: Routledge.

Maira, S. (2004). Imperial feelings: Youth culture, citizenship, and globalization. In M. Suárez-Orozco & D. B. Qin-Hilliard (Eds.), *Globalization, culture, and education in the new millennium* (pp. 203–234). Berkeley: University of California Press.

Malin, H., Ballard, P. J., Attai, M. L., Colby, A., & Damon, W. (2014). *Youth civic development and education: A conference consensus report.* Stanford, CA: Stanford Center on Adolescence & Seattle, WA: Center for Multicultural Education, University of Washington.

McGregor, J. (1993). Effectiveness of role playing and antiracist teaching in reducing student prejudice. *Journal of Educational Research, 86*(4), 215–226.

Moon, S. (2012). Korea, multicultural education in. In J. A. Banks (Ed.), *Encyclopedia of diversity in education* (Vol. 3, pp. 1307–1312). Thousand Oaks, CA: Sage.

Myrdal, G. (with Sterner, R., & Rose, A.) (1944). *An American dilemma: The Negro problem in modern democracy.* New York, NY: Harper & Brothers.

National Bureau of Statistics of the People's Republic of China. (2013). *Zhong hua ren min gong he guo 2012 guo min jing ji he she hui fa zhan tong ji gong bao.* [Statistical communiqué of the People's Republic of China on the 2012 economic and social development]. Retrieved from http://www.stats.gov.cn/tjsj/tjgb/ndtjgb/qgndtjgb/201302/t20130221_30027.html

Nguyen, D. (2012). *Vietnamese immigrant youth: How race, ethnicity, and culture shape sense of belonging.* El Paso, TX: LFB Scholarly Publishing.

Nieto, S. (2009). Multicultural education in the United States: Historical realities, ongoing challenges, and transformative possibilities. In J. A. Banks (Ed.), *The Routledge international companion to multicultural education* (pp. 79–95). New York, NY, & London, United Kingdom: Routledge.

NPR Staff. (2014, August 12). Author explores irony and identity in "A Chinaman's chance." Retrieved from www.npr.org/blogs/codeswitch/2014/08/12/339541058/author-explores-irony-and-identity-in-a-chinamans-chance?utm_medium=RSS&utm_campaign=storiesfromnpr

Nussbaum, M. C. (2002). Patriotism and cosmopolitanism. In M. C. Nussbaum with J. Cohen (Ed.), *For love of country?* (pp. 3–17). Boston, MA: Beacon Press. (Original work published 1994)

Osler, A. (2009). Patriotism, multiculturalism, and belonging: Political discourse and the teaching of history. *Educational Review, 61*(1), 85–100.

Osler, A., & Starkey, H. (2005*). Changing citizenship: Democracy and inclusion in education.* Maidenhead, United Kingdom: Open University Press/McGraw-Hill.

Pettigrew, T. F. (2004). Intergroup contact: Theory, research, and new perspectives. In J. A. Banks & C. A. M. Banks (Eds.), *Handbook of research on multicultural education* (2nd ed., pp. 770–781). San Francisco, CA: Jossey-Bass.

Postiglione, G. A. (2009). The education of ethnic minority groups in China. In J. A. Banks (Ed.), *The Routledge international companion to multicultural education* (pp. 501–511). New York, NY, & London, United Kingdom: Routledge.

Postiglione, G. A. (2014). Education and cultural diversity in multiethnic China. In J. Leibold & C. Yangbin (Eds.), *Minority education in China: Balancing unity and diversity in an era of critical pluralism* (pp. 27–43). Hong Kong, China: Hong Kong University Press.

Riessman, F. (1962). *The culturally deprived child.* New York, NY: Harper & Row.

Rothbart, M., & John, O. P. (1993). Intergroup relations and stereotype change: A social cognitive analysis and some longitudinal findings. In P. M. Sniderman, P. E. Relock, & E. G. Carmines (Eds.), *Prejudice, politics, and the American dilemma* (pp. 1–31). Palo Alto, CA: Stanford University Press.

Schofield, J. W. (2004). Fostering positive intergroup relations in schools. In J. A. Banks & C. A. M. Banks (Eds.), *Handbook of research on multicultural education* (2nd ed., pp. 799–812). San Francisco, CA: Jossey-Bass.

Scott, J. W. (2007). *The politics of the veil.* Princeton, NJ: Princeton University Press.

Slavin, R. E. (1979). Effects of biracial learning teams on cross-racial friendships. *Journal of Educational Psychology, 71,* 381–387.

Slavin, R. E. (1983). *Cooperative learning.* New York, NY: Longman.

Slavin, R. E. (1985). Cooperative learning: Applying contact theory in desegregated schools. *Journal of Social Issues, 41,* 45–62.

Slavin, R. E. (2001). Cooperative learning and intergroup relations. In J. A. Banks & C. A. M. Banks (Eds.), *Handbook of research on multicultural education* (pp. 628–634). San Francisco, CA: Jossey-Bass.

Slavin, R. E., & Madden, N. A. (1979). School practices that improve race relations. *American Educational Research Journal, 16*(2), 169–180.

Smith, E. R., & Mackie, D. M. (1995). *Social psychology.* New York, NY: Worth.

Smitherman, G. (2000). *Talkin that talk: Language, culture, and education in African America.* New York, NY, & London, United Kingdom: Routledge.

Spring, J. (2010). *Deculturalization and the struggle for equality: A brief history of the education of dominated cultures in the United States* (7th ed.). New York, NY: McGraw-Hill.

Steele, D. M., & Cohn-Vargas, B. (2013). *Identity safe classrooms: Places to belong and learn.* Thousand Oaks, CA: Corwin.

Stephan, W. G. (1999). *Reducing prejudice and stereotyping in schools.* New York, NY: Teachers College Press.

Stephan, W. G., & Stephan C. W. (2004). Intergroup relations in multicultural education programs. In J. A. Banks & C. A. M. Banks (Eds.), *Handbook of research on multicultural education* (2nd ed., pp. 782–798). San Francisco, CA: Jossey-Bass.

Suárez-Orozco, M. M. (Ed.). (2007). *Learning in the global era: International perspectives on globalization and education.* Berkeley: University of California Press.

Suárez-Orozco, M. M., & Qin-Hilliard, D. B. (Eds.). (2004). *Globalization: Culture and education in the new millennium.* Berkeley: University of California Press.

Tajfel, H. (1970). Experiments in intergroup discrimination. *Scientific American, 223*(5), 96–102.

Takaki, R. (1993). *A different mirror: A history of multicultural America.* Boston, MA: Little, Brown.

Tomlinson, S. (2009). Multicultural education in the United Kingdom. In J. A. Banks (Ed.), *The Routledge international companion to multicultural education* (pp. 121–133). New York, NY, & London, United Kingdom: Routledge.

Trager, H. G., & Yarrow, M. R. (1952). *They learn what they live: Prejudice in young children.* New York, NY: Harper.

United Nations, Department of Economic and Social Affairs, Population Division, & OECD. (2013, October 3-4). *World migration in figures: A joint contribution by UN-DESA and the OECD to the United Nations High-Level Dialogue on Migration and Development, 3-4 October 2013.* Retrieved from www.oecd.org/els/mig/dioc.htm

United Nations, Department of Economic and Social Affairs, Population Division. (2016). *International migration 2015* (ST/ESA/SER.A/376). Retrieved from www.un.org/en/development/desa/population/migration/publications/wallchart/docs/MigrationWallChart2015.pdf

U.S. Department of State. (2012). Independent states in the world: Fact sheet. Retrieved from www.state.gov/s/inr/rls/4250.htm

Valdés, G. (2001). *Learning and not learning English: Latino students in American schools.* New York, NY: Teachers College Press.

Valencia, R. R. (2010). *Dismantling contemporary deficit thinking: Educational thought and practice.* New York, NY: Routledge.

Valenzuela, A. (1999). *Subtractive schooling: U.S.–Mexican youth and the politics of caring.* Albany, NY: State University of New York Press.

Wan, M. (2004). Ethnic diversity and citizenship education in the People's Republic of China. In J. A. Banks (Ed.), *Diversity and citizenship education: Global perspectives* (pp. 355–376). San Francisco, CA: Jossey-Bass.

Wang, T. (2015). Marginality of rural migrant students in eleven Chinese high schools. *Journal of Ethnic and Cultural Studies, 2*(2), 21–32.

Weiner, M. J., & Wright, F. E. (1973). Effects of undergoing arbitrary discrimination upon subsequent attitudes toward a minority group. *Journal of Applied Social Psychology, 3,* 94–102.

Westheimer, J. (Ed.). (2007). *Pledging allegiance: The politics of patriotism in America's schools.* New York, NY: Teachers College Press.

Westheimer, J., & Kahne, J. (2004). What kind of citizen? The politics of educating for democracy. *American Educational Research Journal, 41*(2), 237–269.

Wong Fillmore, L. (2005). When learning a second language means losing the first. In M. M. Suárez-Orozco, C. Suárez-Orozco, & D. B. Qin (Eds.), *The new immigration: An interdisciplinary reader* (pp. 289–307). New York, NY, & London, United Kingdom: Routledge.

Wood, P. B., & Sonleitner, N. (1996). The effect of childhood interracial contact on adult anti-Black prejudice. *International Journal of Intercultural Relations, 20*(1), 1–17.

Yawkey, T. D., & Blackwell, J. (1974). Attitudes of 4-year-old urban Black children toward themselves and Whites based upon multi-ethnic social studies materials and experiences. *Journal of Educational Research, 67*, 373–377.

Young, I. M. (1989). Polity and group difference: A critique of the ideal of universal citizenship. *Ethics, 99*(2), 250–274.

Young, I. M. (2000). *Inclusion and democracy.* New York, NY: Oxford University Press.

CHAPTER 2

Between Religious/ Ethnic Epistemologies and the Development of Civic Identities in Western Education

Zvi Bekerman

Research across the disciplines shows that schools and education systems serve as primary locations for socialization into collective identities, civic identities, and democratic attitudes and behaviors (Banks, 1997; Galston, 2001; Levy, 2005; Rubin, 2007). Schools embody a framework that strives to offer young people relevant experiences in the realm of political participation and for the development of civic identities. In school, students are exposed to information, interpretation, and practices that tell them about democracy and how it works. Together with other socializing agents, schools are highly influential during a period that is critical to the formation of students' adult personalities, values, attitudes, and behavior patterns as future citizens (Halperin & Bar-Tal, 2006). The classroom in particular serves as a social space in which knowledge, meanings, and identities—ethnic, religious, cultural, and others—are discursively shaped and in which civic identities are continuously negotiated (Pinson, 2007). These negotiations constitute, and are constituted by, the epistemological framings of the coparticipants—teachers and students in the classroom events (Hammer & Elby, 2003; Kienhues, Bromme, & Stahl, 2008).

Epistemologies speak to what counts as knowledge and how it is constructed and evaluated, and as such have implications for all dimensions of life (Hofer, 2000). Beliefs about the nature of knowledge have been shown to influence multiple cognitive processes—comprehension, conceptual change learning, critical evaluation competencies, resolving competing knowledge claims, and theory and evidence coordination (Hofer, 2001; Qian & Alvermann, 2000). Research has also shown the relationships between teacher epistemology, classroom interactions, and related student epistemologies and identities (Johnston, Woodside-Jiron, & Day, 2001; Olafson & Schraw, 2006). While being engaged with classroom narratives, participants acquire, contest, and coconstruct their civic identities. The "unfinished knowledge" (Davies, 2003) of what it means to be a citizen and the ongoing negotiation of civic identities are the foundation for creating a dialogical space of democratic participation in school.

The negotiation of religious, cultural, and civic identities in classrooms is an important problem that focuses and underlies the current discussion on antiracism and marginalization in the public sphere and the concern about the development of civic identities among students who come from immigrant and minority families. By implication it speaks to the question of how classroom discourse and practices define who has the capacity to govern themselves and who lacks such capacities, and how such capacities become effective elements of the formation of political subjects and their subjectivities (Isin, 2012).

For many immigrant and minority students, especially those coming from lower socioeconomic backgrounds, participation in educational institutions of the host/majority societies is a frustrating and mostly unsuccessful experience. Educational theoreticians and practitioners have not been indifferent to this phenomenon and have tried to develop understandings and approaches to alleviate their lot. So far not much success seems to have been achieved. It has become apparent that education, all by itself, cannot offer solace to their plight; without serious structural change—not dependent on educational institutions—the future horizons of this population will stay contracted and in the hands of an unpredictable fate.

In this chapter I will not offer any new solutions; my aim is to widen the discussion in the field of education for us to be able to offer the best we can, given the sociopolitical complexities in which we live. I first review issues related to migrants and minorities in our global world focusing on education. I then consider what seem to me to be the main educational approaches that, from a critical contextual perspective, try to offer partial solutions to the present situation. Finally, I try to link the discussion to issues related to the negotiation of religious and cultural identities in education. My goal is to open up for consideration the importance of focusing on epistemologies—conceptualized as knowledge, beliefs about knowledge, and related values—embedded in particular sociohistorical and cultural contexts represented and interpreted within the frames made available in the intersection between hegemonic and subjugated or alternate formations. Such an approach, I believe, offers a more comprehensive frame for educational considerations than the one accounted for today.

MIGRANTS, MINORITIES, AND EDUCATION

International migration has become a central focus of interest for analysts and policymakers on a variety of subjects, from population aging and public pensions (Bongaarts, 2004) to labor market pressures (DeWaard, Kim, & Raymer, 2012) and education (Brunello & Rocco, 2013).While the era of globalization seems to have encouraged easing restrictions on the movements of goods, services, and capital, international migration—which is also about movements—provokes intense political debate in Western democracies (Breunig, Cao, & Luedtke, 2012). As Hollifield (1998) has argued, migration is the political mirror of trade and finance: while the wealthier states push hard for protection (to keep foreign labor flows out), many poorer states (though rarely explicitly) push for openness. According to United Nations (2013) estimates, the total number of international migrants increased from an estimated 150 million in 2000 to 232 million persons in 2013. Migrants would constitute the fifth most populous country in the world.

It is worth reminding us all that focusing on international migration can give a deceptive picture, for in many countries (e.g., China, India, Brazil) internal migration has reached greater numbers relative to international migration (Castles, 2013). These floating populations moving from peripheral to urban industrialized areas suffer from economic marginalization and legal disadvantages much like migrant populations (Wang, 2015), and their young children suffer from similar disadvantages in the educational systems in which they participate.

Migration (inner or outer) is still often regarded as an exception to sedentary life that is considered to be the rule; and in this sense migration is still not perceived as socially normal. It mostly receives attention when "problematic" social situations—poverty, addiction, delinquency, internal security, unemployment, and political persecution—are revealed against the assumed calmness of the hosting society. While lack of resources are offered as the cause of migration, the "new problems" created in the host society are regarded as side-effects of the migrants' cultural difference, lack of cultural bonding, lack of willingness to integrate, and their "natural" tendency to withdraw into the ethnic community of origin. Thus migration is discursively treated as a problem positioning the migrants (and their culture) at the center of social conflicts that distress the host society. It is only recently that an understanding of migration as a crucial part of modern society has gained increasing ground, for we have come to realize that modern societies are migrant societies (Castles, 2013).

Rather than characterizing migrants and minorities as people needing protection and support to integrate themselves into new surroundings (Cohen, 2001), Western countries characterize them as existential threats (de Haas, 2008), while developing political and legal responses to migration that consist of increased control through bureaucratic systems (Benhabib, 2004). After September 11 the securitization of migration and the construction of migration as a risk has immensely increased (Humphrey, 2013), specifically as it relates to Muslim migrants to Western countries, and has become emblematic of the anxieties of state sovereignty seeking to order, regulate, and integrate the migrant population. Leonard (cited in Humphrey, 2013) suggests that framing migration as a security problem justifies extraordinary legal and policing measures that otherwise would be easily challenged in the liberal political tradition (though they are the product of it) of Western states. Moreover, nationalistic feelings engender negative policies and attitudes against migrant groups and individuals (Wodak & Van Dijk, 2000). These policies and practices lead to hostile treatment of adult migrants and contribute to their social exclusion (Crawley, 2010). Research and first-person accounts reveal varying understandings of migratory experiences among the generations, depending upon whether they or their parents are migrants (Burck, 2007; Cox, 2012).

What lies at the heart of the social and political claim that migrants must integrate is the idea of the national cultural collective of the majority society that describes a specific relationship between the majority and the migrants as members of old or new minorities. While calls for integration might be explicitly mobilized to garner a liberal footing, they frequently conceal assimilative undertones and a drive toward homogeneity in line with normatively positioned "mainstream" perspectives (Bowskill, Lyons, & Coyle, 2007). It is presumed that migrants because of their "foreign" origin are not able to be members of the host society, leading to their quasi- "self-evident" exclusion from the collective "we." It is the majority society's social discourse on integration, directed not to individuals but to culturally homogenized, abstract collectives, that establishes the integration deficit—actual or imagined—of the minority population. All in all, it is methodological nationalism[1] that stands behind these discourses and its social sciences research products (Beck, 2011).

MIGRANT AND MINORITIES IN EDUCATIONAL RESEARCH

Interest in migration is widespread in political, legal, and policy settings (Betts, 2009; Loescher, Betts, & Milner, 2008). Despite the fact that the effects of migration in the labor market have been researched in abundance (Glitz, 2012; Røed & Schøne, 2012), the growing body of research about the impact of immigration on the education system is still scant (Gould, Lavy, & Paserman, 2009). Yet it can easily be assumed that flows of immigration impact educational organizations if only because they change the composition of students in schools and classes, adding to the traditional challenges confronting traditional school systems. It is only recently that migrants and their dependents have become of interest to educational research, allowing for questions regarding the potential influence of an increased share of immigrants in schools and classes on the school performance of natives to be researched (Betts & Fairlie, 2003; Brunello & Rocco, 2013).

Culture in this research context may refer to cultural, ethnic, and religious perspectives that challenge the normative societal and educational assumptions held by the host nation (Palmary, 2007) or challenges to assumptions about young migrant people's learning (Warwick, Neville, & Smith, 2006). Many times young migrants encounter criticisms of their cultural, ethnic, or religious heritages and practices (Bekerman & Geisen, 2011), or denial of their significance and value, which result in oppressive and limiting constructs of young migrant people. Yet the cultures of young migrant people themselves (Kasinitz, Mollenkopf, Waters, & Holdaway, 2008) and of receiving nations (Portes, 2006) are less fixed and more fluid than appearances suggest they are (Cox, 2012).

As immigrant and minority students join native-born students in educational institutions, issues related to race, language, culture, religion, and social status make their appearance and challenge the academic and social participation of immigrant and minority students in these settings. Students from migrant or minority groups face more cultural barriers and have fewer cultural resources in the form of cultural capital to make use of in the hosting educational context (Bourdieu, 1993). Given that socioeconomic status is clearly linked to school quality and teacher quality and given that immigrant families often live in poorer areas and/or in ethnically segregated concentrations, immigrant students tend to participate in schools with fewer resources, which are unable to offer a safe and disciplined climate (Pong & Hao, 2007), thus lowering students' positive attitudes toward school while heightening their sense of alienation (Anderman, 2003).

Immigrant and minority students have been found to have stronger cognitive engagement attitudes toward school but a weaker sense of emotional involvement at school than native students. Native students, who sense a better teacher-student relationship and teacher support, seem to have a weaker attitude toward school but a greater sense of belonging (Chiu, Pong, Mori, & Chow, 2012). These findings are important, for adolescents with a greater sense of belonging at school—which has been linked to cognitive and psychological functioning—often have higher intrinsic motivation and a higher academic performance (Roeser, Midgley, & Urdan, 1996). In a way these studies are paradoxical, for earlier studies (in the United States) have shown immigrant students arriving in schools with positive attitudes (Suárez-Orozco, 2001). In contrast, second-generation immigrant students were found to have a negative attitude—a pattern of generation decline consistent with the "immigrant paradox" in academic achievement in which first-generation immigrant students outperform following generations (Pong & Landale, 2012).

Portes and Rumbaut (2001) did research on second-generation immigrants in the United States focusing on issues of education and employment. In their study they highlight the ways in which identity negotiation mediates patterns of acculturation and academic achievement. They point out that children of immigrants are inescapably engaged in the process of making sense of who they are and finding a meaningful place in the receiving society. Their study highlights the positive effects of what they term *selective acculturation* both on students' self-esteem and academic achievement. In contrast to full assimilation, selective acculturation supports partial retention of parents' home language and norms, thus strengthening self-esteem and supporting academic achievement. They confidently posit that "children who learn the language and culture of their new country without losing those of the old, have a much better understanding of their place in the world" (p. 274). Bishop and Berryman (2006) have also explored the processes of identity negotiation and how they intersect with societal power relations. They concluded that effective education for minorities (the Maori in their case) needs to challenge coercive societal power relations by affirming students' identities in educational settings.

Stereotype threat (Smith & Hung, 2008) is also a main factor affecting the academic performance of minority students. The threat of being poorly judged based on the negative stereotypes attached to minority group membership undercuts the self-esteem and educational performance of minority children (Schofield

& Bangs, 2006). Cummins (2012) synthesized the international research literature on the educational achievement of immigrant and minority language students by articulating three propositions for which there is strong empirical evidence: (1) Print access and literacy engagement play a key role in promoting reading comprehension; (2) the development of bilingual students' first language proficiency plays a positive role in second-language academic development; and (3) societal power relations play a direct causal role in promoting school failure among students from subordinated communities. Cummins' reading of the empirical data stands in strong contrast to the conclusions of recent North American and European reviews, which acknowledge the legitimacy of bilingual education as a policy option but say very little about the role of literacy engagement in promoting reading comprehension.

SOME TRADITIONAL EDUCATIONAL SOLUTIONS

Two main educational approaches, anchored in critical perspectives that recognize the impossibility of detaching education from economic and political processes, have evolved over the last decades to help educators develop effective pedagogical tools to work with students from diverse backgrounds: culturally relevant pedagogy and funds of knowledge. *Culturally relevant pedagogy* is conceptualized as a pedagogical approach that, by using cultural referents to impart knowledge and skills, has the potential for empowering students intellectually, socially, and emotionally (Ladson-Billings, 1995). In its origin this theoretical approach emphasized a wide understanding of what is needed by teachers to implement a culturally sensitive approach—namely, conceptions of self and others, social relations, and conceptions of knowledge—all attuned to the populations involved in the educational setting (Ladson-Billings, 1995). The approach has evolved and been adapted to a variety of settings and disciplines (e.g., in respect to African American students, see Howard, 2001, and Hefflin, 2002); today it would be difficult to find a definition that could easily account for all its different implementations.

Studies have described the difficulties that teachers experience when adopting a culturally relevant stand and culturally relevant pedagogies in their classrooms because of their cultural biases and ethnic prejudices (Cochran-Smith, 2004; Gay, 2002). A small scale study by Young (2010) revealed deep structural issues related to teachers' cultural bias, the nature of racism in school settings, and the lack of support to adequately implement theory into practice, all of which shadow the enthusiasm that accompanied these theoretical developments when they were first developed.

Funds of knowledge offers a conceptual framework that informs educational practice when it encounters student diversity. The concept was originally developed by Velez-Ibanez and Greenberg (1992) and extended from anthropology to education by Moll, Amanti, Neff, and González (1992). It argues that the best way to learn about the lives of people is by getting to know what people do and what they say about what they do (González, 2005). Given that teachers usually align with, recognize, and support middle-class knowledge and expression, students from minority or migrant families suffer serious disadvantages because there is a lack of alignment between their knowledge and the teachers' knowledge. Funds of knowledge suggest a way to overcome these gaps and misfits by encouraging teachers to consider how the knowledge gained from researching the local sites in which students evolve and the resources they use to gain knowledge can be brought into the classrooms to increase the academic achievement of marginalized students.

Recent studies (Hogg, 2011) have shown multiple definitions of funds of knowledge when this conceptualization is applied in varying contexts and when it applies to the understanding of what these funds are and whose knowledge is being accounted for. Oughton (2010) has raised concerns regarding the attempt to develop culturally responsive pedagogies following knowledge gained through a funds of knowledge approach because this activity may risk portraying groups as homogeneous and as possessing fixed cultural traits. Preventing such a development implies a commitment to a critical and reflective position on the part of teachers in order to avoid imposing their own cultural arbitraries on learners, however well intentioned.

The efforts mentioned above are laudable, yet seem not to have been able to offer solutions to the intricate problems they rightfully identified. I will next discuss the intersection between the religious and the civic as these are reflected in both minority and majority sites and chronologies.

On the Civic and the Religious in Education

Within the wider cultural context the development of civic engagement (identity) among youths from nondominant groups poses an ongoing challenge to societal institutions in many Western countries (Banks, 2008; Meer & Modood, 2009). Close to the focus on civic attachment there is a growing recognition among scholars that religion is an important determinant of civic engagement (Gibson, 2008). Though the proper role and influence of religion in the public sphere continues to be contested, it has been widely argued that religion makes valuable contributions to civic participation and that religiously grounded beliefs should be fully welcomed in political decision-making (Kunzman, 2005). Youniss (2011) has posited the relevance of a citizenry actively participating in shaping and responding to policy and government by partaking in civic organizations that represent interests and promote value traditions that have roots in religion, civic movements, social justice, and the like; he suggests that civic education should be more than acquiring a set of facts, learning about rights and obligations, and becoming an informed voter.

The ongoing public debate about the resurgence of religion in the public sphere in contemporary Western societies indicates that, challenged with an increasingly heterogeneous citizenry, "secular" societies have to come to terms with the rights and claims for the public expression of beliefs and practices of religio-cultural minorities, especially today's Muslim minorities (Jews and other minorities suffered similar restrictions in the past), and with the ongoing definition of citizenship and shared civic identities of diverse citizens in these countries.

In all that relates to civic engagement and civic education, a return to cosmopolitanism has been suggested as a possible path to overcome assimilationist national policies (Banks, 2008; Beck, 2009; Nussbaum, 1994/2002), though mostly from theoretical perspectives. The return to cosmopolitanism could be interpreted as working, if not against, at least in parallel to culturally sensitive approaches. To this apparent complexity, I give my attention in the following section because it is the politics, more than the culture, that counts in all that relates to equity and social justice.

Citizenship Contested

Throughout modern history *citizenship*—an elusive, contested, and multifaceted concept (Pinson, 2007)—has been used to describe a variety of phenomena related to legal status, communal membership, and political identity. Civic identities are currently understood as important means toward social cohesion in ethnically, culturally, and religiously diverse societies. As such, they are central to the democratic functioning of such societies (McLaughlin, 1992; Ong, 1996; Phillips, 2010). Of late, the formal conceptualization of citizenship as based on a rights model has been transformed to denote substantive active dimensions in the construction of identities oriented toward the state as a political unit and/or toward transnational or cosmopolitan collectivities (Delanty, 1997).

In Western societies today citizenship and civic identities are contested, and their definition and societal acceptance is tied to ongoing social and political struggles over equality and difference within societies based on social closure (Turner, 2007; Yuval-Davis, 1999). The boundaries of citizenship and civic identities then serve as constant sites for social and political struggles between dominant and nondominant groups in the public sphere and its institutions. Current empirical studies from a range of Western countries indicate that in all that relates to the ongoing exclusion of minorities from the public sphere of Western societies and the alienation of minorities from embracing identities as citizens, it is the adoption of civic identities that presents the central problem that needs to be addressed (Halperin & Bar-Tal, 2006).

Based on the accumulating literature concerned with the transmission and development of young people's understanding of citizenship and civic identities, there is evidence that the development of civic identities is linked to other salient social identities. Empirical studies on civic identities among minority youths suggest that the formation of civic identities of youths whose coexisting identities have been "rejected" appears to be troubled (Heitmeyer, 2005; Heitmeyer & Anhut, 2008). Kahanec and Tosun (2009) found that perceived negative attitudes of natives negatively affected the citizenship interest of immigrants across several cohorts. Alternate and intertwining social identities include religious identity, ethnic background, nationality (Yuval-Davis, 1999), cultural–civilizational heritage, and political orientation. These intertwined identities may either align neatly, appear in combinations, or appear to exclude each other.

Western countries today have rising numbers of citizens who are born into religio-cultural communities other than the dominant, especially Muslim communities (but also Jewish, Christian neo-Pentecostal, and Christian Charismatic). The claims of Muslim communities, for example, for the public expression of their beliefs and practices in the "secular" institutions of society has led to the emergence of a public debate over how to handle the "religious" in the institutions, civic society, and public sphere of "postsecular" society (Amir-Moazami, 2005; Fischer, Hotam, & Wexler, 2012). The current public concern with the resurgence of the religious in the public sphere in contemporary Western societies forces us to refocus our attention not just on the cultural but on the intersection of civic and religio-cultural identities (Dalsheim, 2010; Hagan & Ebaugh, 2003; Kastoryano, 2004; Peri, 2012; Salvatore, 2006).

Citizenship as Hegemonic

To discuss the master narratives of citizenship in general and as they relate to the religious, the concept of *hegemony* is helpful (Bourdieu, 1993; Gramsci, 1971; Lears, 1985; Lemish, 2010; Mouffe, 1988; Roseberry, 1994; Sayer, 1994). Hegemonic formations represent ensembles of relatively stable social forms and relations; they are the socially articulated result of the reciprocal reaction of different social groups to each other (Mouffe, 1988). The master narratives of Western countries today have been shown to be built on and synthesize accumulating hegemonic discourses about the civilizational, cultural, religious, ethnic, and political heritage of the dominant groups of society (Asad, 2003; Mignolo, 2003). While hegemony is never conclusively established and is continually contested (Bakhtin, 1981; Gramsci, 1971), analyses of discourse and institutional practices indicate that the hegemonic formations momentarily established within and across the West erase the ethnic, cultural, and religious diversity of their citizens and subsume the heterogeneous citizenries and their various worldviews to the hegemonic narratives. These narratives are overtly secular and rationalist, but latently civilizational, racialized, and religious.

The hegemonic formation of citizenship and related concepts (democracy, rationality, liberalism, and secularism) engenders a civilizational narrative, in which the West and its history is portrayed in its continuity with Judeo-Christian traditions and Occidental civilization. While these contours of a Judeo-Christian tradition have been called a "fictitious amalgam" almost synonymous to the similarly vague notion of "Western values," this amalgam is a dominant hegemonic formation that entails an otherizing and re-Orientalizing of Islam (Salvatore, 2006). Based on a view of the inherited historical conflicts with Islam, "Western civilization" and "Islamic civilization" are presented as essentialized and opposed entities whose traits are conferred to their populations (Featherstone, 2009; Goody, 2006; Said, 1979), and the impossibility of value consensus between these entities is one of its core claims (Huntington, 1996). By extension, it is arguable that this formation ascribes essentialized political values onto those entities: democratic values onto those categorized to be Western and Judeo-Christian, and fundamentalist values onto those categorized as Muslim (similar phenomena can be identified in fundamentalist trends within the Christian and Jewish tradition as well) (Bekerman & Neuman, 2001; Lawrence, 1995).

An important aspect of the civilizational master narrative is a cultural narrative which positions "Western culture" as opposed to, for example, "Muslim-oriental culture" (Said, 2000); as such, it represents one variation of a cultural–civilizational discourse specified and customized to national and regional contexts (Dumont, 1986; Grosfoguel & Mielants, 2006). Entailed in the civilizational–cultural narrative is also an implicit religious dimension that is based on the alleged "Judeo-Christian" civilizational roots of society. Importantly, as competing narratives are not mutually exclusive, the religious dimension in the construction of "Western" versus "Islamic civilizations" coexists today with a narrative of the "West" as secular.

A secular narrative in which the "West" is portrayed as the heir of Enlightenment and, as such, secular and rationalist (Asad, 2003) represents a second hegemonic formation of citizenship in European countries today. Building on the civilizational narrative, secularity is portrayed as a logical and modern continuation of Judeo-Christian traditions and Occidental civilization (Mignolo, 2003). Media discourses and public debates across the West struggle with a modern and secular self-understanding that needs to be guarded against the threat of a backlash into the religious. The hierarchical construction of the religious and the secular as linear progression in historical time is contrasted by both historical and philosophical views on "secular" societies, which cannot attest to a negation of the religious in contemporary society (Fischer et al., 2012). In contrast, the tacit endurance of religious ideas, and hence the intertwining of religion and democracy in Western societies, has been amply documented (Asad, 2003; Özyürek, 2005).

The transformation of former theological concepts into "democratic" social and political concepts is at the center of this political–theological intertwining (Diner, 2000; Fischer et al., 2012). Accordingly, empirical studies show that in different national settings, the segregation of religion and state is executed to different degrees (e.g., French laïcité, Germany as "in-between-state") (Amir-Moazami, 2005). In the literature there is, however, a consensus that the "dialectic of secularization" (Goldstein, 2009), an admixture of secular and religious notions, is embedded within the secular imperative of contemporary "Western" societies itself.

The current resurgence of the religious in contemporary European societies may best be understood as a public contestation of hitherto implicit, yet manifest, religious guiding principles around which European societies and their institutions—which discriminate against religious minorities—were organized. With the demands of religious minorities for participation in the public sphere, the secular master narrative has faced a breakdown of the clear-cut divide between the religious and the modern, and the secular and the theological (Fischer et al., 2012). Western civil societies are then struggling with the question of how to integrate religious minorities into the institutions of their societies.

Moreover, the hegemonic formation of citizenship is based on the master narrative of ethnicity. Though citizenship is seen as separate from nationality or ethnicity, in this narrative citizenship is implicitly linked to a racializing discourse (blood ties, *jus sanguinis*), which assigns people to memberships in different groups based on their discordance from the blood of their parents (Aktürk, 2011; Herzog, 1997; Sand, 2009). The ethnic master narrative sees an ethnic nation sharing a common descent, and it is the ethnic nation, not the citizenry, that shapes the symbols, laws, and policies of the state.

The narrative distinguishes strongly between members of the ethnic nation and nonmembers. Social closure to new members characterizes ethnic nations, though various means of immigration are possible (e.g., via marriage to a member of the ethnic nation, birth as a mixed offspring, and religious conversion) (Turner, 2007). Nonmembers of the ethnic nation are regarded as less desirable and as a serious threat to the survival and integrity of the ethnic nation. This threat is phrased in terms of "biological dilution, demographic swamping, cultural downgrading, security danger, subversion, and political instability" (Smooha, 2002, p. 478).

Based on these hegemonic formations, contemporary master narratives of citizenship are built on different variations of intersecting and accumulating discourses of religion, ethnicity, culture, civilization, and political orientation. As such, they are rich spheres of ideational stuff that allow us to move across lines when considering minority/majority encounters.

HOW IS THIS RELEVANT TO OUR DISCUSSION?

In the West the civic often masks the religious. It should come then as no surprise that migrants and minorities express distrust and/or sense a strong clash between their unarticulated perception, civic religious Western perspectives, and their own religious traditions (Janmaat, 2008; McLaren, 2012; Vlas & Gherghina, 2012). Moreover, the literature shows that there is an intimate tie between social identities, social relationships, and epistemological beliefs (Schommer, 1994; Schommer-Aikins, 2004). The idea of how knowledge is negotiated or how one judges the quality of knowledge is affected by how one relates to other people—the degree of perceived closeness between people (social relationships), as well as the degree of perceived status differences among people (class, minoritization). The settings in which identities, belonging, and dominant–nondominant relations are being negotiated thus have implications for the voicing of epistemological positions and vice versa.

Religious epistemologies, as other private epistemologies, have implications for all dimensions of life as they speak to what counts as knowledge and how knowledge is constructed and evaluated (Hofer, 2004). Beliefs about the nature of knowledge have been shown to influence comprehension, cognitive processing, conceptual change learning, and the competency to critically evaluate information, resolve competing knowledge claims, and coordinate theory and evidence (Hofer & Pintrich, 1997; King & Kitchener, 1994; Kuhn, 1991; Qian & Alvermann, 2000; Schommer, 1994). To date, the question whether the construction of epistemological beliefs can be influenced through direct instruction is open for research. What is evident, however, is that epistemological beliefs share with other belief systems characteristics such as affective components, limited adherence to logic, difficulty in changing, and powerful influence on thinking (Schommer-Aikins, 2004). Unlike knowledge systems, epistemological belief systems "do not require general or group consensus regarding the validity and appropriateness of their beliefs. Individual beliefs do not even require internal consistency within the belief system. This nonconsensuality implies that belief systems are by their very nature disputable, more inflexible, and less dynamic than knowledge systems" (Pajares, 1992, p. 311). In sum, epistemological beliefs are often unreflected, they are "comfortable" and not easy to change, and their general fuzziness adds to the challenge of addressing them (Schommer, 1994). This might help explain the essentializing tendency found even in those who hold to culturally sensitive perspectives.

Religious Epistemologies Subjugated

Religious epistemologies often contradict secular epistemic traditions on what counts as authoritative knowledge, how competing knowledge claims may be resolved, and how theory and evidence can be coordinated. Students who hold these epistemologies are often judged as irrational, premodern, or anti-Western by their nonreligious peers and teachers (Gottlieb, 2008). However, as research has shown, the developmental progression of epistemological reasoning from prereflective (including religious reasoning) to reflective thinking (seeing knowledge as constructed) posited by early research is not as linear as it had been assumed (Kuhn, Cheney, & Weinstock, 2000). Research shows that cognitively sophisticated and mature individuals subscribe to religious epistemological beliefs that would have been described as immature or naive by early research (Gottlieb, 2008). There is a great variability of how people of different ages reason (King & Kitchener, 2004), and religious epistemologies are included in this variability, independent of intellectual ability or maturity. Nevertheless, today religious epistemologies represent a type of "subjugated knowledges . . . that have been disqualified as inadequate to their task or insufficiently elaborated: naive knowledges, located low down on the hierarchy, beneath the required level of cognition or scientificity" (Foucault, 1980, p. 82).

Needless to say, when embarking on a study of the religious/civic/communal epistemologies of minorities, and now majorities too, it is of utmost importance to differentiate between religious epistemologies as relatively stable belief systems as expressed by nonexpert "novices" (Chen & Pajares, 2010; Smith, diSessa, & Roschelle, 1993–1994) and the many contemporary trends in contemporary religious interpretation that express diverse ideological tendencies within religious culture including but not limited to "traditional," "moderate," "liberal," and "progressive" orientations. Minority students and majority teachers (and students too) may be assumed, thus, to come to the classroom with diverse interpretive frames that allow for quite different negotiations of what counts as knowledge (Stahl, 2011). It is arguable that various religious positions are represented among these participants and that, in fact, many are "dwelling between labels." This is where our claims might have an important contribution, the fissure between "traditional" epistemologies and overtly secular classroom discourse may be the most urgent to address in contemporary educational practice.

Legitimizing Epistemologies

The incommensurability of "traditional" religious epistemologies and secular hegemonic discourse is situated in a historic construction of what counts as legitimate knowledge that has its roots in the era of Enlightenment (Mignolo, 2009). Because the overlap with secular "scientific" knowledge systems appears to be higher, in public debates there is a tendency to engage more interlocutors who represent "progressive" or "reform" strands of religious hermeneutics (AlSayyad & Castells, 2002; Inglehart, 2007). The discursive erasure of "traditional" religious epistemologies from the public sphere is philosophically and ethically contested, yet a social fact. We posit that, linked to the ongoing process of re-religionization and retraditionalization (Hagan & Ebaugh, 2003; Peri, 2012), it is especially the incommensurable positions encountered in everyday classroom discourse and practice that are most important to explore and to understand today. We hypothesize that in studying how incommensurable epistemologies encounter each other, several possibilities exist: erasure (as in the public sphere); cultural relativism, that is, regarding these as autochthonous and insular entities in their own right; and what Mignolo (1995) has called "plurotopic hermeneutics." We posit that, as today's cultures and epistemologies begin to mingle and translation between them becomes inevitable (Isin, 2012), what is ideally required in classrooms is "an interactive concept of knowledge and understanding that reflects on the very process of constructing (e.g., putting in order) that portion of the world to be known" (Mignolo, 2003, p. 15). The emphasis on the negotiations of what counts as legitimate knowledge is not new and has partially been the sphere of activity of the educational approaches mentioned above. Focusing on the civic/religious is just more inclusive because it allows for multiple memberships to intersect, memberships that belong at once to multiple sites and chronologies, and because—what is more important—its focus can be (should be) minority/majority hybrid.

Entailed in this process is the collaborative negotiation of new conceptions of what counts as legitimate knowledge in the public sphere and its institutions and how this knowledge is linked to notions of civics and citizenship. This process may include "undoing knowledge" as it involves deorientalizing and decolonizing the ways in which legitimate knowledge has been instituted through scientific and educational practices (Mignolo, 2003); "uncovering knowledge" that has been masked and disqualified by hegemonic discourse (Foucault, 1980); and "reinventing knowledge," which includes forging new conceptions of unconcealed knowledges (Isin, 2012; Mignolo, 2009). All three are directly linked to understandings of who has the right to speak as a citizen and how, and with this they speak to ways in which civic identities can be enacted through creative microacts of citizenship while not focusing only on minority migrant "cultures."

Widening the Research Agenda

As our discussion of the intertwining hegemonic formations of citizenship discourse has shown, dominant students, teachers, and especially the curriculum draw on intersecting civilizational, secular, and ethnic narratives. Hence, in the classroom various religious and secular epistemologies and identities are in conflict, and due to their very nature, it is not argumentative force that can decide this epistemic conflict in the classroom. How then do students and teachers negotiate this impasse? We hypothesize that, in a context in which hegemonic formations of citizenship discourse intertwine religious, cultural, ethnic, and political identities, religious/cultural epistemologies will be seen to index (i.e., vary according to context features) these other social identities framed by this discourse in the discursive space of the classroom.

As the concern of research and policy is shifting away from the either–or question whether it is religious minorities that have to change or societal institutions, that is, whether the process toward societal integration of a diverse population into one civic body works via assimilation of the minority or a perceived loss of "cultural identity" of the dominant society, we need to develop research attentive to processes that might enhance or constrain the transformation of newly emerging civic/religious/cultural identities. This research would explore the conditions provided for youths—from dominant and nondominant groups—to navigate these identities, and the ways how, under these conditions, students are able to construct "transversal" (Yuval-Davis, 1999) identities as both minorities and as citizens of their countries. Attention needs to be paid to how the negotiation of civic identities and religio-cultural identities and epistemologies plays out in the everyday practices of and artifacts in schools and classrooms.

More specifically, in educational contexts in which diverse cultural, religious, and secular paradigms compete for hegemony we need to uncover how minority youths' religious epistemologies are represented in the discursive space of the classroom and its related artifacts (such as curriculum, imagery). We need to explore the hegemonic formations of religious and secular–occidental civilizational paradigms and practices in the classroom, as well as the discursive construction of religious minorities and their epistemologies (e.g., possibly as premodern and naive) by peers, teachers, and curricula.

When focusing on the prism of religious epistemologies, we need to explore how minority and majority students—and their teachers—negotiate what counts as knowledge in this contested space. How is authority of knowledge invoked, negotiated, and argued for? How does negotiation, construction, and contestation of knowledge happen? Is there space for the voice of minority youths whose views do not align with the hegemonic narrative? If yes, which conditions, understandings, and classroom practices characterize these classrooms? If not, what appears to hinder the development of a dialogic space?

We also need to ask, how do religious minority students interpret the negotiation of epistemological authority and how do they connect this to their identities as citizens of the countries they live in? How do students perceive the construction of an equal and open dialogic space in their classrooms? How do students relate their experiences about the (non)validity of their religious epistemologies to their status as citizens of the country?

The above is a call to widen our present discussion on the need to sensitize teachers, curriculum, and educational practice to include an appreciation of the civic and the religious/cultural and the epistemologies that encompass them all in educational work. The civic covers wide spectrums of knowledge and activity. It is in a sense transdisciplinary and it is also fundamentally political, thus not allowing (hopefully) the denial of the political in education. In this way it is a sphere of activity that fits the emancipatory critical approaches that identified those who urged educators and education to adopt culturally sensitive approaches. The civic as analyzed above is intimately related to the religious, thus allowing for the drawing of new boundaries. "Modern" and "traditional" are now positioned in a common ground, a relaxing imagined hierarchies if seriously considered. And, if this is indeed so, the emphasis on the civic and religious might help in some small way to prevent cultural essentialization—*culturally we are all not only civic/communal but also religious; we are similar*. We all play on a common stage that needs to be critically approached. We need to understand not just the cultural backyard of the migrant but ours as well.

Our analytical approach needs to be more inclusive. Our traditional attempts to recognize and legitimate others' cultural practice need to be complemented by an analysis of our own cultural milieu focusing on the civic/political and its immediate outcomes as these shape our present lives (in the polis). Doing so might help open a better dialogue in which we all become suspects but also possible collaborators, not in the defense of a nonexistent fixed culture but instead in the work of shaping a better present.

POSTSCRIPT

The National Academy of Education workshop that was the genesis of this book was an intellectually rich environment where I encountered a variety of theoretical and methodological approaches, which ultimately sharpened my questioning about what can be expected in practical terms from research in education and about which type of research is the one that I favor when considering what I think can be done. Clearly, all serious research has much to contribute to our knowledge;

thus what I question is not any specific research approach. If macrosociological research shows that a rather small number of immigrant or minority students have better chances to be included and integrated in a host/majority student's classroom than when they outnumber the majority/powerful students, this is important knowledge. If we know that an immigrant has better chances to learn the host society language when living in the midst of the host society and not in segregated neighborhoods, this is also important information. Of no less importance is understanding that the better predictors of educational success are the parent's level of education or the rate of incarceration. Yet, this knowledge—all of which has been repeatedly documented in the research literature—seems not to have been able to successfully influence educational policy. Moreover, many of the categories that are used by this research (such as immigrant, ethnicity, nationality, and bilingual) seem to be assumed to be normal. *Methodological nationalism* understood as the assumption that the nation/state/society is the natural social and political form of the modern world stands at the basis of this uncritical approach. So not only has macroresearch not succeeded in influencing policy, but it risks fixing the same categories and constructs that constitute the problem that it is trying to solve.

There are other risks that need to be considered in educational research today, and these relate to what I would call, for lack of better concepts, "methodological psychologism" and "methodological schoolism." The main assumptions (and following suggested correctives) of educational research rise from a psychological paradigm that assumes the existence of a universal solipsistic individual detached from context and historical development. These psychological perspectives seem to be supported by philosophical idealistic approaches that ultimately rest on transcendental premises that do not always fit a scientific empirical commitment. Even when context and historical development are accounted for, the realities of massive educational policies cannot seriously acknowledge them. Last, education understood mostly as schooling disregards that schools are technologies that have evolved through centuries and deploy specific patterns of knowledge (as compartmentalized), strategies and activities (focusing on the individual and its cognition) that reflect specific sociopolitical underpinnings, which tint all their undertakings.

The National Academy of Education workshop allowed for only a limited treatment of these issues; much more time and effort are needed to revise them in depth while trying to uncover their implications for vulnerable immigrant and minority groups in educational settings. My own work tries to focus on these issues, assuming they flow from an epistemological Western perspective that goes unacknowledged, thus sustaining its power and not allowing for potential change. I focus on the intersection between civic and religious/cultural education, which I realize are narrow concepts many times open to misinterpretation. It was clear that in the workshop setting "religious/cultural education" was suspect of hiding support for much of what liberal humanist perspectives find to be aberrations. Even if it were (which clearly is not what I have in mind), denying them is not a solution but is the problem itself. If, as discussed in the workshop, "reactive ethnicity" partially explains the "rejection" of immigrant minority groups by the (threatened) host society, this reaction may very well work in both directions. I do not believe the clash between the reactive ethnicity of both the host and the migrant/minority societies can be dealt with in full in education, but I believe that education can become a sphere where we can help students realize how these clashes are constructed, upon which constructed naturalized assumptions they rest, and through which practices they are put into play.

Civic education—not as representing a compartmentalized subject of studies, but as a conglomerate of interconnected fields of practical knowledge—might be the area that needs to be researched, first to realize how, as implemented today, it supports and at times accentuates ethnic reactivity and then to ask ourselves which educational strategies and practices might need to be implemented to sooth these tensions. In this sense my goals are modest and focused on what goes on in the practical educational arena, which is the place where I think our research might achieve some small success.

NOTE

1. The social sciences tendency to conceptualize social phenomena around the boundaries of the nation-state creates a set of blinders for the social sciences that makes it difficult to capture some crucially important forms of social interaction and structure.

REFERENCES

Aktürk, S. (2011). Regimes of ethnicity: Comparative analysis of Germany, the Soviet Union/Post-Soviet Russia, and Turkey. *World Politics, 63*(1), 115–164.

AlSayyad, N., & Castells, M. (Eds.). (2002). *Muslim Europe or Euro-Islam: Politics, culture, and citizenship in the age of globalization.* Lanham, MD: Lexington Books.

Amir-Moazami, S. (2005). Muslim challenges to the secular consensus: A German case study. *Journal of Contemporary European Studies, 13*(3), 267–286.

Anderman, L. H. (2003). Academic and social perceptions as predictors of change in middle school students' sense of school belonging. *Journal of Experimental Education, 72*(1), 5–22.

Asad, T. (2003). *Formations of the secular: Christianity, Islam, modernity.* Stanford, CA: Stanford University Press.

Bakhtin, M. M. (1981). Discourse in the novel (C. Emerson & M. Holquist, Trans.). In M. Holquist (Ed.), *The dialogic imagination: Four Essays* (pp. 259–422). Austin, TX: University of Texas Press.

Banks, J. A. (1997). *Educating citizens in a multicultural society.* New York, NY: Teachers College Press.

Banks, J. A. (2008). Diversity, group identity, and citizenship education in a global age. *Educational Researcher, 37*(3), 129–139.

Beck, U. (2009). Critical theory of world risk society: A cosmopolitan vision. *Constellations, 16*(1), 3–22.

Beck, U. (2011). Cosmopolitanism as imagined communities of global risk. *American Behavioral Scientist, 55*(10), 1346–1361.

Bekerman, Z., & Geisen, T. (2011) *International handbook of migration, minorities and education: Understanding cultural and social differences in processes of learning*. Dordrecht, The Netherlands: Springer.

Bekerman, Z., & Neuman, Y. (2001). Joining their betters rather than their own: The modern/postmodern rhetoric of Jewish fundamentalist preachers. *Journal of Communication Inquiry, 25*(2), 184–199.

Benhabib, S. (2004). *The rights of others: Aliens, residents and citizens*. Cambridge, United Kingdom: Cambridge University Press.

Betts, A. (2009). *Forced migration and global politics*. West Sussex, United Kingdom: Wiley Blackwell.

Betts, J. R., & Fairlie, R. W. (2003). Does immigration induce "native flight" from public schools into private schools? *Journal of Public Economics, 87*(5–6), 987–1012.

Bishop, R., & Berryman, M. (2006). *Culture speaks: Cultural relationships and classroom learning*. Wellington, New Zealand: Huia Publishers.

Bongaarts, J. (2004). Population aging and the rising cost of public pensions. *Population and Development Review, 30*(1), 1–23.

Bourdieu, P. (1993). *Sociology in question*. London, United Kingdom: Sage.

Bowskill, M., Lyons, E., & Coyle, A. (2007). The rhetoric of acculturation: When integration means assimilation. *British Journal of Social Psychology, 46*(4), 793–813.

Breunig, C., Cao, X., & Luedtke, A. (2012). Global migration and political regime type: A democratic disadvantage. *British Journal of Political Science, 42*(04), 825–854.

Brunello, G., & Rocco, L. (2013). The effect of immigration on the school performance of natives: Cross country evidence using PISA test scores. *Economics of Education Review, 32*, 234–246.

Burck, C. (2007). *Multi-lingual living: Explorations in language and subjectivity*. Basingstoke, Hampshire, United Kingdom: Palgrave Macmillan.

Castles, S. (2013). The forces driving global migration. *Journal of Intercultural Studies, 34*(2), 122–140.

Chen, J. A., & Pajares, F. (2010). Implicit theories of ability of grade 6 science students: Relation to epistemological beliefs and academic motivation and achievement in science. *Contemporary Educational Psychology, 35*(1), 75–87.

Chiu, M. M., Pong, S.-L., Mori, I., & Chow, B. W.-Y. (2012). Immigrant students' emotional and cognitive engagement at school: A multilevel analysis of students in 41 countries. *Journal of Youth and Adolescence, 41*(11), 1409–1425.

Cochran-Smith, M. (2004). Defining the outcomes of teacher education: What's social justice got to do with it? *Asia-Pacific Journal of Teacher Education, 32*(3), 193–212.

Cohen, S. (2001). *States of denial: Knowing about atrocities and suffering*. Cambridge, United Kingdom: Polity Press.

Cox, P. (2012). Beyond limits and limitations: Reflections on learning processes in contexts of migration and young people. In Z. Bekerman & T. Geisen (Eds.), *International handbook of migration, minorities and education: Understanding cultural and social differences in processes of learning* (pp. 35–52). Dordrecht, The Netherlands: Springer.

Crawley, H. (2010). "No one gives you a chance to say what you are thinking": Finding space for children's agency in the UK asylum system. *Area, 42*(2), 162–169.

Cummins, J. (2012). The intersection of cognitive and sociocultural factors in the development of reading comprehension among immigrant students. *Reading and Writing, 25*(8), 1973–1990.

Dalsheim, J. (2010). On demonized Muslims and vilified Jews: Between theory and politics. *Comparative Studies in Society and History, 52*(03), 581–603.

Davies, I. (2003). *Education and conflict: Complexity and chaos*. London, United Kingdom: Routledge-Falmer.

de Haas, H. (2008). The myth of invasion: The inconvenient realities of African migration to Europe. *Third World Quarterly, 29*(7), 1305–1322.

Delanty, G. (1997). Models of citizenship: Defining European identity and citizenship. *Citizenship Studies, 1*(3), 285–303.

DeWaard, J., Kim, K., & Raymer, J. (2012). Migration systems in Europe: Evidence from harmonized flow data. *Demography, 49*(4), 1307–1333.

Diner, D. (2000). *Beyond the conceivable: Studies on Germany, Nazism, and the Holocaust*. Berkeley, CA: University of California Press.

Dumont, L. (1986). Are cultures living beings? German identity in interaction. *Man, 21*(4), 587–604.

Featherstone, M. (2009). Occidentalism: Jack Goody and comparative history. *Theory, Culture & Society, 26*(7–8),1–15.

Fischer, S., Hotam, Y., & Wexler, P. (2012). Democracy and education in postsecular society. *Review of Research in Education, 36*, 261.

Foucault, M. (1980). *Power and knowledge: Selected interviews and other writings, 1972–1977*. New York, NY: Pantheon Books.

Galston, W. A. (2001). Political knowledge, political engagement, and civic education. *Annual Review of Political Science, 4*(1), 217–234.

Gay, G. (2002). Preparing for culturally responsive teaching. *Journal of Teacher Education, 53*(2), 106–116.

Gibson, T. (2008). Religion and civic engagement among America's youth. *The Social Science Journal, 45*(3), 504–514.

Glitz, A. (2012). The labor market impact of immigration: A quasi-experiment exploiting immigrant location rules in Germany. *Journal of Labor Economics, 30*(1), 175–213.

Goldstein, W. S. (2009). Secularization patterns in the old paradigm. *Sociology of Religion, 70*(2), 157–178

González, N. (2005). Beyond culture: The hybridity of funds of knowledge. In N. González, L. C. Moll, & C. Amanti. (Eds.), *Funds of knowledge: Theorizing practices in households, communities, and classrooms* (pp. 29–46). Mahwah, NJ: Lawrence Erlbaum.

Goody, J. (2006). *The theft of history*. Cambridge, United Kingdom: Cambridge University Press.

Gottlieb, E. (2008). Arguments as venues for cultural education: A comparison of epistemic practices at general and religious schools in Israel. In Z. Bekerman & E. Kopelowitz (Eds.), *Cultural education—cultural sustainability: Minority, diaspora, indigenous, and ethno-religious groups in multicultural societies* (pp. 285–303). New York, NY: Routledge.

Gould, E. D., Lavy, V., & Paserman, M. D. (2009). Does immigration affect the long-term educational outcomes of natives? Quasi-experimental evidence. *Economic Journal, 119*(540), 1243–1269.

Gramsci, A. (1971). *Selections from the prison notebooks* (Q. Hoare & G. Nowell Smith, Eds. & Trans.). New York, NY: International.

Grosfoguel, R., & Mielants, E. (2006). The long-durée entanglement between Islamophobia and racism in the modern/colonial capitalist/patriarchal world-system: An introduction. *Human Architecture: Journal of the Sociology of Self-Knowledge, 1*, 1–12.

Hagan, J., & Ebaugh, H. R. (2003). Calling upon the sacred: Migrants' use of religion in the migration process. *International Migration Review, 37*(4), 1145–1162.

Halperin, E., & Bar-Tal, D. (2006). Democratic values and education for democracy in the state of Israel. *Democracy and Security, 2*(2), 169–200.

Hammer, D., & Elby, A. (2003). Tapping epistemological resources for learning physics. *Journal of the Learning Sciences, 12*(1), 53–90.

Hefflin, B. R. (2002). Learning to develop culturally relevant pedagogy: A lesson about cornrowed lives. *Urban Review, 34*(3), 231–250.

Heitmeyer, W. (Ed.). (2005). *Deutsche Zustände [German Conditions]*. Frankfurt, Germany: Suhrkamp.

Heitmeyer, W., & Anhut, R. (2008). Disintegration, recognition, and violence: A theoretical perspective. *New Directions for Youth Development: Theory, Practice and Research* (Special Issue: Youth, Violence, and Social Disintegration), *119*, 25–37.

Herzog, T. (1997). Hybrids and Mischlinge: Translating Anglo-American cultural theory into Germany. *German Quarterly, 70*(1), 1–17.

Hofer, B. K. (2000). Dimensionality and disciplinary differences in personal epistemology. *Contemporary Educational Psychology, 25*, 378–405.

Hofer, B. K. (2001). Personal epistemology research: Implications for learning and teaching. *Journal of Educational Psychology Review, 13*(4), 353–383.

Hofer, B. K. (2004). Introduction: Paradigmatic approaches to personal epistemology. *Educational Psychologist, 39*(1), 1–3.

Hofer, B. K., & Pintrich, P. R. (1997). The development of epistemological theories: Beliefs about knowledge and knowing and their relation to learning. *Review of Educational Research, 67*, 88–140.

Hogg, L. (2011). Funds of knowledge: An investigation of coherence within the literature. *Teaching and Teacher Education, 27*(3), 666–677.

Hollifield, J. F. (1998). Migration, trade, and the nation-state: The myth of globalization. *UCLA Journal of International Law and Foreign Affairs, 3*, 595–636.

Howard, T. C. (2001). Powerful pedagogy for African American students: A case of four teachers. *Urban Education, 36*(2), 179–202.

Humphrey, M. (2013). Migration, security and insecurity. *Journal of Intercultural Studies, 34*(2), 178–195.

Huntington, S. P. (1996). *The clash of civilizations and the remaking of world order*. New York, NY: Simon & Schuster.

Inglehart, R. F. (2007). The worldviews of Islamic publics in global perspective. In M. Moaddel (Ed.), *Values and perceptions of the Islamic and Middle Eastern publics* (pp. 25–46). New York, NY: Palgrave Macmillan.

Isin, E. F. (2012). Citizenship after orientalism: An unfinished project. *Citizenship Studies, 16*(5–6), 563–572.

Janmaat, J. G. (2008). The civic attitudes of ethnic minority youth and the impact of citizenship education. *Journal of Ethnic and Migration Studies, 34*(1), 27–54.

Johnston, P., Woodside-Jiron, H., & Day, J. (2001). Teaching and learning literate epistemologies. *Journal of Educational Psychology, 93*(1), 223.

Kahanec, M., & Tosun, M. S. (2009). Political economy of immigration in Germany: Attitudes and citizenship aspirations. *International Migration Review, 43*(2), 263–291.

Kasinitz, P., Mollenkopf, J. H., Waters, M. C., & Holdaway, J. (2008). *Inheriting the city: The children of immigrants come of age.* New York, NY: Russell Sage Foundation.

Kastoryano, R. (2004). Religion and incorporation: Islam in France and Germany. *International Migration Review, 38*(3), 1234–1255.

Kienhues, D., Bromme, R., & Stahl, E. (2008). Changing epistemological beliefs: The unexpected impact of a short-term intervention. *British Journal of Educational Psychology, 78*(4), 545–565.

King, P. M., & Kitchener, K. S. (1994). *Developing reflective judgment: Understanding and promoting intellectual growth and critical thinking in adolescents and adults.* San Francisco, CA: Jossey-Bass.

King, P. M., & Kitchener, K. S. (2004). Reflective judgment: Theory and research on the development of epistemic assumptions through adulthood. *Educational Psychologist, 39*(1), 5–18.

Kuhn, D. (1991). *The skills of argument.* Cambridge, United Kingdom: Cambridge University Press.

Kuhn, D., Cheney, R., & Weinstock, M. (2000). The development of epistemological understanding. *Cognitive Development, 15*, 309–328.

Kunzman, R. (2005). Religion, politics and civic education. *Journal of Philosophy of Education, 39*(1), 159–168.

Ladson-Billings, G. (1995). Toward a theory of culturally relevant pedagogy. *American Educational Research Journal, 32*, 465–491.

Lawrence, T. (1995). *The defenders of God.* Columbia: University of South Carolina Press.

Lears, T. J. J. (1985). The concept of cultural hegemony: Problems and possibilities. *American Historical Review, 90*(3), 567–593.

Lemish, P. (2010). Civic and citizenship education in Israel. *Cambridge Journal of Education, 33*(1), 53–72.

Levy, G. (2005). From subjects to citizens: On educational reforms and the demarcations of the "Israeli-Arab." *Citizenship Studies, 9*, 271–291.

Loescher, G., Betts, A., & Milner, J. (2008). *United Nations High Commissioner for Refugees: The politics and practice of refugee protection into the 21st century.* New York, NY: Routledge.

McLaren, L. M. (2012). The cultural divide in Europe: Migration, multiculturalism, and political trust. *World Politics, 64*(02), 199–241.

McLaughlin, T. H. (1992). Citizenship, diversity and education: A philosophical perspective. *Journal of Moral Education, 21*(3), 235–250.

Meer, N., & Modood, T. (2009). The multicultural state we're in: Muslims, "multiculture" and the "civic re-balancing" of British multiculturalism. *Political Studies, 57*(3), 473–497.

Mignolo, W. D. (2003). *The darker side of the renaissance: literacy, territoriality, and colonization* (2nd ed.). Ann Arbor, MI: The University of Michigan Press.

Mignolo, W. D. (2009). Epistemic disobedience, independent thought, and decolonial freedom. *Theory, Culture, Society, 26*, 159.

Moll, L. C., Amanti, C., Neff, D., & González, N. (1992). Funds of knowledge for teaching: Using a qualitative approach to connect homes and classrooms. *Theory into Practice, 31*(2), 132–141.

Mouffe, C. (1988). Hegemony and new political subjects: Toward a new concept of democracy. In C. Nelson & L. Grossberg (Eds.), *Marxism and the interpretation of culture* (pp. 89–101). Urbana. IL: University of Illinois Press.

Nussbaum, M. C. (2002). Patriotism and cosmopolitanism. In M. C. Nussbaum with J. Cohen (Ed.), *For love of country?* (pp. 3–17). Boston, MA: Beacon Press. (Original work published 1994)

Olafson, L., & Schraw, G. (2006). Teachers' beliefs and practices within and across domains. *International Journal of Educational Research, 45*(1), 71–84.

Ong, A. (1996). Cultural citizenship as subject-making: Immigrants negotiate racial and cultural boundaries in the United States. *Current Anthropologist, 37*(5), 737–762.

Oughton, H. (2010). Funds of knowledge: A conceptual critique. *Studies in the Education of Adults, 42*(1), 63–78.

Özyürek, E. (2005). The politics of cultural unification, secularism, and the place of Islam in the new Europe. *American Ethnologist, 32*(4), 509–512.

Pajares, M. F. (1992). Teachers' beliefs and educational research: Cleaning up a messy construct. *Review of Educational Research, 62,* 307–332.

Palmary, I. (2007). Gender, race and culture: Unpacking discourses of tradition and culture in UNHCR refugee policy. *Annual Review of Critical Psychology, 6,* 125–133.

Peri, Y. (2012). The "Religionization" of Israeli society. *Israel Studies Review, 27*(1), 1–30.

Phillips, D. (2010). Minority ethnic segregation, integration and citizenship: A European perspective. *Journal of Ethnic and Migration Studies, 36*(2), 209–225.

Pinson, H. (2007). Inclusive curriculum? Challenges to the role of civic education in a Jewish and democratic state. *Curriculum Inquiry, 37*(4), 351–382.

Pong, S.-L., & Hao, L. (2007). Neighborhood and school factors in the school performance of immigrants' children. *International Migration Review, 41*(1), 206–241.

Pong, S.-L., & Landale, N. S. (2012). Academic achievement of legal immigrants' children: The roles of parents' pre- and postmigration characteristics in origin-group differences. *Child Development, 83*(5), 1543–1559.

Portes, A. (2006, June). Institutions and development: A conceptual re-analysis. *Population and Development Review, 32,* 233–262.

Portes, A., & Rumbaut, R. G. (2001). *Legacies: The story of the immigrant second generation.* Berkeley, CA: University of California Press.

Qian, G., & Alvermann, D. (2000). Relationship between epistemological beliefs and conceptual change learning. *Reading and Writing Quarterly, 16*(1), 59–74.

Røed, M., & Schøne, P. (2012). Does immigration increase labour market flexibility? *Labour Economics, 19*(4), 527–540.

Roeser, R. W., Midgley, C., & Urdan, T. C. (1996). Perceptions of the school psychological environment and early adolescents' psychological and behavioral functioning in school: The mediating role of goals and belonging. *Journal of Educational Psychology, 88*(3), 408–422.

Roseberry, W. (1994). Hegemony and the language of contention. In G. M. Joseph & D. Nugent (Eds.), *Everyday forms of state formation: Revolution and the negotiation of rule in modern Mexico* (pp. 355–366). Durham, NC: Duke University Press.

Rubin, B. (2007). "There's still not justice": Youth civic identity development amid distinct school and community contexts. *Teachers College Record, 109*(2), 449–481.

Said, E. W. (1979). *Orientalism.* London, United Kingdom: Penguin Books.

Said, E. (2000). "Latent and manifest orientalism." In A. L. Macfie (Ed.), *Orientalism: A reader* (pp. 111–114). Edinburgh, Scotland: Edinburgh University Press.

Salvatore, A. (2006). Public religion, ethics of participation, and cultural dialogue. In A. Aziz Said, M. Abu-Nimer, & M. Sharify-Funk (Eds.), *Contemporary Islam: Dynamic, not static* (pp. 83–100). London, United Kingdom: Routledge.

Sand, S. (2009). *The invention of the Jewish people*. New York, NY: Verso.

Sayer, D. (1994). Everyday forms of state formation: Some dissident remarks on "hegemony." In G. M. Joseph & D. Nugent (Eds.), *Everyday forms of state formation: Revolution and the negotiation of rule in modern Mexico* (pp. 367–378). Durham, NC: Duke University Press.

Schofield, J. W., & Bangs, R. (2006). Conclusions and further perspectives. In J. W. Schofield (Ed.), *Migration background, minority-group membership, and academic achievement: Research evidence from social, educational, and developmental psychology* (AKI Research Review 5; pp. 93–102). Berlin, Germany: Programme on Intercultural Conflicts and Societal Integration, Social Science Research Center.

Schommer, M. (1994). An emerging conceptualization of epistemological beliefs and their role in learning. In R. Garner & P. A. Alexander (Eds.), *Beliefs about text and instruction with text* (pp. 25–40). Hillsdale, NJ: Lawrence Erlbaum

Schommer-Aikins, M. (2004). Explaining the epistemological belief system: Introducing the embedded systemic model and coordinated research approach. *Educational Psychologist, 39*(1), 19–29.

Smith, C., & Hung, L.-C. (2008). Stereotype threat: Effects on education. *Social Psychology of Education, 11*(3), 243–257.

Smith, J. P., diSessa, A. A., & Roschelle, J. (1993–1994). Misconceptions reconceived: A constructivist analysis of knowledge in transition. *Journal of the Learning Sciences, 3*(2), 115–163.

Smooha, S. (2002). The model of ethnic democracy: Israel as a Jewish and democratic state. *Nations and Nationalism, 8*(4), 475–503.

Stahl, E. (2011). The generative nature of epistemological judgments: Focusing on interactions instead of elements to understand the relationship between epistemological beliefs and cognitive flexibility. In J. Elen, E. Stahl, R. Bromme, & G. Clarebout (Eds.), *Links between beliefs and cognitive flexibility* (pp. 37–60). Dordrecht, The Netherlands: Springer.

Suárez-Orozco, M. (2001). Globalization, immigration, and education: The research agenda. *Harvard Educational Review, 71*(3), 345–366.

Turner, B. S. (2007). Citizenship studies: A general theory. *Citizenship Studies, 1*(1), 5–18.

United Nations. (2013, September 11). *Number of international migrants rises above 232 million, UN reports*. Retrieved from http://www.un.org/apps/news/story.asp?NewsID=45819&Cr=migrants&Cr1=#.V2HWLPkrKUk

Velez-Ibanez, C. G., & Greenberg, J. B. (1992). Formation and transformation of funds of knowledge among U.S.–Mexican households. *Anthropology and Education Quarterly, 23*(4), 313–335.

Vlas, N., & Gherghina, S. (2012). Where does religion meet democracy? A comparative analysis of attitudes in Europe. *International Political Science Review, 33*(3), 336–351.

Wang, T. (2015). Marginality of rural migrant students in eleven Chinese high schools. *Journal of Ethnic and Cultural Studies, 2*(2), 21–32.

Warwick, I., Neville, R., & Smith, K. (2006). My life in Huddersfield: Supporting young asylum-seekers and refugees to record their experiences of living in Huddersfield. *Social Work Education, 25*(2), 129–137.

Wodak, R., & Van Dijk, T. (2000). *Racism at the top: Parliamentary discourses on ethnic issues in six European states*. Klagenfurt, Austria: Drava.

Young, E. (2010). Challenges to conceptualizing and actualizing culturally relevant pedagogy: How viable is the theory in classroom practice? *Journal of Teacher Education,* *61*(3), 248–260.

Youniss, J. (2011). Civic education: What schools can do to encourage civic identity and action. *Applied Developmental Science, 15*(2), 98–103.

Yuval-Davis, N. (1999). The multi-layered citizen: Citizenship in the age of globalization. *International Feminist Journal of Politics, 1,* 119–136.

CHAPTER 3

Language and Immigrant Integration in an Age of Mass Migration

Shifts and Changes in Teaching and Learning Destination Languages

Guadalupe Valdés

The importance of acquiring a societal language for all immigrants has been clearly established by the literature on migration. There is no debate about the benefits of acquiring the destination language for the integration and adaptation of new arrivals. Chiswick and Miller (2007), for example, argue that language skills are a form of human capital that play an important role in determining immigrant social and economic status. How destination languages are best acquired and what role needs to be played by established educational systems in receiving societies in providing instruction to new immigrants, however, is a matter of debate. There is much concern, for example, about the ability of these established systems to deliver language instruction to adult immigrants with varying educational and linguistic backgrounds as well as to provide an education to both their newly arrived and native-born children who are in the process of acquiring the societal language. It is generally agreed that formal classroom instruction and the involvement of the educational system is needed in supporting the linguistic integration of both adults and their children (Batalova & Fix, 2010; Xi, Hwang, & Cao, 2010). This position is supported by research on the acquisition of societal languages by immigrants (e.g., Chiswick & Miller, 2007) revealing that, because there is limited exposure to the societal language in ethnic enclaves where immigrants reside, systematic formal instruction is required.

Unfortunately, the challenge facing immigrant-receiving countries in providing formal language instruction is complicated and exacerbated by the instability of our knowledge about the design of formal language instruction for both newly arrived and established immigrants. Moreover, a number of economic, political, educational, and theoretical shifts are currently intersecting in perhaps unanticipated ways with the reality of mass migratory flows. While there is some disagreement about the stability of migration flows, Abel and Sander (2014) conclude that the largest movements are occurring between South and West Asia, from Latin to North America, and within Africa. Migration flows originating in Asia and Latin America are more spatially focused than are flows to and from Europe from almost all regions of the world. Zetter (2015), on the other hand, points out that there is currently a blurring of voluntary and forced migration. Much current displacement responds to a combination of drivers, including conflict, poor governance, political instability, and resource scarcity. Many forced migrants, moreover, are leaving their immediate home regions and "relying on wider patterns of mobility, both on the regional and global scale, to ensure their access to livelihoods and safety" (Zetter, 2015, p. 1). These groups include both skilled and unskilled labor migrants (Skeldon, 2013) with very different educational backgrounds. Recent research reveals, for example, that one in every three international migrants age 15 and above has a limited education. Moreover, according to OECD figures on world migration (UN-DESA & OECD, 2015), emigration rates of the highly educated vary widely from country to country. For example, in 2010–2011, the total population emigrating from Mexico was 11,249 and the highly educated emigrant population was 867. By comparison, the emigrant population for India in 2010–2011 was 3,441 and the highly educated emigrant population was 2,080.

In spite of these differences in the educational backgrounds of different groups, there is no debate about the importance, for both immigrants and displaced individuals, of acquiring the destination language. Language skills are important for everyday living, for entering the workforce, and for participating in civic society. The challenge for receiving societies is developing effective educational language policies and practices that can support the acquisition of the societal language by individuals of many different linguistic and educational backgrounds.

In this chapter I examine the challenges involved in the teaching and learning of destination languages to new arrivals. I focus on what is referred to as *instructed second-language (L2) acquisition*, that is, on both theories about language and language acquisition and the practices and approaches directed at creating the conditions and circumstances necessary for the development of *elective* bilingualism[1] in traditional classroom settings. I begin with a discussion of naturally occurring bilingualism and multilingualism in order to establish important aspects of language use and acquisition across the world and to emphasize the fundamental differences between natural and artificial language acquisition contexts. I then describe significant theoretical shifts taking place in the field of second-language acquisition (SLA), the research field that informs the teaching and learning of second languages. I include an in-depth discussion of the four fundamental questions raised about the teaching and learning of second languages that are a product of these theoretical shifts: (1) What needs to be acquired in second-language learning? (2) How are second languages acquired? (3) What is the end point of second-language acquisition? and (4) How is language proficiency to be assessed? In the examination of this fourth question, I include an overview of the challenges raised by current thinking about language proficiency assessment. Following the examination of changing perspectives on second-language acquisition, I move to a very general discussion of learner differences in adult and school-age immigrants and the implications of these differences for program design and for the development of a knowledge base for teacher preparation. I conclude with a number of observations about the need for those engaged in the study of immigration to develop a nuanced understanding of the possible outcomes of language instruction and the role that conceptualizations of language can play in designing programs for immigrants and their children.

BILINGUALISM/MULTILINGUALISM AND MASS MIGRATION

Bilingualism/multilingualism is a common human condition that is both an individual and a societal characteristic. The condition of acquiring and using more than one language in everyday life comes about as a result of language contact, that is, of the interaction between people who speak different languages. Bi/multilingualism emerges as a consequence of commerce and trade, invasion, conquest, colonization, and migration. It is the movement of peoples for numerous reasons (trade, conquest, migration) that brings about the need to communicate with other individuals who do not speak the same language. Currently, the successful development of bi/multilingualism is seen as increasingly important around the world because of the rise of immigration and because of the challenge of integrating new arrivals (Leikin, Schwarz, & Tobin, 2012).

Over the last several decades, research on bi/multilingualism has increasingly focused on the economic, political, social, cultural, and linguistic changes brought about by the process of globalization and mass migration. The complexity of the changes ushered in by transnational population flows and the accompanying impact on language use emanating from new communication technologies, movement of goods and capital, transnational contact and recontact, and new and return migration have moved the field to a new critical examination of previously unquestioned issues. New discourses on bilingualism examine *superdiversity* (Blommaer & Rampton, 2012), *transidiomatic practices* (Jacquemet, 2005), *metrolingualism* (Otsuji & Pennycook, 2010), *translanguaging* (Canagarajah, 2011; Creese & Blackledge, 2010; García, 2009) and the acquisition of language repertoires used for a variety of purposes in complex, non-monolingual-like combinations by multicompetent individuals (Cook, 1992, 1996). Much attention, therefore, is being given to the nature of languages themselves, and many questions such as the following are being raised: Are languages discrete and bounded entities as described by linguistic theory (Heller, 2007), or are they inventions and products of the construction of nation-states (Makoni & Pennycook, 2007)? Are monolingual norms (i.e., standards of language use typical of monolinguals) legitimate (Wei, 2010) or even useful in an age of complex multilingualism and diversity?

Both individual and societal bilingualism have been studied extensively from the perspectives of sociolinguistics, psycholinguistics, and linguistics. The scholarly examination of bilingualism/multilingualism is now encyclopedic in nature,[2] and much is known about how and why groups of people become bilingual, how they maintain and/or abandon their original languages in a new context, how languages are processed and stored in the brain by bilingual individuals, and about the ways in which languages themselves change and do not change as a result of being used interchangeably by the same speakers.

Recently a number of scholars have examined other issues that are central to bi/multilingualism. Much attention has been given, for example, to the role of language in the construction of national identities through the established perspective of one language and one nation in what some have referred to as a postnational scenario (e.g., Pujolar, 2007). In an era of increasing migration, moreover, other scholars have examined these processes extensively. Leikin, Schwartz, and Tobin (2012), for example, draw from the case of Israel to document the challenge to the original Hebrew monolingual nation-building ideology posed by the massive arrival of immigrants from the former Soviet Union. Finally, new discourses on bi/multilingualism in the age of globalization have characterized English as a "killer" language (Skutnabb-Kangas, 2000) and have argued that because of its role and increasing importance as a lingua franca (MacKenzie, 2012; Pennycook, 1994), it threatens multilingualism across the world.

From the perspective of the scholarship on societal bi/multilingualism, formal language instruction is not considered essential to the development of communicative and functional resources in additional languages. Research carried out in a variety of settings over time has established that languages can be and *are* acquired in noninstructed settings by ordinary people in the course of observing, overhearing, and attempting to engage in communication over time. All humans have the capacity of developing both productive and receptive proficiencies in multiple oral languages through ordinary interactions with speakers of those languages without instruction. There are many documented examples of multilingual settings around the world in which the normal state of affairs is the acquisition and use of several languages by the majority of individuals. Scholars agree that natural or circumstantial bi/multilingualism develops in individuals and communities when one language alone does not suffice to meet real or perceived communicative needs. People add to their communicative repertoires and become bi/multilingual (i.e., users of more than one language) in order to understand and be understood by those persons with whom they want to interact. Such bi/multilingualism does not depend on instruction, on classes, on courses and textbooks. It depends, as Wong Fillmore (1985a, 1985b) pointed out, on individuals having access to proficient speakers of the target language who speak a target language[3] well, and who are willing to use it frequently in interactions with them.

Unfortunately, in many receiving societies, access to proficient speakers of the societal language is limited. As a result, spontaneous and informal second-language acquisition cannot take place. Formal instructional settings, then, become the only context in which new immigrants can be systematically exposed to this new language. I return to this point below in the section titled "Learner Differences: Challenges of Designing Language-teaching Programs."

A SHIFTING TERRAIN: CHANGING THEORETICAL PERSPECTIVES

Increasing global migratory flows have brought attention to various matters involving the integration of skilled immigrants, including the challenge of recognizing foreign qualifications in receiving countries (Hawthorne, 2013), the difficulty of addressing skills deficits in workforce development (Benton, 2013), and the complexity of preparing the children of immigrants for academic success (Crosnoe, 2013). All of these issues directly involve one fundamental barrier to integration: the acquisition of the destination language by these new immigrants and their children. They pose deep challenges to established education systems that are being called upon to take on tasks and engage in instruction for which traditional teachers were not prepared. Such challenges are intensified in a rapidly shifting world terrain that involves both global educational reforms and changing theoretical perspectives on language itself.

Changing Theoretical Perspectives

The fact that destination language programs for immigrants have only been *moderately* successful (McHugh, Gelatt, & Fix, 2007)[4] suggests that a careful examination of rationales and theoretical assumptions underlying the design of such programs is strongly warranted. A key shift with which I am concerned, then, is one that can potentially inform educational policies governing the design of language instruction for new immigrants in important ways. This shift involves changing theoretical perspectives about language itself and about the ways in which second languages are acquired. It is noteworthy because it directly calls into question widely accepted views of language goals and outcomes that now inform the design, implementation, and evaluation of language-teaching programs for newly arrived immigrants.

In the last decade, the field of second-language (L2) acquisition (conventionally referred to as SLA) and the theories informing the field of applied linguistics have shifted rapidly, and there are many ongoing theoretical debates that many believe will fundamentally alter established approaches to language instruction. For example, recent scholarship, particularly from the perspectives of the "social turn" (Block, 2003) and the "multilingual turn" (May, 2013) in the field of SLA has raised the following fundamental questions:

1. What needs to be acquired in L2 acquisition?
   - Is it an internal grammatical system and a set of structures and forms or the ability to use language for a variety of purposes?
2. How are second languages acquired?
   - Is L2 acquisition an individual cognitive process that is similar for most L2 learners?
   - Is it the "learning" of bits and pieces of language conforming to the target language (as spoken by "idealized" native speakers)?

- Is L2 acquisition a highly variable, "mediated, social semiotic activity" acquired through experience and use?

3. What is the end state of L2 acquisition?

- Is "native-like" mastery or "complete acquisition" of the target language possible?
- Does L2 acquisition result in two "full" discrete language systems kept separate in use?
- Does L2 acquisition lead to the development of grammatical resources termed multi-competence (Cook, 1992) and to the acquisition of linguistic repertoires that grow and change to meet communicative needs without reaching, as Larsen-Freeman (2006) suggested, a native-like end point or ultimate attainment?

4. How then is language proficiency to be assessed? How will progress and development be measured if monolingual norms of complexity, accuracy, and fluency are no longer considered a valid measure of acquisition?

In the sections that follow, I address each of these questions in some detail.

What Needs to Be Acquired in L2 Acquisition?

Fundamental to all language program design is an underlying theoretical stance about the nature of language. Whether stated or not, the general public, program funders, language instructors, and students themselves have internalized beliefs and ideas about what language is and is not, what good language sounds like, and what needs to be "learned" when individuals study a second language. Much attention has been given to such beliefs (known as *language ideologies*) in the fields of anthropology and sociolinguistics (e.g., Kroskrity, 2004, 2010; Woolard, 1998), and scholars generally agree that such values and beliefs ideologies are strongly held and generally unexamined by both ordinary users of language and language-teaching professionals. In the case of immigrants, there are strong negative ideologies directed, for example, at accented speech (Lippi-Green, 2012) and at other aspects of the spoken and written language of newcomers that are considered non-native-like by members of the receiving society.

The design of language-teaching programs involves the process of curricularizing language (Valdés, 2015), that is, treating language as if it were an ordinary academic subject or skill, the elements of which can be ordered and sequenced, practiced and studied, learned and tested in artificial contexts within which learners of the target language outnumber proficient speakers. This process determines what is taught (program goals and outcomes), who teaches (how teachers are prepared and hired), what approaches and materials are used in instruction, how learners are categorized and classified (e.g., beginners, advanced), and what counts as learning (i.e., what is assessed and what units of academic credit are attached to such learning). The process, moreover, is directly informed by educational language policies (language requirements, unit-credit options), that are enacted at multiple levels (e.g., state, school district, and school or community and school) depending on how programs are organized.

Answering the question, What needs to be acquired in L2 acquisition? is fundamental to program design and depends directly on conceptualizations of the nature of language itself and of what it means to be fluent or proficient in a first and second language. Conceptualizations of language include notions about language and definitions of language, both of which may be informed by the study of or exposure to established bodies of knowledge, by facts about existing and developing theories in applied or theoretical linguistics, by research data on the teaching and learning of second languages, and/or by personal experiences with language and language instruction. Seedhouse (2010) argues that in applied linguistics (the field that informs L2 teaching and learning) it is essential to make conceptualizations of language evident as well as to make explicit conceptualizations of "learning" because all discussions of learning in second-language acquisition depend directly on definitions of language. When there are arguments about language learning, it is often because different pedagogies and approaches are rooted in conflicting conceptualizations of language that, as Cook (2010) points out, are unfortunately unwinnable because different views cannot account for particular aspects of language that the other side denies even exist. To illustrate his point, Cook (2010) lists different definitions of language including a human representation system, a set of actual and potential sentences, a social phenomenon, the knowledge in the mind of an individual, and a set of observable actions that people use in order to do things.

Surprisingly, perhaps, for students of migration, applied linguists and language instructors define language in many different ways. These perspectives are not the same and give rise to dramatically different expectations about teaching, learning, and assessing languages. As Seedhouse (2010) contends, however, researchers in the field of SLA may not be aware that they are starting with vastly different conceptualizations of language and that it is these differences in conceptualization that have led to existing debates in the field. The same is true for educational researchers, practitioners, and policymakers.

The same point had been made previously by van Lier (2004, p. 26) who also categorized a number of different common assumptions underlying conceptualizations of language. This listing of assumptions is summarized in Table 3.1. It is important to emphasize that van Lier contended that all of these assumptions involve "half truths that can easily lead to questionable teaching and learning practices" (p. 27).

As will be noted, many of the assumptions listed in Table 3.1 commonly underlie competing perspectives on what it means for second-language learners to "learn" or "know" the second language. Both the storage and the componential assumptions take the position that language can be subdivided into component elements that can be taught, practiced, learned, and assessed in a predictable and established order. Whether the elements are words or sentence frames or verb

Table 3.1. Seven Common Assumptions About Language

Assumption	Conceptualization of Language and Language Learning
Computational	Language is information exchange consisting of inputs and outputs.
Storage	Language is a fixed code, which is learned by internalizing knowledge and skills.
Either–Or	Language consists of two separate aspects: form (structure) and meaning (function).
Componential	Language consists of building blocks (pronunciation, vocabulary, grammar, and meaning, including discourse and pragmatics).
Correctness	Language use can be classified as correct or incorrect, standard or nonstandard, native or nonnative.
Warring Languages	Languages are systems that compete with other like systems in human brains for attention and storage.
Separateness	Language is autonomous, separate from all other aspects of human characteristics or experience.

Note: van Lier, L. (2004). *The ecology and semiotics of language learning: A sociocultural perspective*. Boston, MA: Kluwer Academic.

groups, the assumption is the same: Language is an academic subject that can be taught and learned effectively in a classroom setting.

How Are Second Languages Acquired?

Like many other scholarly fields, the field of SLA is characterized by debates and disagreements that are part of continuing research and theory development. Specifically SLA investigates

> the human capacity to learn languages other than the first, during late childhood, adolescence or adulthood, and once the first language or languages have been acquired. It encompasses the study of naturalistic and formal language acquisition in second, foreign and heritage learning contexts. It seeks to understand universal, individual and social forces that influence what gets acquired, how fast, and *how well* [emphasis added] by different people under different circumstances. (Ortega, 2009, p. 10)

Table 3.2. Cognitivist and Social-Oriented Positions on Language and SLA

	Mainstream Perspectives	Alternative Perspectives
What needs to be acquired in L2 acquisition?	The internal grammatical system. A set of structures and forms.	The ability to use language for a variety of purposes in real-life communication.
How are L2s acquired?	L2 acquisition is an individual cognitive process. Learners move through the process in similar ways.	Language is learned through experience and use. The process of acquisition is nonlinear and variable.
What is the end state of L2 acquisition?	"Native-like" mastery or "complete acquisition" of the target language and/or two discrete language systems are kept separate in use.	The linguistic repertoire grows and changes to meet communicative needs without a native-like "end point."

New perspectives and reexaminations of established views reflect contributions to the growing understanding of language acquisition and language development and, of course, raise questions about previous understandings as well as about established language-teaching pedagogies and theories that underlie these instructional approaches.

Until the mid- to late 1990s, it was generally agreed that second-language learning/acquisition is an individual, cognitive process that takes place in the mind of individual learners. What is to be acquired is the grammatical system of the target language, primarily a set of structures and forms. Students were assumed to follow a linear common acquisition process when exposed to instruction and it was expected that the end goal for all students of a second language was to become as similar as possible to native speakers of the target language. Researchers spent a great deal of energy and time trying to understand exactly why ultimate attainment was largely unsuccessful, that is, why very few second-language learners became native-like.

Beginning in the mid-1990s, the "social turn" in applied linguistics shifted the thinking of many in the field to a view of L2 acquisition as a social process that takes place in interactions between learners and speakers of the target language. Table 3.2 summarizes the key differences between these two theoretical perspectives. The cognitivist view has been dominant in the field and is often referred to as "mainstream SLA." Socially oriented theories, following Atkinson (2011), can be referred to as "alternative SLA."

As I emphasize in Table 3.2, the fundamental difference between cognitivist and social views of second-language acquisition has to do with their contrasting views about exactly what it is that has to be acquired in the process of learning a language other than the first. Cognitivist-oriented researchers are focused on understanding how speakers of one language internalize the grammatical system of another language. They want to know, for example, how learners develop an implicit grammar of a second language, how they process input (the language that they hear and read), what the developing linguistic system looks like at different stages, what kinds of errors learners make with different structures at different points of acquisition, and whether direct instruction on grammatical structures can change the pace of acquisition of those structures. Socially oriented researchers, by comparison, are concerned with the ways in which second-language learners learn "how to mean," that is, with the ways in which learners, by interacting with speakers of the L2, are able to develop and use evolving/imperfect grammatical, sociolinguistic, textual, and pragmatic systems to carry out numerous communicative actions. Most important, all socially oriented approaches reject the essential notion of the cognitivist orientation, namely, language as an individual process, the goal of which is the acquisition of the grammatical system.

It is important to note that while I have contrasted two main perspectives here, there is an important epistemological diversity currently present in the field (Ortega, 2013) that includes a number of theories, for example, emergentism, connectionism, dynamic systems, and complexity theory, as well as usage-based theories of various types. There has also been extensive methodological advancement in the field, as well as a broadening of the populations studied by SLA researchers.

What Is the End Point of L2 Acquisition?

Answers to the third question, What is the end point of L2 acquisition? are very possibly ones that can most directly call into question existing notions about the outcomes of language instruction. As summarized in Table 3.2, common existing views about the end state of the L2 acquisition process have been informed by mainstream SLA. The end point of L2 acquisition for all learners has been assumed to be the internalization of the implicit grammatical system of the monolingual "native" speaker. Such native-like, ultimate attainment, though seldom achieved by most L2 learners (Han, 2004), has nevertheless been established as the goal of L2 instruction, and learners have been evaluated primarily in terms of their acquisition of forms, structures, or communicative behaviors thought to be characteristic of educated speakers raised from birth in a monolingual environment. Monolingual competence and monolingual performance have been seen as the norm, and deviations from this norm have been labeled using terms such as *incomplete acquisition, fossilization*, and *interlanguage*. In the last decade, however, work carried out by various researchers on the nature of bilingualism (Auer, 2007; Grosjean, 1998; Wei, 2013), as well as the roles of socialization (Duff & Talmy, 2011), interaction (Kasper & Wagner, 2011), and language variability (e.g., de Bot,

Lowie, & Verspoor, 2007; Larsen-Freeman, 2010, 2012; Larsen-Freeman & Cameron, 2008) in second-language acquisition has raised many questions about a number of these and other commonly accepted assumptions about L2 acquisition and bilingualism.

Two alternative theories in particular, chaos/complexity theory (C/CT) (Larsen-Freeman, 2002; Larsen-Freeman & Cameron, 2008) and dynamic systems theory (DST) (de Bot, Lowie & Verspoor, 2007), have raised pivotal questions about the nature of language acquisition and about the centrality of variability in the second-language acquisition process. Complexity theory (which was first proposed to explain physical science phenomena) attempts to understand how multiple interacting parts of nonlinear, self-organizing, complex adaptive systems (neurons in the brain, fauna in an ecosystem) operate. Drawing from the theoretical perspectives of C/CT and DST, second-language acquisition is seen as a complex adaptive process, which is itself self-organizing and intrinsically variable. Interacting elements constantly change, and language forms are considered to emerge in language use. Individual variability is considered central and, as Larsen-Freeman (2006) has argued, there is no clearly definable and common end state in the process of second-language acquisition for all learners.

The common notion that the goal of all L2 learning is to become native-like has been discredited primarily due to scholarship on bilingualism from linguistic and sociolinguistic perspectives. It is now established that bilinguals are specific speaker–hearers (Grosjean, 1989) who are not two monolinguals in one. Rather, they use their multiple linguistic repertoires in a variety of ways in order to meet their communicative needs. Bilinguals do not normally have the same levels of proficiency in all language modalities (speaking, listening, reading, and writing) in each of their languages, and as a result there is increasing concern about the construct of language proficiency as it has been used to measure bilingualism by researchers (Hulstijn, 2012). As Wei (2010) points out, it has become increasingly obvious that bilinguals should be compared only to other bilinguals and not to monolinguals in any one of their languages.

May (2013) refers to these changes in perspective as the "multilingual turn" in applied linguistics that has come about as a natural consequence of the increasingly globalized world in which the teaching of English is now taking place. According to May (2013) and Ortega (2013), dissatisfaction with and concern about the tendency to view individuals acquiring a second language as failed native speakers, however, has been present in SLA for some time. A number of other scholars have also criticized monolingual assumptions and the narrow views of language experience they imply, beginning in the early 1990s (Amin, 2004; Canagarajah, 1999a; Davies, 1991, 2003; Doerr, 2009; Doerr & Kumagai, 2009; Kramsch, 1997), but Ortega (2013) contends that mainstream SLA research communities still do not fully understand the ideological or empirical consequences of the native-speaker norms and assumptions they rely upon in their work in spite of the extensive work carried out on this topic (Canagarajah, 1999a, 1999b; Cook, 1999; Doerr, 2009; Leung, Harris, & Rampton, 1997; Piller, 2002; Rampton, 1990; Toker, 2012).

Importantly, for those charged with developing instructional arrangements for the teaching and learning of second languages as well as constructing language proficiency progressions in order to measure language acquisition, current scholarship reflects much unease about the lack of longitudinal studies in SLA (Ortega & Iberri-Shea, 2005) that might inform our understanding of naturally occurring L2 acquisition trajectories. Researchers working from the tradition of corpus linguistics, for example, argue for authentic collections of learner language as the primary data and the most reliable information about learners' evolving systems. In a special edition of the *Modern Language Journal* on "learner corpora" (that is, on samples of learner language over time), the editor (Hasko, 2013) argues, "A 'typical' L2 developmental profile is an elusive target to portray, as L2 development is not linear or evenly paced and is characterized by complex dynamics of inter- and intralearner variability, fluctuation, plateaus, and breakthroughs" (p. 2).

In sum, the state of knowledge about stages of acquisition in L2 learning does not support precise expectations about the sequence of development of second languages or support the types of assessments that are often mandated by language policies in immigrant-receiving countries. Constructing developmental sequences and progressions is an exacting and difficult process that some have characterized as a minefield because of its potential impact on the lives of learners.

Assessing L2 Proficiency: A Fundamental Challenge

As pointed out above, a fundamental challenge in developing instructional arrangements for teaching a second language is the assessment of language development and language growth. Assessing language proficiency, however, is a complicated and difficult endeavor. As Fulcher and Davidson (2012) contend, the practice of language testing "makes an assumption that knowledge, skills and abilities are stable and can be 'measured' or 'assessed.' It does it in full knowledge that there is error and uncertainty," and strives to make "the extent of the error and uncertainty transparent" (p. 2) Within recent years, there has been an increasing concern within the language testing profession about the degree to which that uncertainty is actually made transparent to test users at all levels as well as the general public. Shohamy (2001), for example, has raised a number of important issues about ethics and fairness of language testing with reference to language policy. Attention has been given, in particular, to the impact of high-stakes tests, to the uses of language tests for the management of language-related issues in many national settings (Spolsky, 2009), and to the special challenges of standards-based testing (Cumming, 2008). Cumming (2008), for example, makes the following very strong statement about the conceptual foundations of language assessments:

> A major dilemma for comprehensive assessments of oracy and literacy are the conceptual foundations on which to base such assessments. On the one hand, each language assessment asserts, at least implicitly, a certain conceptualization of language and of

language acquisition by stipulating a normative sequence in which people are expected to gain language proficiency with respect to the content and methods of the test. *On the other hand, there is no universally agreed upon theory of language or of language acquisition nor any systematic means of accounting for the great variation in which people need, use, and acquire oral and literate language abilitie*s [emphasis added]. (p. 10)

Given this dilemma, educational systems nevertheless develop their own sets of standards. These standards—developed as part of a policymaking consensus process—are generally based on the professional perspectives of educators or on the personal experiences and views of other members of standards-writing committees and not on empirical evidence or on second-language acquisition theories. According to Cumming, second-language proficiency assessments, as currently constructed by most educational systems, can therefore only tell us where a student scores with reference to the hypothesized sequence of development on which the assessment is based. Such scores are useful because, given educational policies and regulations, they allow educators to classify and categorize students and, in theory, to provide them with instructional supports appropriate for them while they acquire the societal language. Many would argue that in a world of imperfect systems, nation-states are doing the very best they can.

While that may well be the case, it is important to consider what Bialystok (Bialystok & Peets, 2010), one of the most distinguished researchers on child bilingualism in the world, has to say about categorizations:

Our ordinary conversational means for describing people's language experience perpetuates a fiction so compelling that we accept the description as a meaningful category. We talk as though being bilingual, or being a language learner, or being literate in a language is an identifiable state with objective criteria and stable characteristics. Our faith in these descriptions as reliable and valid categories extends to education, where such categories are used to classify children and place them in various instructional programs, and to research, where experimental designs are built around the objective of uncovering the unique profile for members of the respective categorical groups. Practically, these approaches are useful and allow educational practice and research inquiry to proceed, producing outcomes that are largely positive. Theoretically, however, the categories are elusive, with individual variation with a category sometimes as great as that between two individuals in different categories. (p. 134)

Identifying and classifying immigrant students in terms of their second-language proficiencies is a requirement of many existing policy mandates across the world. Such a requirement assumes that accurate language categorizations can be created and students identified who fit into such categories. If Bialystok and Peets (2010) are correct, however, much harm can come to students if we expect consistent growth and development that is known to be highly variable among learners and if we create policies and practices that can only lead to a narrowly defined and rarely attained success for the majority of adult immigrants and their children.

LEARNER DIFFERENCES: CHALLENGES OF DESIGNING
LANGUAGE-TEACHING PROGRAMS

According to Chiswick and Miller (2007), destination language proficiency is a function of three factors: exposure, efficiency and economic incentives. What this means from an applied linguistics/SLA perspective is that in order to develop functional proficiency, immigrants must have access to the language in either natural or instructed settings. It also means that learner characteristics such as age of arrival, school attainment, and ability to invest time, energy, and money in language tuition matter a great deal. In this section of the chapter, I focus on the design of language-teaching programs and on the multiple challenges that are involved in responding to often-contradictory beliefs and expectations about the outcomes of language instruction.

In an ideal world, it would be possible for newly arrived immigrants to be exposed to the societal language in real-life settings and to be involved in frequent interactions with proficient speakers of the language who would engage with them for a variety of purposes, both work-related and personal. They would live in neighborhoods and communities in which they would interact with such speakers every day. They would work next to them, attend sporting events with them, and spend time with them on weekends. In the real world, however, immigrants frequently have little exposure (outside of their own family networks) to the majority language. Few long-term, proficient speakers of the target language live in the areas where new immigrants cluster in overcrowded inexpensive housing, carry out menial jobs, and send their children to "undesirable" schools in which the majority of students are also learners of the new language.

Providing the right amount and degree of exposure to the destination language, then, becomes one of the primary functions of formal language classes. For immigrants and their children, however, these classes may or may not provide much actual exposure to language used for real-life purposes. They may only provide very limited access to language in the form of grammar drills and exercises on bits and pieces of disconnected language. As pointed out above, the problem is that language programs designed for immigrants are informed by a variety of mechanisms (e.g., adult immigrant language standards, language proficiency examinations) as well as by unexamined language ideologies, societal beliefs about immigrant integration, and expectations established by educational practices, testing and accountability policies, and funding mechanisms. These designs and the entire educational apparatus that governs them are difficult to change or modify.

For example, learner characteristics are a major consideration in the design of formal language programs, and most educational systems attempt to respond in some way to the main types of learner differences presented in Table 3.3.

Adult Learners

In the case of adults, the most important distinction to be made in the design of language-teaching programs is that between immigrants who have been educat-

Table 3.3. Types of Immigrant L2 Learners

Adults	School-age Children
High education and high literacy in L1	Preschool
Low education and low literacy in L1	Children acquiring initial literacy
	Children with age-appropriate schooling in L1
	Children with limited or interrupted education in L1

ed in their own countries and who have acquired high literacy skills and those who have not. The "success rate" of high education/high literacy learners in most traditional programs is well known in the United States. These are the learners who, whether they begin their instructional journey in survival-focused community-based English as a second language (ESL) programs, or in grammar-based classes in adult schools, or in noncredit examination-oriented community college programs, meet the expected learning outcomes hypothesized by program designers. Because such immigrants have been successful at "doing school," they are comfortable studying language as a generic school subject. If their ESL program conceptualizes language as componential, that is, as consisting of building blocks (pronunciation, vocabulary, grammar, and meaning, including discourse and pragmatics) that they must learn in bits and pieces following a textbook sequence, they have no difficulty with this orientation. They will learn the bits and pieces as required and do well on language proficiency examinations that test such knowledge. More important, because this group of adult learners brings highly developed L1 literacy skills to the acquisition of literacy in a second language, they can transfer underlying literacy components to the societal language. These skills will provide them advantages in the new society, give them additional exposure to the target language from proficient speakers who interact with them in the workplace, and allow them to do well on language proficiency measures including increasingly challenging citizenship tests, which are a growing element of national policies in immigrant-receiving countries (Hogan-Brun, Mar-Molinero, & Stevenson, 2009; McNamara & Shohamy, 2008; Shohamy, 2009, 2012; Spotti & Van Avermaet, 2009).

As shown in Table 3.3, this is not the case for adults who have had limited education and have limited or no literacy skills.[5] These individuals—precisely because of their limited literacy skills—struggle in even survival-language courses taught by supportive community organizations. If the courses are textbook based and assume literacy and a certain degree of metalinguistic sophistication in order to make sense of grammatical categories such as tense, grammatical gender, and number and to profit from teachers' grammatical corrections, these students do not do well. Proceedings from the yearly symposia conducted by the international forum on Low-Educated Second Language and Literacy Acquisition (LESLLA) document the unique struggles of these adults in traditional language classes.[6] It is argued that current instruction in second languages is not informed by research on this particularly vulnerable group of adult learners.

Limited-education and limited-literacy adult learners also struggle in L2 language classes because all instruction is generally being carried out through a language that they do not understand. Lukes (2009), for example, documents the frustration of Latino immigrants in New York City who were not able to understand grammatical explanations and class directions carried out exclusively in English. Over the course of several years, these individuals followed the well-documented process of enrolling and dropping out of Level 1 ESL multiple times. The assumption that a second language is best learned through the target language itself is deeply ingrained in the language-teaching profession. It is particularly well established in TESOL (the professional group that focuses on teaching English as a second language). Within TESOL the superiority of the monolingual "native-speaking" teacher was traditionally assumed (Canagarajah, 1999b; Phillipson, 1992), and English-only practices were often defended by arguing that the heterogeneity of the learners made the use of students' first languages impractical. In English-speaking countries, moreover, strong ideologies of language, popular attitudes, and educational policies discourage the use of non-English languages in instruction, even as a temporary support for both child and adult learners (Cummins, 2008).

Adult learner characteristics intersect in important ways with language-teaching program goals. McHugh and Challinor (2011), for example, argue that generic or umbrella language programs designed for initial survival and basic interaction do not meet the needs of individuals who must develop workplace language proficiency. Tarone and Bigelow (2011) agree and point out that SLA theory—in all of its many variations—has focused only on a narrowly defined type of language learner. Very little is known about limited literacy adult immigrant students and the ways in which they acquire a second language.[7] Most generic language-teaching programs follow what are known as grammatical syllabi, that is, programs of study and instructional plans that present structures and forms in some ordered sequence and assume that L2 acquisition involves the internalization (or the skilled use) of these structures. The sequencing and contextual use of the elements taught are determined to a great degree by the assessment instruments that will be used to measure what is considered by established policies to constitute language proficiency development. The establishment of cost-effective, accessible, and tailored language-teaching programs designed to combine work-focused, tailored language instruction and work skills training for specific workplaces proposed by McHugh and Challinor (2011) is an attractive and important possible solution.

Of necessity, workplace programs would need to vary depending on the backgrounds of individuals seeking different types of employment. It is widely known that the spectrum of adult individuals who hope to participate in the labor force in new host societies includes well-educated individuals referred to by Gunnarsson (2013) as "bilingual professionals" who work in other countries physically or virtually and who are capable users of the particular language used in those labor spheres. It also includes low-paid migrants who work in what Roberts (2010) describes as entry-level jobs that are "insecure, isolated, in poor and noisy conditions, and organized into ethnic work units" (p. 217). These latter individuals have little opportunity to master the new language at work, and, if they have limited literacy and experience in schools, they will have little success in generic umbrella courses following a traditional grammar approach to instruction. For these learners, the implementation of work-focused language programs designed from the beginning to build on current understandings of the L2 acquisition process is essential. More important, appropriate assessments also need to be designed that effectively evaluate the growth and development of the functional proficiencies needed in the workplace as opposed to grammatical accuracy, complexity, or fluency that are based on unrealistic notions of uniform progress by all learners toward native-like attainment.

School-age Learners

As is the case with adult language learners, school-age learners can also be grouped into a number of categories having to do with their age, educational background, recency of arrival, and access to the societal language in their family and community. For school-age learners, however, the intersections between learner characteristics and available language-teaching programs and program goals are much more complex. For example, in the United States, ESL programs for adults ordinarily take place as self-contained courses organized by different groups and agencies. Language instruction for school-age learners, however, is governed by legal mandates (e.g., *Lau v Nichols*, a Supreme Court Decision), by prohibitions (e.g., Proposition 227 in California, which prohibits bilingual education), by accountability requirements established by federal statute (e.g., the No Child Left Behind Act [NCLB] which, until the passage in 2015 of the Elementary and Secondary Education Act, now referred to as the Every Student Succeeds Act [ESSA], mandated the identification, assessment, and reclassification of English language learners), and by new education reform movements (e.g., Common Core State Standards, New Generation Science Standards) and their accompanying subject matter and computer-based assessments. While a thorough description of these many interacting factors is beyond the scope of this chapter,[8] I identify a number of key questions that are raised by the changing theoretical understandings in SLA, applied linguistics, and the study of bi/multilingualism about our current understandings of school language instruction:

1. What is a realistic and theoretically defensible goal for the "successful attainment" of English for school-age students?

2. If native-like proficiency is rarely attainable by most human beings, how can educators and the general public be persuaded that children can learn and function in society with less than perfect English?
3. If native-like proficiency is rarely attainable, and the learning trajectories of all learners vary in numerous ways, what types of language assessments can be constructed to measure movement and progress in individual students across time?
4. What is the role of language instruction in supporting school-age children's learning?
5. How have more recent theoretical perspectives informed what we currently accept as "best practices" in teaching and testing young learners?
6. What is the quality of the evidence about these accepted "best practices" and their use with different ages of schoolchildren (e.g., the use of grammar-focused instruction with very young children)?
7. What types of instructional arrangements can support both subject-matter learning and second-language development for school learners?

The challenges of designing new types of programs in school settings that can support L2 acquisition in ways that are informed by new knowledge are extraordinarily difficult. Beliefs about the ways that language is learned and about what is, and is not, correct language are firmly established in both public views about bilingualism as well as in time-honored school practices. Atomistic views of bilingualism (Cenoz, 2013) in which each language is seen as separate and unconnected to the other language used by the same individual are unquestioned even among bilingual speakers themselves. More recently, educators have focused on "academic language," a variously defined construct that is assumed to be essential for adequate standardized test performance (Snow & Uccelli, 2009; Solomon & Rhodes, 1995). As Bonfiglio (2010) originally argued and Flores (2013) recalled more recently, the formation of nation-states and the European colonization of the world gave rise to ideologies of language that consider languages to be enumerable, separate, and representative of the nation itself. Flores, for example, contends that, in education, broadly accepted notions of "academic language" would be better described as "the idealized context-embedded practices of the American bourgeoisie" (p. 276). Undoubtedly, it will be difficult for immigrant-receiving countries to transcend such deeply embedded notions; but if they are to be successful in promoting the integration of new immigrants, they must recognize and work to understand the actual and potential bi/multilingual realities of entering immigrants, refugees, and their children.

A LANGUAGE TEACHER'S KNOWLEDGE BASE FOR TEACHING LANGUAGE TO IMMIGRANT LANGUAGE LEARNERS

Throughout this chapter I have emphasized that traditional views of language instruction, perspectives on the goals and outcomes of language tuition, and the end state of second-language learning are currently in flux. In the sections above, I have made the following points: (1) Second-language acquisition is a highly variable and individual process; (2) it is not linear; (3) ultimate attainment for most L2 learners does not result in monolingual-like language—even when the L2 is acquired by very young children (Ortega, 2009); and (4), as Larsen-Freeman (2013) contends, teaching may not result in learning.

Many questions about teachers of language[9] and their preparation are raised by these views. What we know, however, is that changing teaching and teachers' views about what they teach and how and about the characteristics of their students is not an easy task. Currently, many accepted views that were part of second-language teacher preparation programs are being rejected by theorists and researchers (e.g., Freeman & Johnson, 1998) and, to some degree by teacher educators, those individuals most involved in the preparation of future language teachers. Much, however, has remained the same. The cognitivist perspective is still dominant in language-teaching textbooks and the many recently available webinars and online instructional professional development sites for teachers. On many of these sites, language is defined as vocabulary, and "teaching" language is considered to require direct and explicit teaching of grammatical structures and drilling and repetition of what are now called "sentence frames," which harken back to the audiolingual era.[10] Most second-language teachers at both K–12 and adult levels are prepared in the tradition of "language-as-subject" instruction (Larsen-Freeman & Freeman, 2008) in which they view their "content" as the grammar of the language that they teach. Freeman and Johnson (1998) conjecture that language teacher preparation programs still primarily emphasize a body of knowledge about language (phonology, morphology, and syntax), a set of teaching methods, and limited field experiences. Vinogradov (2013) maintains, moreover, that language teachers draw extensively from their own experiences as language learners and often believe that language teaching is a "matter of knowing the language and knowing a bit about language teaching" (p. 16).

In this currently shifting landscape surrounding both immigration reform and educational reform, there is much concern in English-speaking countries about the role of ESL teachers in the light of much-discussed new language proficiency examinations and citizenship tests for adult immigrants and the implementation of standards-based instruction and accompanying testing regimes for school-age learners. It is important, then, to advocate for the further development of a knowledge base for language teacher education previously begun by scholars who have been concerned about the particular challenges of teaching second languages as a part of established educational systems (Larsen-Freeman, 1990; Freeman & Johnson, 1998; Vinogradov, 2013). Such a knowledge base would embrace the areas of knowledge and specific elements already proposed by these researchers, as well as other critical areas that I have described in this chapter. Moreover, it can then be examined, debated, and discussed in professional organizations and conferences, and over time elements of this knowledge base might inform the thinking of teacher educators and of teachers themselves. Table 3.4 includes a listing of areas and elements that are congruent with the discussion presented in

Table 3.4. A Knowledge Base for L2 Teacher Preparation

Areas of Knowledge	Sample Elements
Themselves as teachers	• Their own beliefs and knowledge about teaching and learning • Their own learning processes as they learn how to teach
Language in the world	• The development of bilingualism and multilingualism in real-life settings • Changing perspectives on the second-language acquisition process • Contributions and limitations of the various subfields that inform language teaching • Debates and disagreements within these subfields
Schools and students	• The social and political processes that surround immigrant language instruction • The social context of schools
Immigration and education	• Immigrant students, their experiences and characteristics • The social and political processes that inform immigrant language instruction
Pedagogy	• The pedagogical processes of language teaching and learning • The pedagogical processes of teaching literacy to adult and school-age children with limited educations
Assessment	• Formative and summative assessments of L2 proficiency

this paper and might be included in an initial version of such a knowledge base.

The areas covered by the proposed knowledge base can clearly not be covered in preservice teacher education programs. Difficult choices would need to be made about the sequencing of essential points and key elements. Most important, from the perspective of the teaching of newly arrived child and adult immigrants, language teacher preparation must endeavor to connect theory, practice, and research. As Larsen-Freeman (1990) pointed out, most language teachers "teach in a manner consistent with their own oft implicit and somewhat idiosyncratic, 'small-t' theories" (p. 261). If language teaching is to incorporate changing theoretical perspectives, teachers need to be supported in examining and reflecting on the outcomes of their practice in the context of the actual needs and challenges of using language in a new society. In so doing they must be invited to engage with new knowledge about the development of bi/multilingualism in an age of super diversity.

CONCLUSION

The importance of acquiring the destination language for all immigrants has been clearly established. There is no debate about the benefits of this language for the integration and adaptation of new arrivals. Language skills are important for everyday living, for entering the workforce, and for participating in civic society. They are also important in meeting existing requirements for citizenship that involve demonstrating the acquisition of language proficiency in the host language. In this chapter I have argued that the ways in which second languages are best acquired by adult and child learners are a matter of debate. The theoretical shifts taking place in the field of SLA, moreover, raise many questions about business-as-usual approaches to providing language instruction

I have deliberately focused on shifting theories of second-language acquisition in a book dedicated to the examination of global migratory flows because language matters. I have attempted to make clear the difficulties of measuring language, the problems with assuming that native-like proficiencies in a second language can be attained by most immigrants—or indeed, most human beings. I have also emphasized the importance of learner differences in the planning and design of language-teaching programs. Most important, I have argued that language assessments that are based on consensus views of acquisition progressions will provide little information about the actual learning and development of the host language, but they can and will serve to create categories that will label and exclude particular individuals or groups of individuals. Working with and through established educational systems, moreover, is a difficult process. At every level these systems work slowly. New theories are unlikely to change practice.

In concluding, I want to emphasize that language is a "loaded weapon" (Bolinger, 1980). It is an instrument that can be used for the inclusion and exclusion of groups and individuals in ways that limit their potential and their future. It is important that the research community that focuses on migration have realistic expectations about L2 instruction and about both theories about language and language acquisition and the practices and approaches directed at creating the conditions and circumstances necessary for the development of functional bilingualism in new immigrants and their children. An understanding of what is really possible for the majority of individuals who acquire a second language is essential in crafting policies, designing programs, and investigating the success or failure of immigrant integration.

NOTES

1. Valdés and Figueroa (1994) contrast *elective bilinguals* (individuals who make a conscious choice to acquire a second language generally in instructed settings) with *circumstantial bilinguals* (individuals who acquire an additional language in the course of everyday life by interacting with fluent speakers).

2. For a broad overview of this scholarship, the reader is directed to two recent handbooks: Bhatia & Ritchie (2012) and Hickey (2010).

3. The term *target language* is used in the language-teaching field to refer to a language that an individual seeks to acquire as a second language.

4. Programs of various types designed for the children of immigrants have also been only moderately successful. For comprehensive discussions of the many factors involved in the education of bilingual/multilingual students, the reader is referred to Wright, Boun, and García (2015).

5. The contrast I have set up here between highly educated immigrants and members of sending populations who have not had the opportunity to acquire such an education in their home countries unfortunately does not focus on the many other life skills and strengths that these individuals bring with them. However, formal education and the lack of it is a key factor in the teaching and learning of language in classroom settings, so program designers must be aware of the population for whom their programs are intended. One size does not fit all. There is much work to be done in identifying the best ways that such life skills can be built on in acquiring a destination language outside the classroom.

6. Proceedings are available on the LESLLA website (http://www.leslla.org/). It should be noted that this organization uses the term *low-educated* which others might consider to be a deficit label.

7. There has been some work conducted by communities themselves on the strategies (based on first-language literacy) used by new immigrants in acquiring English (e.g., Kalmar, 2015).

8. For recent discussions of some of these issues, the reader is referred to Linquanti and Cook (2013) and Uro and Barrio (2013).

9. I am differentiating here between teachers who teach language as an academic subject and teachers who primarily teach other content (math, biology, history) and only incidentally focus on language.

10. *Audiolingualism* (based on behaviorist theory) was a popular language-teaching approach—now generally discredited—that used repetition of basic patterns to promote mechanical habit-formation. It was thought that the drilling of such patterns would lead to eventual fluency and to grammatical accuracy.

REFERENCES

Abel, G. J., & Sander, N. (2014). Quantifying global international migration flows. *Science*, *343*(6178), 1520–1522. Retrieved from www.sciencemag.org/content/343/6178/1520. short

Amin, N. (2004). Nativism, the native speaker construct, and minority immigrant women teachers of English as a second language. In L. D. Kamhi-Stein (Ed.), *Learning and teaching from experience: Perspectives on nonnative English-speaking professionals* (pp. 61–80). Ann Arbor: University of Michigan Press.

Atkinson, D. (2011). Introduction: Cognitivism and second language acquisition. In D. Atkinson (Ed.), *Alternative approaches to second language acquisition* (pp. 1–23). New York, NY: Routledge.

Auer, P. (2007). The monolingual bias in bilingualism research, or: Why bilingual talk is (still) a challenge for linguistics. In M. Heller (Ed.), *Bilingualism: A social approach.* (pp. 320–339). New York, NY: Palgrave.

Batalova, J., & Fix, M. (2010). A profile of limited English proficient adult immigrants. *Peabody Journal of Education, 85*(4), 511–534.

Benton, M. (2013). *Maximizing potential: How countries can address skills deficits within the immigrant workforce.* Washington, DC: Migration Policy Institute.

Bhatia, T. K., & Ritchie, W. C. (2012). *The handbook of bilingualism and multilingualism.* Malden, MA: Wiley-Blackwell.

Bialystok, E., & Peets, K. F. (2010). Bilingualism and cognitive linkages: Learning to read in different languages. In M. Shatz & L. C. Wilkinson (Eds.), *The education of English language learners: Research to practice* (pp. 133–151). New York, NY: Guilford Press.

Block, David. (2003). *The social turn in second language acquisition.* Washington, DC: Georgetown University Press.

Blommaert, J., & Rampton, B. (2012). Language and superdiversity. MMG Working Paper. Retrieved from http://hdl.handle.net/11858/00-001M-0000-000E-7CFE-9

Bolinger, D. L. M. (1980). *Language: The loaded weapon.* London, United Kingdom: Longman.

Bonfiglio, T. P. (2010). *Mother tongues and nations: The invention of the native speaker.* Boston, MA: De Gruyter.

Canagarajah, A. S. (1999a). Interrogating the "native speaker fallacy": Non-linguistic roots, non-pedagogical results. In G. Braine (Ed.), *Non-native educators in English language teaching* (pp. 77–92). Mahwah, NJ: Lawrence Erlbaum.

Canagarajah, A. S. (1999b). *Resisting linguistic imperialism in English teaching.* Oxford, United Kingdom: Oxford University Press.

Canagarajah, A. S. (2011). Translanguaging in the classroom: Emerging issues for research and pedagogy. *Applied Linguistics Review, 2,* 1–28

Cenoz, J. (2013). Defining multilingualism. *Annual Review of Applied Linguistics, 33,* 3–18.

Chiswick, B. R., & Miller, P. W. (2007). *The economics of language: International analyses.* New York, NY: Taylor & Francis.

Cook, V. (1992). Evidence for multi-competence. *Language Learning, 42*(4), 557–591.

Cook, V. (1996). Competence and multi-competence. In G. Brown, K. Malmkjaer, & J. Williams (Eds.), *Performance and competence in second language acquisition* (pp. 57–69). Cambridge, United Kingdom: Cambridge University Press.

Cook, V. (1999). Going beyond the native speaker in language teaching. *TESOL Quarterly, 33*(2), 185–209. doi:10.2307/3587717/abstract

Cook, V. (2010). Prolegomena to second language learning. In P. Seedhouse, S. Walsh, & C. Jenks (Eds.), *Conceptualizing "learning" in applied linguistics* (pp. 6–22). New York, NY: Palgrave.

Creese, A., & Blackledge, A. (2010). Translanguaging in the bilingual classroom: A pedagogy for learning and teaching? *Modern Language Journal, 94*(1), 103–115.

Crosnoe, R. (2013). *Preparing the children of immigrants for early academic success.* Washington, DC: Migration Policy Institute.

Cumming, A. (2008). Assessing oral and literate abilities. In E. Shohamy & N. H. Hornberger (Eds.), *Encyclopedia of language and education: Vol. 7. Language testing and assessment* (pp. 3–17). Boston, MA: Springer.

Cummins, J. (2008). Teaching for transfer: Challenging the two solitudes assumption in bilingual education. In J. Cummins (Ed.), *Encyclopedia of language and education: Vol. 5. Bilingual Education* (pp. 65–75). Boston, MA: Springer.

Davies, A. (1991). *The native speaker in applied linguistics*. Edinburgh, United Kingdom: Edinburgh University Press.

Davies, A. (2003). *The native speaker: Myth and reality*. Tonawanda, NY: Multilingual Matters.

de Bot, K., Lowie, W., & Verspoor, M. (2007). A dynamic systems theory approach to second language acquisition. *Bilingualism: Language and Cognition, 10,* 7–21.

Doerr, N. M. (Ed.). (2009). *The native speaker concept: Ethnographic investigations of native speaker effects*. Berlin, Germany: De Gruyter.

Doerr, N. M., & Kumagai, Y. (2009). Towards a critical orientation in second language education. In N. M. Doerr (Ed.), *The native speaker concept: Ethnographic investigations of native speaker effects* (pp. 299–317). Berlin, Germany: De Gruyter.

Duff, P. A., & Talmy, S. (2011). Language socialization approaches to second language acquisition: Social, cultural, and linguistic development in additional languages. In D. Atkinson (Ed.), *Alternative approaches to second language acquisition* (pp. 95–116). New York, NY: Routledge.

Flores, N. (2013). Silencing the subaltern: Nation-state/colonial governmentality and bilingual education in the United States. *Critical Inquiry in Language Studies, 10*(4), 263–287.

Freeman, D., & Johnson, K. E. (1998). Reconceptualizing the knowledge base of language teacher education. *TESOL Quarterly, 32*(3), 397–417.

Fulcher, G., & Davidson, F. (2012). *The Routledge handbook of language testing*. New York, NY: Routledge.

García, O., with Beardsmore, H. B. (2009). *Bilingual education in the 21st century: A global perspective*. Malden, MA: Wiley–Blackwell.

Grosjean, F. (1989). Neurolinguists, beware! The bilingual is not two monolinguals in one person. *Brain and Language, 36,* 5–15.

Grosjean, F. (1998). Studying bilinguals: Methodological and conceptual issues. *Bilingualism: Language and Cognition, 1*(2), 131–149.

Gunnarsson, B.-L. (2013). Multilingualism in the workplace. *Annual Review of Applied Linguistics, 33,* 162–189.

Han, Z. (2004). *Fossilization in adult second language acquisition*. Clevedon, United Kingdom: Multilingual Matters.

Hasko, V. (2013). Capturing the dynamics of second language development via learner corpus research: A very long engagement. *Modern Language Journal, 97*(S1), 1–10.

Hawthorne, L. (2013). *Recognizing foreign qualifications: Emerging global trends*. Washington, DC: Migration Policy Institute.

Heller, M. (2007). Bilingualism as ideology and practice. In M. Heller (Ed.), *Bilingualism: A social approach*. New York, NY: Palgrave Macmillan

Hickey, R. (Ed.). (2010). *The handbook of language contact*. Malden, MA: Wiley.

Hogan-Brun, G., Mar-Molinero, C., & Stevenson, P. (2009). *Discourses on language and integration: Critical perspectives on language testing regimes in Europe* (Vol. 33). Amsterdam, The Netherlands: John Benjamins.

House, J. (2003). English as a lingua franca: A threat to multilingualism. *Journal of Sociolinguistics, 7*(4), 556–578.

Hulstijn, J. H. (2012). The construct of language proficiency in the study of bilingualism from a cognitive perspective. *Bilingualism: Language and Cognition, 15*(2), 422–433.

Jacquemet, M. (2005). Transidiomatic practices: Language and power in the age of globalization. *Language & Communication, 25*(3), 257–277.

Kalmar, T. M. (2015). *Illegal alphabets and adult biliteracy: Latino migrants crossing the linguistic border,* (2nd ed.). New York, NY: Routledge.

Kasper, G., & Wagner, J. (2011). A conversation-analytic approach to second language acquisition. In D. Atkinson (Ed.), *Alternative approaches to second language acquisition* (pp. 117–142). New York, NY: Routledge.

Kramsch, C. (1997). The privilege of the nonnative speaker. *PMLA, 112*(3), 359–369.

Kroskrity, P. V. (2004). Language ideologies. In A. Duranti (Ed.), *A companion to linguistic anthropology* (pp. 496–517). Oxford, United Kingdom: Blackwell.

Kroskrity, P. V. (2010). Language ideologies: Evolving perspectives. In J. Jurgen, J.-O. Ostman, & J. Verschueren (Eds.), *Society and language use* (pp. 192–211). Amsterdam, Netherlands: John Benjamins.

Larsen-Freeman, D. (1990). On the need for a theory of language teaching. In J. E. Alatis (Ed.), *Linguistics and language pedagogy: The state of the art* (pp. 261–270). Georgetown University Round Table on Languages and Linguistics. Washington, DC: Georgetown University Press.

Larsen-Freeman, D. (2002). Language acquisition and language use from a chaos/complexity theory perspective. In C. Kramsch (Ed.), *Language acquisition and language socialization: Ecological perspectives* (pp. 33–46). London, United Kingdom: Continuum.

Larsen-Freeman, D. (2006). Second language acquisition and the issue of fossilization: There is no end, and there is no state. In Z. Han & T. Odlin (Eds.), *Studies of fossilization in second language acquisition* (pp. 189–200). Clevedon, United Kingdom: Multilingual Matters.

Larsen-Freeman, D. (2010). Having and doing: Learning from a complexity theory perspective. In P. Seedhouse, S. Walsh, & C. Jenks (Eds.), *Conceptualizing "learning" in applied linguistics* (pp. 52–68). New York, NY: Palgrave.

Larsen-Freeman, D. (2012, November). Chaos/complexity theory for second language acquisition. *The Encyclopedia of Applied Linguistics.* doi: 10.1002/9781405198431. wbeal0125

Larsen-Freeman, D. (2013, March). *The standards and second language development: A complexity theory perspective.* Paper presented at the TESOL International Convention & English Language Expo, Dallas, Texas.

Larsen-Freeman, D., & Cameron, L. (2008). *Complex systems and applied linguistics.* New York, NY: Oxford University Press.

Larsen-Freeman, D, & Freeman, D. (2008). Language moves: The place of "foreign languages in classroom teaching and learning. *Review of Research in Education, 32, 147–186.*

Leikin, M., Schwartz, M., & Tobin, Y. (2012). Current issues in bilingualism: A complex approach to a multidimensional phenomenon. In M. Leikin, M. Schwartz, & Y. Tobin (Eds.), *Current issues in bilingualism: Cognitive and socio-linguistic perspectives* (pp. 1–18). Dordrecht, The Netherlands: Springer.

Leung, C., Harris, R., & Rampton, B. (1997). The idealised native speaker, reified ethnicities, and classroom realities. *TESOL Quarterly, 31*(3), 543–560. doi/10.2307/3587837/ abstract

Linquanti, R., & Cook, G. (2013). *Toward a "common definition of English learner": Guidance for states and state assessment consortia in defining and addressing policy and technical issues and options.* Washington, DC: Council of Chief State School Officers.

Lippi-Green, R. (2012). *English with an accent* (2nd ed.). New York, NY: Routledge.

Lukes, M. M. (2009). "We thought they had forgotten us": Research, policy, and practice in the education of Latino immigrant adults. *Journal of Latinos and Education, 8*(2), 161–172.

MacKenzie, I. (2012). English as a lingua franca in Europe: Bilingualism and multicompetence. *International Journal of Multilingualism, 9*(1), 83–100.

Makoni, S. B., & Pennycook, A. (2007). *Disinventing and reconstituting languages.* Clevedon, United Kingdom: Multilingual Matters.

May, S. (2013). Disciplinary divides, knowledge construction and the multilingual turn. In S. May (Ed.), *The multilingual turn: Implications for SLA, TESOL and bilingual education.* New York, NY: Routledge.

McHugh, M., & Challinor, A. E. (2011). *Improving immigrants' employment prospects through work-focused language instruction.* Washington, DC: Migration Policy Institute.

McHugh, M., Gelatt, J., & Fix, M. (2007). *Adult English language instruction in the United States: Determining need and investing wisely.* Washington, DC: Migration Policy Institute.

McNamara, T., & Shohamy, E. (2008). Language tests and human rights. *International Journal of Applied Linguistics, 18*(1), 89–95.

Ortega, L. (2009). *Understanding second language acquisition.* London, United Kingdom: Hodder Education.

Ortega, L. (2013). Ways forward for a bi/multilingual turn in SLA. In S. May (Ed.), *The multilingual turn: Implications for SLA, TESOL and bilingual education* (pp. 32–54). New York, NY: Routledge.

Ortega, L., & Iberri-Shea, G. (2005). Longitudinal research in second language acquisition: Recent trends and future directions. *Annual Review of Applied Linguistics, 25,* 26–45.

Otsuji, E., & Pennycook, A. (2010). Metrolingualism: Fixity, fluidity and language in flux. *International Journal of Multilingualism, 7*(3), 240–254.

Pennycook, A. (1994). *The cultural politics of English as an international language.* London, United Kingdom: Longman.

Pennycook, A. (2011). Critical and alternative directions in applied linguistics. *Australian Review of Applied Linguistics, 33*(2), 16.1–16.16.

Phillipson, R. (1992). *Linguistic imperialism.* Oxford, United Kingdom: Oxford University Press.

Piller, I. (2002). Passing for a native speaker: Identity and success in second language learning. *Journal of Sociolinguistics, 6*(2), 179–208. Retrieved from onlinelibrary.wiley.com/doi/10.1111/1467-9481.00184/full

Pujolar, J. (2007). Bilingualism and the nation-state in the post-national era. In M. Heller (Ed.), *Bilingualism: A social approach* (pp. 71–95). New York, NY: Palgrave.

Rampton, M. B. H. (1990). Displacing the "native speaker": Expertise, affiliation, and inheritance. *ELT Journal, 44*(2), 97–101. doi: 10.1093/elt/44.2.97

Roberts, C. (2010). Language socialization in the workplace. *Annual Review of Applied Linguistics, 30*(1), 211–227.

Seedhouse, P. (2010). A framework for conceptualizing learning and applied linguistics. In P. Seedhouse, S. Walsh, & C. Jenks (Eds.), *Conceptualizing "learning" in applied linguistics* (pp. 240–256). New York, NY: Palgrave.

Shohamy, E. G. (2001). *The power of tests: A critical perspective on the uses of language tests.* Harlow, United Kingdom: Longman.

Shohamy, E. G. (2009). Language tests for immigrants: Why language? Why tests? Why citizenship? In G. Hogan-Brun, C. Mar-Molinero, & P. Stevenson, P. (Eds.), *Discourses on language and integration: Critical perspectives on language testing regimes in Europe* (pp. 45–59). Amsterdam, Netherlands: John Benjamins.

Shohamy, E. G. (2012). *Language policy: Hidden agendas and new approaches.* New York, NY: Routledge.

Skeldon, R. (2013). *Global migration: Demographic aspects and its relevance for development.* New York, NY: Department of Economic and Social Affairs. Retrieved from www.un.org/en/development/desa/population/migration/publications/technicalpapers/index.shtml

Skutnabb-Kangas, T. (2000). *Linguistic genocide in education or worldwide diversity and human rights.* Mahwah, NJ: Lawrence Erlbaum.

Snow, C. E., & Uccelli, P. (2009). The challenge of academic language. *The Cambridge Handbook of Literacy,* 112–133. dx.doi.org/10.1017/CBO9780511609664.008

Solomon, J., & Rhodes, N. C. (1995). *Conceptualizing academic language* (Research Report No. 15). Washington, DC: National Center for Research on Cultural Diversity and Second Language Learning.

Spolsky, B. (2009). *Language management.* Cambridge, United Kingdom: Cambridge University Press.

Spotti, M., & Van Avermaet, P. (2009). *Language testing, migration and citizenship: Cross-national perspectives on integration regimes.* New York, NY: Continuum.

Tarone, E., & Bigelow, M. (2011, September). *A research agenda for second language acquisition of preliterate and low literate adult and adolescent readers.* Paper presented at the 7th symposium of Low Educated Second Language and Literacy Acquisition (LESLLA), Minneapolis, MN.

Toker, E. B. C. (2012). What makes a native speaker? Nativeness, ownership, and global Englishes. *Minnesota Review, 2012*(78), 113–129.

UN-DESA & OECD. (2015). *World Migration in Figures.* United Nations: Department of Economic and Social Affairs. Retrieved from http://www.oecd.org/els/mig/dioc.htm

Uro, G., & Barrio, A. (2013). *English language learners in America's great city schools .* Washington, DC: Council of the Great City Schools.

Valdés, G.. (2015). Latin@s and the intergenerational continuity of Spanish: The challenges of curricularizing language. *International Multilingual Research Journal, 9*(4), 253–273.

Valdés, G., & Figueroa, R. (1994). *Bilingualism and testing: A special case of bias.* Norwood, NJ: Ablex.

van de Craats, I., Kurvers, J., & Young-Scholten, M. (Eds.). (2006). *Low-educated second language and literacy acquisition: Proceedings of the inaugural symposium, Tilburg University, August 2005.* Utrecht, The Netherlands: LOT.

van Lier, L. (2004). *The ecology and semiotics of language learning: A sociocultural perspective.* Boston, MA: Kluwer Academic.

Vinogradov, P. (2013). Defining the LESLLA teacher knowledge base. In T. Tammelin-Laine, L. Nieminen, & M. Martin (Eds.), *Low-educated second language and literacy acquisition: Proceedings of the 8th symposium,* University of Jyväskylä, [2012] (pp. 9–24). Jyväskylä, Sweden: Jyväskylä University Printing House. Retrieved from https://jyx.jyu.fi/dspace/handle/123456789/41907

Wei, L. (2010). The nature of linguistic norms and their relevance to multilingual development. In M. Cruz-Ferreira (Ed.), *Multilingual Norms* (pp. 397–404). Frankfurt, Germany: Peter Lang.

Wei, L. (2013). Conceptual and methodological issues in bilingualism and multilingualism research. In T. K. Bhatia & W. C. Ritchie (Eds.), *The handbook of bilingualism and multilingualism* (2nd ed., pp. 26–51). Oxford, United Kingdom: Wiley Blackwell.

Wong Fillmore, L. (1985a, July). *Second language learning in children: A proposed model.* Paper presented at a conference on Issues in English Language Development for Minority Language Education, Arlington, VA.

Wong Fillmore, L. (1985b). When does teacher talk work as input? In S. Gass & C. Madden (Eds.), *Input in second language acquisition* (pp. 17–50). Rowley, MA: Newbury.

Woolard, K. A. (1998). Introduction: Language ideology as a field of inquiry. In B. B. Schieffelin, K. A. Woolard, & P. A. Kroskrity (Eds.), *Language ideologies: Practice and theory* (pp. 3–47). New York, NY: Oxford University Press.

Wright, W. E., Boun, S., & García, O. (Eds.). (2015). *The handbook of bilingual and multilingual education.* New York, NY: Wiley.

Xi, J., Hwang, S.-S, & Cao, Y. (2010). Ecological context and immigrants' earnings: English ability as a mediator. *Social Science Research, 39*(4), 652–661.

Zetter, R. (2015). *Protection in crisis: Forced migration and protection in a global era.* Washington, DC: Migration Policy Institute.

Part II

IMMIGRATION, EDUCATION, AND CITIZENSHIP: CASE STUDIES

CHAPTER 4

Immigrant Students in the United States

Addressing Their Possibilities and Challenges

Carola Suárez-Orozco and Amy K. Marks

American educational settings are encountering ever more diverse students. As the foreign-born U.S. population has increased in recent decades, so too has the number of their children. Currently 25% of U.S. children under age 18 (18.7 million children) have an immigrant parent. This growth has been rapid—in 1970 the population of immigrant-origin children was 6% of all children. It reached 20% by 2000 and is projected to be 33% by 2050 (Pew Research Center, 2013). These children are an integral part of the national tapestry. Most of the expansion of the immigrant-origin youth population has been in the second generation—citizen children born to foreign-born parents. Notably, this increase has occurred at a faster rate than the birth rate of children who are not of immigrant origin. In order to serve these diverse students well, educators will need to have a broad understanding of who they are, what their strengths are, and what some of their challenges are.

Schools are the first contexts in which immigrant-origin students are likely to have sustained contact with members of the host society. School is a space where they begin to learn the rules of engagement of their new land as well as to comprehend the messages of reception of their hosts. Further, schools are the single most important elevator of social mobility in a knowledge-intensive economy. Thus the ways in which schools succeed or fail have clear implications for immigrants as well as for our society.

Here we provide an overview of the educational possibilities and challenges for immigrant students as they navigate their way into their new land. We outline how the social and educational contexts of reception that immigrant families and students encounter have significant implications for these students and consider how family resources and challenges also play an important role in framing educational trajectories. We provide some insights into ways in which schools often misalign with immigrant students' needs. As not all schools are created equal, we conclude with insights into how schools can serve as bridges to opportunity for their immigrant-origin students.

RECOGNIZING THE POSSIBILITIES AND CHALLENGES
OF IMMIGRANT STUDENTS

Immigrant youth in the United States are more diverse then ever before, arriving from multiple points of origin: 89% originate from Latin America, Asia, Africa, Oceania, or the Caribbean, while 11% migrate from Europe or Canada. Some are the children of educated professional parents, while others have illiterate parents. Some receive excellent schooling in their countries of origin, while others leave educational systems that are in shambles. Some are refugees escaping political, religious, and social strife or environmental catastrophes (see APA 2010 report on refugee children; Lustig et al., 2004; Masten & Narayan, 2012). Others are motivated by the promise of better jobs, while still others frame their migrations as an opportunity to provide better education for their children (Hagelskamp, Suárez-Orozco, & Hughes, 2010). Some are documented migrants, while millions are unauthorized migrants (see Bean & Lowell, 2007; Suárez-Orozco, Yoshikawa, Teranishi, & Suárez-Orozco, 2011). Some join well-established communities with robust social supports, while others move from one migrant setting to another (Ream, 2005). The educational outcomes of immigrant youth will vary considerably, depending upon their constellation of resources (Portes & Rumbaut, 2006; Suárez-Orozco, Suárez-Orozco, & Todorova, 2008).

Whether or not immigrant students will be successful educationally is determined by a convergence of factors: the social context of reception (economic realities, immigration policies, and the social mirror), family capital (such as poverty, parental education, and authorization status), student resources (their socioemotional assets and their facility in acquiring a second language), and the kinds of schools that immigrant students encounter (school segregation, the language instruction they are provided, how well prepared their teachers are to provide services to them). This complex constellation of variables serves to undermine or, conversely, to bolster students' academic integration and adaptation.

Immigrant families arrive in their new land with distinct social and cultural resources (Perreira, Harris, & Lee, 2006). Their high aspirations (Fuligni, 2001; Portes & Rumbaut, 2006), dual frames of reference (Suárez-Orozco & Suárez-Orozco, 1995), optimism (Kao & Tienda, 1995), dedicated hard work, positive attitudes toward school (Suárez-Orozco & Suárez-Orozco, 1995), and ethic of family support for advanced learning (Li, 2004) contribute to the fact that some immigrant youth educationally outperform their native-born peers (Perreira, Harris, & Lee, 2006). On the other hand, many immigrant youth encounter a myriad of challenges—economic obstacles, xenophobia,[1] language difficulties, family separations, underresourced neighborhoods and schools—as they struggle to gain their bearings in an educational system that may put them on a downward trajectory (García Coll & Marks, 2011; Portes & Zhou, 1993; Suárez-Orozco, Suárez-Orozco, & Todorova, 2008; Suárez-Orozco, Abo-Zena, & Marks, 2015).

THE SOCIAL CONTEXTS OF RECEPTION

The contexts in which an immigrant family settles shape the cultural adaptation experiences of its children. Here we consider three contexts that arguably matter most for immigrant student education.

Economic Realities

Securing work is a paramount motivation for many immigrants, and the work setting is extremely important in understanding the immigrant experience. The broader economic context shapes the experience of immigration in a variety of ways: the types of jobs that are available, the stability of jobs, and the opportunities to move up a status mobility ladder (Suárez-Orozco & Suárez-Orozco, 2013). The stability and quality of jobs, along with parents' status mobility, in turn have implications for immigrant students. How often students change schools and how well members of immigrant communities are represented in the school system are but a few of the variables linking parents' work with their children's educational experiences and successes (García Coll & Marks, 2009). While skilled immigrants have been rapidly moving up into the top tiers of the work hierarchy (Hanson, 2010), many others, particularly those with lesser skills, have stagnated since the Great Recession of 2008 (Suárez-Orozco & Suárez-Orozco, 2013).

Immigration Policies

In recent decades in the United States, immigration policy has largely focused on border control, with little consideration given to a national integration policy for new immigrants (M. Suárez-Orozco & Suárez-Orozco, 2013), which is a sharp contrast to Canada's policies. Since 1988, when the amnesty provisions of the Immigration Reform and Control Act of 1986 ended, U.S. immigration policy has restricted pathways to citizenship for the undocumented (Motomura, 2008). What in the public imagination are clearly demarcated lines of *legal* and *illegal* are in fact states of *liminal legality* (Suárez-Orozco, Yoshikawa, et al., 2011). Many families, children, and youth exist in a state of ambiguous documentation, fall out of legal status, or live in families of mixed status in which some members are documented while others are not (Kanstrom, 2010; Menjívar, 2006; Suárez-Orozco, Yoshikawa, et al., 2011). Furthermore, during the past decade, the United States became a "deportation nation," deporting 400,000 individuals a year (Kanstrom, 2010). Concurrently, as attitudes toward undocumented immigrants have grown increasingly harsh, a wave of state and local laws has targeted undocumented immigrants (Preston, 2011). Long backlogs, deep bureaucracy, and high rates of denials and deportations have cemented growing numbers of transnationally separated and mixed-status families (Suárez-Orozco, Yoshikawa, et al., 2011). These contexts of reception have significant implications for students' development and academic experiences (Suárez-Orozco, Yoshikawa, et al., 2011; Yoshikawa, 2011).

The Social Mirror

In addition to economic and policy contexts of reception, the social welcome mat profoundly influences the development of immigrant-origin children. Immigrants' identities are shaped by their ethos of reception. The *social mirror*—the general social and emotional atmosphere and the collective representations of immigrants that new arrivals encounter upon their settlement in the new country—is an important context of immigration (Suárez-Orozco & Suárez-Orozco, 2001). In the 1980s a comprehensive look at the experiences of Punjabi immigrants in rural California painted a troubling picture of the effects of negative social mirroring on academic challenges—from intense peer interactions around race to struggles within the community on how to support (or reject) Punjabi families in schools (Gibson, 1988). More recently, and during times of socioeconomic and political anxiety, there is continued evidence that immigrants embody nativists' fear of the unknown. The recent rapid increase in immigration; the terrorist attacks on September 11, 2001; the persistence of unauthorized immigration; and the deep economic recession have aligned to arouse U.S. citizens' unease concerning immigrants of color. Xenophobia has been on the rise, especially as directed toward newer immigrants and toward Muslims (Sirin & Fine, 2008) and Latinos (Chavez, 2008). There is ample evidence of negative media coverage of immigration (Massey, 2010), an increase in hate crimes against immigrants (Leadership Conference on Civil Rights Education Fund, 2009), and exclusionary legislation enacted on municipal, state, and federal levels (Carter, Lawrence, & Morse, 2011). Furthermore, since the new immigrants are predominantly of non-European origin, their children will remain visible minorities for generations, subject to the ongoing racial climate of the nation. What are the developmental and educational implications of such a social reception? (García Coll & Magnuson, 1997; Suárez-Orozco & Suárez-Orozco, 2001.)

FAMILY-OF-ORIGIN ISSUES

The family is a context of development that is critical for shaping the experiences of children in both positive and negative ways. Here we consider three negative issues that may matter most for immigrant youth's challenges in their educational experiences.

Poverty

More than half of children with immigrant parents live in circumstances of poverty (Hernandez & Napierala, 2012). Further, for immigrant-origin children, official calculations of family poverty fail to consider the economic complications of their families' transnational lives. Many immigrant families, particularly those who recently arrived, maintain dual economic ties, making remittances to spouses and other family members in the country of origin for medical, educational, and other basic expenses (Levitt & Schiller, 2004). Thus, already thin resources are stretched further.

Poverty is a significant risk factor for poor educational outcomes (Luthar, 1999; Milner, 2013). Children raised in circumstances of socioeconomic deprivation are vulnerable to an array of distresses, including difficulties concentrating and sleeping, anxiety, and depression, as well as a heightened propensity for delinquency and violence. Those living in poverty often experience the stress of major life events as well as the stress of daily hassles that significantly impede academic performance (Luthar, 1999). Poverty frequently coexists with other factors that augment risks—such as single-parenthood and residency in neighborhoods plagued by violence, gang activity, and drug trade—as well as school environments that are segregated, overcrowded, and poorly funded (Luthar, 1999). Poverty is also associated with high rates of housing mobility and concurrent school transitions, which are disruptive to educational performance (Gándara & Contreras, 2009; Milner, 2013). Although some immigrant students come from privileged backgrounds, large numbers suffer today from the challenges associated with poverty (Hernández, Denton, & Macartney, 2007; Mather, 2009; United Nations Development Programme, 2009).

Undocumented Status

An estimated 11.1 million immigrants live in the United States without authorization, and of that population, 78% are from Mexico and Latin America (Pew Research Center, 2013). Among the undocumented population in the United States, 1.1 million are children or adolescents (Suárez-Orozco, Yoshikawa, et al., 2011). Undocumented youth often arrive after multiple family separations and traumatic border crossings (Suárez-Orozco, Todorova, & Louie, 2002). In addition, there are an estimated 4.5 million U.S.-citizen children living in households headed by at least one undocumented immigrant (Passel, 2006). Unauthorized children and youth in households with other unauthorized members live with anxiety and fear of being separated from family members if they or someone they love is apprehended or deported (Capps, Castañeda, Chaudry, & Santos, 2007); such psychological and emotional duress can take a heavy toll on the academic experiences of children growing up in these homes. Further, while unauthorized youth legally have equal access to K–12 education, they do not have equal access to healthcare, social services, or jobs (Gándara & Contreras, 2009; Suárez-Orozco, Yoshikawa, et al., 2011). In addition, undocumented students with dreams of higher education will find their legal status stands in the way of their access to these opportunities (Suárez-Orozco, Suárez-Orozco, & Todorova, 2008). Thus immigrant-origin students who are unauthorized or who come from unauthorized families suffer from both a particular burden of unequal access and the psychological burdens of growing up in the shadows of unauthorized status (Suárez-Orozco, Yoshikawa, et al., 2011).

Family Educational Background

Parental education matters tremendously for children's academic pathways. Highly literate parents are better equipped to guide their children in studying, accessing, and making meaning of educational information. Children with more educated parents are exposed to more academically oriented vocabulary and interactions at home, and younger children tend to be read to more often from books that are valued at school (Rueda, August, & Goldenberg, 2006). These parents understand the value of and have the resources to provide additional books, home computers, Internet access, and tutors that less educated parents cannot supply. They are also more likely to seek information about how to navigate the educational system in the new land.

Unfortunately, many immigrant parents have had limited schooling. Moreover, low parental education is compounded by parents' limited skills in the new land's language, which are related to the support children receive for learning the language of instruction at home (Castro, Páez, Dickinson, & Frede, 2011). Such disadvantaged backgrounds will have implications for the students' educational transition; unsurprisingly, youth arriving from families with lower levels of education tend to struggle academically while those who come from more literate families with strong language skills often flourish (Kasinitz, Mollenkopf, Waters, & Holdaway, 2008). It is worth noting, however, that these patterns do not hold true for all immigrant families and communities. There are many examples of immigrant parents who provide educational socialization in the home despite having a low level of education themselves (Roy & Roxas, 2011).

Immigrant parents, however, often do not possess the kind of "cultural capital" that serves middle-class mainstream students well (Perreira et al., 2006); not knowing the dominant cultural values of the new society limits immigrant parents' abilities to provide an upward academic path for their children. Oftentimes parental involvement is neither a cultural practice in their countries of origin nor an activity that their financial situation in this country would permit. They come from cultural traditions in which parents are expected to respect teachers' recommendations rather than to advocate for their children (Delgado-Gaitan, 2004). In addition, not speaking English and having limited education may make them feel inadequate. Lack of documentation may cause them to worry about exposure to immigration raids (Capps, Castañeda, et al., 2007) if they were to have contact with their children's school. Moreover, low-wage, low-skill jobs with off-hour shifts typically do not provide much flexibility for parents to obtain child care and attend parent–teacher conferences. The impediments to these parents' abilities to come to the school are multiple, but they are frequently interpreted by teachers and principals as the parents' "not valuing" their children's education.

Nevertheless, immigrant parents often frame the family narrative of migration around providing better educational opportunities for their children (Suárez-Orozco, Suárez-Orozco, & Todorova, 2008). Although they may care deeply about their children's education and may urge their children to work hard in school so that they will not have to perform hard physical labor as they do, immigrant parents frequently do not have firsthand experience with the host country's school system or their own native country's educational system (López, 2001). Thus they often have limited capacities (including limited social networks) to help their children successfully "play the educational game" in their new land.

STUDENT-LEVEL ISSUES

Socioemotional Challenges

Migration is a transformative process with profound implications for the family as well as the potential for lasting impact on socioemotional development (García Coll & Magnuson, 1997; Suárez-Orozco & Suárez-Orozco, 2001). By any measure, immigration is one of the most stressful events a family can undergo (Falicov, 1998; Suárez-Orozco & Suárez-Orozco, 2001), removing family members from predictable contexts—community ties, jobs, and customs—and stripping them of significant social ties—extended family members, best friends, and neighbors. New arrivals who experienced trauma (either prior to migrating or as events secondary to the "crossing") may remain preoccupied with the violence and may also feel guilty about having escaped while loved ones remained behind (Amnesty International, 1998; Lustig et al., 2004). Those who are undocumented face the growing realities of workplace raids that can lead to traumatic and sudden separations (Capps, Castañeda, et al., 2007; Suárez-Orozco, Yoshikawa, et al., 2011).

The dissonance in cultural expectations and the cumulative stressors, together with the loss of social supports, lead to elevated affective and somatic symptoms (Alegría et al., 2007; Mendoza, Joyce, & Burgos, 2007). Due to their own struggles in adapting to a new country, many immigrant parents may be relatively unavailable psychologically, posing a developmental challenge to their children (Suárez-Orozco & Suárez-Orozco, 2001). Immigrant parents often may turn to their children when navigating the new society; they are frequently asked to take on responsibilities beyond their years, including sibling care, translation, and advocacy (Faulstich-Orellana, 2001), sometimes undermining parental authority but also often stimulating precocious development (Suárez-Orozco & Suárez-Orozco, 2001). Additionally, immigrant children and youth face the challenges of forging an identity and sense of belonging to a country that may reflect an unfamiliar culture while also honoring the values and traditions of their parents (Berry, Phinney, Sam, & Vedder, 2006). Nonetheless, many immigrant-origin children demonstrate extraordinary resilience and resourcefulness as they navigate their developmental journey (Suárez-Orozco & Suárez-Orozco, 2001; Suárez-Orozco, Suárez-Orozco, & Todorova, 2008; Suárez-Orozco, Abo-Zena, & Marks, 2015).

Challenges of Language Acquisition

Many immigrant children struggle with acquiring academic English. Among pre-kindergarten to 5th-grade immigrant children in the United States, 62% of foreign-born children were found to speak English less than "very well," while 43% of the U.S.–born children of immigrants and 12% of children of U.S.–born were categorized as such (Capps, Fix, et al., 2005). It is well established that the complexity of oral and written academic English skills generally requires between 5 and 7 years of optimal academic instruction for a student to develop academic second-language skills comparable to those of native English speakers (Collier, 1995; Cummins, 1991, 2000).

Many immigrant students from strife-ridden or poverty-stricken countries enter schools in their new lands with little or no schooling, and they may not read or write well in their native languages (Hernández et al., 2007). Research in second-language acquisition suggests that when students are well grounded in their native language and have developed reading and writing skills in that language, they are able to efficiently apply that knowledge to the new language when provided with appropriate instructional supports (August & Shanahan, 2006; Hakuta, Butler, & Witt, 2000). Many immigrant students do not enter schools with this advantage, however. Further, English language learner (ELL) students often cannot receive support for learning English from their parents (Capps, Fix, et al., 2005). These students also have limited opportunities for sustained interactions with highly proficient native English-speaking peers in informal situations—contact that is strongly predictive of academic second-language proficiency outcomes (Carhill, Suárez-Orozco, & Páez, 2008; Jia & Aaronson, 2003).

Less developed academic English proficiency, however, can mask the actual knowledge and skills of immigrant second-language learners (SLLs), which they are unable to express and demonstrate. Even when second-language learners are able to participate and compete in mainstream classrooms, they often read more slowly than do native speakers, may not understand double entendres, and simply have not been exposed to the same words and cultural information as native-born middle-class peers. Their academic language skills may also not allow them to be easily engaged with academic content and to perform well on "objective" assessments designed for native English speakers. Thus it is not surprising that limited English proficiency is often associated with poor performance on standardized tests, lower GPAs, repeating grades, and low graduation rates (Ruiz-de-Velasco, Fix, & Clewell, 2001).

Further, the strong emphasis on high-stakes assessments in the United States—first with No Child Left Behind and now with the Common Core—presents a particular challenge for ELLs (Menken, 2008). There is considerable debate about whether and how educational assessments, and high-stakes assessments in particular, may lead to unequal outcomes for English language learners (APA, 2012; Menken, 2008; Solórzano, 2008). Standardized tests used to screen for learning differences or for making policy decisions were largely designed for and normed with middle-class populations (Agbenyega & Jiggetts, 1999) or were adapted from work with those populations (Birman & Chan, 2008). Such tests assume exposure to mainstream cultural knowledge and fail to recognize culture-of-origin content knowledge (Rhodes, Ochoa, & Ortiz, 2005; Solano-Flores, 2008). This perspective can lead to underestimation of students' abilities and competencies.

In a climate of high-stakes educational assessment, school districts are sometimes pressured to prematurely reclassify students from English language learners to fluent English proficient (Escamilla, Mahon, Riley-Bernal, & Rutledge, 2003). In other cases, immigrant students suffer as "long-term ELLs" (Olsen, 2014). With poorly implemented school assessments and an assortment of language-learning policies, there is wide variability among districts and states in this classification. Seldom is reclassification tied to the research evidence on what it takes for a student to attain a level of academic-language proficiency required to be competitive on standardized assessments (Cummins, 2000; Kieffer, Lesaux, Rivera, & Francis, 2009). As higher stakes have become attached to standardized tests, this issue has heightened consequences for English language learners and the schools that serve them.

SCHOOL CONTEXTS

Schools, while offering great potential, are all too often out of sync in serving immigrant-origin students. Here we consider three such ways.

Segregation

Segregation in neighborhoods and schools has negative consequences for the academic success of minority students (Massey & Denton, 1993; Orfield & Lee, 2006). Nationally, immigrants tend to settle in highly segregated and deeply impoverished urban settings and attend the most segregated schools of any group in the United States today—in 1996, only 25% of immigrant students attended majority-White schools (Orfield & Lee, 2006). In 2010, these segregation trends persisted with 79.1% of Hispanic students, and only 15.9% of White students, in attendance at minority-majority schools (Krogstad & Fry, 2014). Immigrants who settle in predominantly minority neighborhoods often have virtually no direct, systematic, or intimate contact with middle-class White Americans. This situation in turn affects the quality of the schools their children attend and the networks that are useful for accessing desirable colleges and jobs (Orfield, 2002; Portes & Rumbaut, 2006).

Segregation of immigrant-origin students often involves their isolation at the levels of race/ethnicity, poverty, and language—aptly named "triple segregation" (Orfield & Lee, 2006, p. 4). These three dimensions of segregation have been associated with reduced school resources and a variety of negative educational outcomes, including low expectations for students, their difficulties learning English, their lower achievement, greater school violence, and higher dropout rates (Gándara & Contreras, 2009). Such school contexts undermine immigrant students' capacity to concentrate, their sense of security, and their ability to access positive trajectories of performance (Suárez-Orozco, Suárez-Orozco, & Todorova, 2008).

Second-Language Instruction

The majority of immigrant students must learn a new language as part of their journey to their new land; thus second-language instruction is a critical component necessary to ensure their academic success (Batalova, Fix, & Murray, 2007). Frequently, students are typically placed in some kind of second-language instructional setting as they enter their new schools (Gándara & Contreras, 2009). Students are then transitioned out of these settings in various schools, districts, and states, often with very little rhyme or reason for the transition (Callahan, 2005; Suárez-Orozco, Suárez-Orozco, & Todorova, 2008; Thomas & Collier, 2002). Research considering the efficacy of second-language instruction and bilingual programs reveals contradictory results (Callahan & Gándara, 2004, 2014; Callahan, Wilkinson, Muller, & Frisco, 2009). This outcome should not be surprising given that there are models of bilingual and language-assistance programs featuring a wide array of practices as well as philosophical approaches (Thomas & Collier, 2002; Callahan & Gándara, 2004) across districts. Well-designed and well-implemented programs produce good educational results and buffer at-risk students from dropping out by easing transitions, providing academic scaffolding, and furnishing a sense of community (Padilla et al., 1991; Callahan & Gándara, 2004, 2014). There is significant disparity in the quality of instruction among settings, however. Although it has been well demonstrated that high-quality programs produce excellent results, not surprisingly, districts plagued with problems (August & Hakuta, 1997; Thomas & Collier, 2002) produce less than optimal results. Many bilingual programs face real challenges in their implementation, including inadequate resources, uncertified personnel, and poor administrative support.

Teacher Expectations

In schools that serve immigrant students we commonly find cultures of low teacher expectations; what is sought and valued by teachers is student compliance rather than curiosity or cognitive engagement (Suárez-Orozco, Suárez-Orozco, & Todorova, 2008). Low expectations from their teachers shape the experiences and outcomes of these students in fundamental ways beyond simply exposing them to low educational standards (Weinstein, 2002). Classrooms and schools typically sort students into those who are thought to be talented versus those who are thought to be less so. These expectations may be based on impressions of individual capabilities, but often they are also founded upon stereotypical beliefs about students' racial, ethnic, and socioeconomic backgrounds (e.g., "Asian students are smart and hardworking" while "Latino students are social"). Students are well aware of the perceptions that teachers have of them; well-regarded students receive ample positive social mirroring (or reflections and feedback) about their capacity to learn and thus are more likely to redouble their efforts. Students who are found wanting on any combination of these characteristics, however, tend to either become invisible in the classroom or be actively disparaged. Under these circumstances, only the most resilient of students remain engaged (Suárez-Orozco, Suárez-Orozco, & Todorova, 2008). Immigrant students from families that do not always share the culture of their teachers are particularly susceptible to such negative expectations and poor outcomes (Suárez-Orozco & Suárez-Orozco, 2001).

IMPLICATIONS FOR ADAPTATIONS OVER TIME

Findings from the Longitudinal Immigrant Student Adaptation Study

How are schools doing in helping newcomers adapt over time? The Longitudinal Immigration Student Adaptation (LISA) study[2] took a longitudinal mixed-methods approach to document patterns of adaptation among 407 recently arrived immigrant youth from Central America, China, the Dominican Republic, Haiti, and Mexico. Ecological (Brofenbrenner & Morris, 1998) and segmented-assimilation (Portes & Zhou, 1993) theories informed the conceptual framing of this study. (For details about the study see Suárez-Orozco, Suárez-Orozco, & Todorova, 2008).

Five trajectories emerged from the latent growth analyses (see Figure 4.1). Approximately a quarter of the participants did remarkably well, maintaining high achievement through the course of the 5 years of the study. However, the academic performance of nearly two-thirds of the sample declined over the course of the study. Approximately a quarter of the participants were "Slow Decliners," demonstrating waning in performance of approximately half a grade over 5 years. For many "Slow Decliners," a premature transition into a demanding academic setting led to a downward trend in grades. More alarming was the grade-and-a-half drop that "Precipitous Decliners" (who constituted 27.8% of the sample) experienced. Multinomial logistic regressions indicated that these students struggled with multiple school and background impediments. They attended low-quality schools and had poor English language proficiency. In addition, "Precipitous Decliners" were the most likely of all the groups to report psychological symptoms at both the beginning and end of the study—clearly, these issues took their toll. Many had difficult premigratory histories (experiencing hardship abroad and long separations from parents) and had arrived to complicated circumstances (difficult reunifications, less than optimal neighborhoods and schools) once they entered their new land. Students who had initially been engaged in their schoolwork had difficulty maintaining this engagement for long in far from optimal and often hostile school environments.

Another 14.4% of participants—the "Low Performers"—started out with low performances that declined further over time. Low-achieving students tended to

Figure 4.1. Trajectories of 5 Academic Pathways from the LISA Study

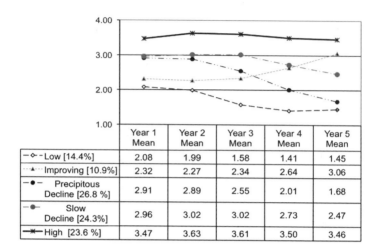

	Year 1 Mean	Year 2 Mean	Year 3 Mean	Year 4 Mean	Year 5 Mean
– ◇ – Low [14.4%]	2.08	1.99	1.58	1.41	1.45
···▲··· Improving [10.9%]	2.32	2.27	2.34	2.64	3.06
– ● – Precipitous Decline [26.8 %]	2.91	2.89	2.55	2.01	1.68
– ● – Slow Decline [24.3%]	2.96	3.02	3.02	2.73	2.47
–✳– High [23.6 %]	3.47	3.63	3.61	3.50	3.46

Note: This figure presents levels of student GPA over time for each of the 5 academic pathway groups in the LISA study. The first group (diamonds) of low achievers comprised 14.4% of the sample, while high achievers (x's) comprised 23.6% of the sample. Other pathways captured both growth (Improving group) as well as decline (both slow and precipitous). X-axis legend is GPA (4=A; 3=B, 2=C, 1=D).

arrive in their new land with a series of significant challenges. The quantitative data showed that these students had families with the least resources—the poorest and most segregated schools, the weakest English skills, interrupted schooling, lengthy family separations, undocumented status, and barren social worlds. These students readily admitted to having the least sustained academic engagement and the most interest in turning to the world of work.

The remaining 11% of the students—the "Improvers"—started out quite low but over the course of time, overcame their initial "transplant shock" and reached nearly the same levels of achievement as the "High Achievers." The majority of these students had sustained some sort of premigratory trauma. They had experienced long family separations and problematic initial family reunifications. To their advantage, they tended to settle into schools that provided them with a healthy fit with their developmental needs (Eccles et al., 1993). Over time, many found mentors and community supports that guided them in their journeys in their new land and that arguably contributed to their academic engagement (Suárez-Orozco, Suárez-Orozco, & Todorova, 2008).

The quarter of the sample of "High Achievers" demonstrated a constellation of advantages in family capital and family structure associated with academic achievement (Bourdieu & Passeron, 1977; Sirin & Rogers-Sirin, 2005). They had started out as high performers and maintained high achievement throughout the 5 years of the study. Relative to the other groups, the parents of "High Achievers" reported the highest levels of education and no or short family separations. These students reported having multiple social supports, the strongest English language skills, and the most engagement in their studies. They also attended schools that were the least segregated and had the fewest students qualifying for free lunches. Thus, perhaps not surprisingly, the data revealed that overall, students with the most school, familial, and individual resources tended to perform better academically over time.

The Immigrant Paradox

As scholars consistently observe the promise and successes of newcomer immigrant students in large-scale studies such as the LISA, a pattern of findings has emerged highlighting the resiliency of newcomer immigrants. The phenomenon is known as the *immigrant paradox,* a pattern by which newcomer and less-acculturated immigrant students fare better in their academic attitudes, achievements, and trajectories than their more highly acculturated or U.S.–born peers (Marks, Seaboyer, & García Coll, 2015). It is seemingly a paradox because newcomers and less-acculturated youth tend to be poorer, on average, and to have fewer social resources than their peers who have resided in the United States longer or who were born in the United States (as discussed above). However, most scholars today would agree that these patterns are not so paradoxical upon close inspection: Newcomer immigrant students bring many resiliency assets to their studies, including optimism and the ability to build supportive relationships within the school setting (Suárez-Orozco, Rhodes, & Milburn, 2009), which help facilitate the achievement of their educational goals. Recent studies have shown that bilingualism is also protective for newcomers; sharing both their family's language from its culture of origin and the English language at home facilitates strong behavioral well-being such as lower adolescent risk behavior, which in turn supports academic achievement.

Nevertheless, there is a downside to the paradox as well. Though newcomers may fare well initially, the longer students reside in the United States, the greater risk they have for lowered academic performance and outcomes. This phenomenon was seen, for example, in the LISA study described above, in which after the first year of the study, many newcomer students declined from their initial levels of academic achievement. Further, evidence of the paradox in education is mixed. The paradox holds more strongly, for example, in adolescence than in early childhood, with mixed findings based on the type of academic outcome assessed (García Coll & Marks, 2011). Further differences in the paradox exist when looking across countries of origin and region of U.S. settlement as well. Many Asian-origin students, for example, have shown evidence of an academic achievement paradox whereas for many Latino students, the paradox is more consistently demonstrated in attitude and behavior-related domains.

SCHOOLS AS "SITES OF POSSIBILITIES"?

These data illuminate the cumulative challenges immigrant youth encounter and the ways in which their educational environments misalign with their socioemotional and educational needs. Understanding how social contextual, familial, individual, and school variables contribute to varying patterns of academic trajectories for recently arrived youth is important; focusing on schools is essential due to the mutable nature of this setting. Working to develop and implement practices to bridge the gap between immigrant students' challenges and their educational environments is a crucial step toward helping these newest students achieve their potential.

Newcomer immigrant students with limited resources often enter the poorest and most segregated schools, which have the very least to offer students most in need of support. These schools typically offer run-down facilities and less access to basic supplies like textbooks as well as high rates of teacher and principal turnover (Suárez-Orozco, Suárez-Orozco, & Todorova, 2008). In many such schools, we observed low standards and aspirations for the students and frequent exchanges of disparaging comments. Many of these schools were sites of gang activities and/or bullying, and the adults on site demonstrated little connection with their students or the parents they ostensibly served (for detailed descriptions of these "less than optimal schools," see Suárez-Orozco, Suárez-Orozco, & Todorova, 2008). Rather than acting as "sites of possibilities" (Fine & Jaffe-Walter, 2007), all too many schools were failing to meet the needs of their newcomer students.

The effects of immigration are not confined to mere changes of geography. The political upheaval, ethnic or religious persecution, and traumas experienced prior to migration add burdens for many youth beyond the dislocations and necessary adjustment of immigration. Separations from parents for lengthy periods of time occur in a majority of migratory journeys. Some students face the added stress of undocumented status. To be most successful, educators serving the recently arrived immigrant students must be aware of the issues their students may be facing. However, very few of the teachers or administrators we spoke with were aware of the unique constellation of risks that burden some immigrant youth and their families.

Social relationships and interactions with schoolmates, teachers, and counselors, along with the flow of informational capital (Perreira et al., 2006; Pianta, 1999; Ryan, Stiller, & Lynch, 1994), play a significant role in shaping academic outcomes for youth with limited opportunities (Stanton-Salazar & Dornbusch, 1995). For recently arrived immigrants, positive relationships with family, community, and school members serve to create a sense of well-being in school. Formal and informal relationships with supportive adults and mentors can help recently arrived immigrants by providing them with crucial information about the educational system as well as explicit academic tutoring, homework assistance, and college pathway scaffolding. Programs developed with the needs of this target population in mind can play an important role in easing their transition to their new land (Roffman, Suárez-Orozco, & Rhodes, 2003; Suárez-Orozco, Suárez-Orozco, &

Todorova, 2008). However, our ethnographies and case studies demonstrate that not all schools are created equal in facilitating such connections. Although all too many were disconnected from their students and parents, some were islands of opportunity. This finding led to the Promising Practices Project—determining just what were the common denominators of schools that were "sites of opportunity" (Fine & Jaffe-Walter, 2007).

SCHOOL PRACTICES CONDUCIVE TO POSITIVE OUTCOMES FOR IMMIGRANT-ORIGIN YOUTH

Immigrant-origin students bring to schools a variety of hopes and dreams along with academic and linguistic challenges. Although it is not a challenge to critique the myriad of ways that schools fail to meet the needs of these students, it is more difficult to identify promising practices that serve them well (Lucas, 1997; Walqui, 2000). We sought to shed light on the strategies that teachers, students, and administrators develop as they attempt to meet the educational challenges of preparing immigrant-origin youth for this global era in two distinct social, political, and educational contexts.[3] All schools were public schools and had to have a reputation within the broader educational community for being innovative and attaining superior outcomes on standard performance indicators when compared with other schools with high proportions of low-income immigrant students (e.g., student stability rates, graduation rates, recruitment of highly qualified teachers, and retention of teachers) (see Suárez-Orozco, Martin, Alexandersson, Dance, & Lunneblad, 2013).

We were guided by the question of what school-based practices were being implemented in innovative, promising school settings to both ease the transition and integration and foster the academic performances of immigrant-origin youth. Using a multiple case study approach (Yin, 2003) across schools, we sought to identify approaches and strategies implemented in the various school sites that would serve to ease the adaptation and meet the educational needs of immigrant-origin youth. We began with overarching conceptual categories based on previous research in the field. As part of the iterative process of fieldwork, we added new practices as we encountered them and determined whether these practices occurred across sites.

Promising Practices for All Students

We found that some practices were sound, promising, or innovative for immigrant-origin students whether they were second-generation, newcomers, or second-language learners. Arguably, some of these practices are simply sound for students in general, regardless of whether they are of immigrant origin.

All four schools practiced reforms founded on progressive multicultural education (Banks & Banks, 2016; Nieto, 2010). Interdisciplinary, project-based, and student-centered approaches to curriculum and instruction were central to teaching and learning across the schools. All four schools utilized an integrated curriculum in some form, and two schools placed particular emphasis on integrating technology into the curriculum. The four schools attempted to create curricula that are relevant to the lives of their diverse students. The schools used decentralized pedagogical strategies designed to place the student at the center of learning to deliver content, moving away from traditional teacher lectures for at least part of the time. The schools sought multiple strategies to assess their students and ways to prepare them for high-stakes testing. All of the schools implemented some kinds of academic supports to help students be successful. Finally, all access of the schools placed particular focus on postsecondary school.

Particularly Promising Practices for Immigrant-Origin Students

Other practices were very specific to the needs of newcomer students and second-language learners, serving to ease their negotiation of the cultural transition and learning a new language.

Negotiating cultural transitions. The schools were highly strategic in their approaches to helping newcomer youth adjust to their new environs. As new students come in, teacher teams meet to discuss each one, and a series of assessments are conducted and discussed in order to develop the best plan for him or her. Teachers try to meet with as many of the parents as possible. Parents are asked to bring prior education and health records in person at the beginning of the school year. Information gleaned during these conferences is then shared when teachers meet across the teams working with each student. The ongoing transition is primarily the responsibility of the advisory program, which helps students adjust to their new school under the guidance of an advisor who is looking out for them. One of the guidelines for forming advisory groups is to have a newcomer/beginning learner of the new language in the same group as at least one student who shares the same native language and is also proficient in the new language so that the more advanced new language speaker can translate. In advisory groups, students discuss a variety of topics ranging from difficulties with a class and missing families and friends back home to boyfriend/girlfriend issues. Further, aligned with the language-intensive and student-centered learning approaches, instructional tasks, in particular writing tasks, encourage students to share their personal experiences in both their old and new countries and in the transition from one to the other.

Supports for gaps in interrupted schooling and literacy. Some students enter secondary school with limited prior education or significant interruptions in their schooling. These may occur for a variety of reasons, including socioeconomic or gender inequities in original educational access, political strife, or hiccups in the migratory process. Whatever the cause of an interruption in schooling, the consequence is often students who are overage and underskilled and who have considerable catching up to do in the classroom. Addressing this situation takes creativity, flexibility, and sustained effort on the part of school administrators and teachers. Understanding was shown for these students' circumstances. Sensitivity was exhibited toward the overage students; support was given while encouragement was provided to allow as much independence and peer support as possible. Students with interrupted formal education (SIFE) received the same supports provided to other newcomer students and more. Particular emphasis was placed on literacy. Typically, these students take longer than the standard 4 years to graduate from high school—often stretching to 7 years. With the right amount of scaffolding, the daunting tasks of learning a new language, acquiring literacy, mastering content knowledge of a new culture, accruing graduation-credit courses, and passing high-stakes tests are achievable for many students who would have given up in another setting.

Second-language learning. All the promising schools we observed had systematic second-language acquisition policies and practices. These schools recognized that many of their students, particularly those entering secondary school with little background in the language of instruction, required systematic and effective long-term curriculum plans for language education. Thus, second-language instruction for immigrant students is most successful when learners are placed in a progressive and systematic program of instruction that first identifies a student's incoming literacy and academic skills (Christensen & Stanat, 2007). Research shows that consistency of instruction is essential for students as frequent transitions place them at a considerable disadvantage (Christensen & Stanat, 2007; Gándara & Contreras, 2009). Second-language learning is most successful when high-quality second-language instruction is provided with continued transitional academic supports—like tutoring, homework help, and writing assistance—as the language learners integrate into mainstream programs (Christensen & Stanat, 2007). In order to ensure a smooth transition between grades as well as the continual development of skills, teachers need to both understand and conform to the instructional model adopted by the school or district (Sugarman & Howard, 2001). Further, assessment of skills development should be done annually using portfolio assessment as well as testing in order to measure progress and adjust interventions (Christensen & Stanat, 2007).

Teaching across content areas. In addition to developing communicative proficiency in the new language, SLLs need to simultaneously build content literacies; many of these students also have low cognitive academic language proficiency (CALP) skills. Second-language acquisition programs (e.g., bilingual education, self-contained SLL programs) primarily focus on literacy development in terms of language proficiency, with only limited attention given to academic second-language acquisition in content areas (August & Hakuta, 1997). It is a challenge for students to learn content across the academic disciplines while at the same time acquiring new language and literacy skills, and the task poses an instructional challenge for many teachers as well (August & Hakuta,1997; NCES, 2000). Teachers in the exemplary schools receive extensive training in language-intensive curriculum; language learning is embedded across the entire curriculum. Writing is not simply an activity for language-arts classes. Students are pushed daily to write and use their developing language skills in every class.

Language-learning accommodations. Students are encouraged to use their first language to help them learn the second language, even if those addressed do not know the students' mother tongue. Informally, students are encouraged to translate for the newest immigrants, read and write in their first language during silent reading times, and carry bilingual dictionaries, but they are gently prodded toward their new language over time. The mother tongue is thus used strategically to aid the development of the new one. Assignments are continually modified to make them accessible to students, providing much-needed scaffolding for newcomer students as they make the transition to their new educational setting.

Promising Practices in Sum

The schools we studied are rich with innovations that allow youth to develop the ethics, skills, sensibilities, and competencies needed to identify, analyze, and solve problems from multiple perspectives (Suárez-Orozco, Martin, et al., 2013). Across schools we found a commitment to marginalized and disadvantaged students (Suárez-Orozco, Martin, et al., 2013). The schools offer a stimulating, rigorous, and relevant curriculum but also provide a number of supplemental resources (e.g., after-school programs, tutoring, high-stakes test preparation, homework help, explicit college-entry information, and so forth) to at-risk students in order to ease their educational transition and ameliorate their outcomes. Teachers make their pedagogies transparent, and there is a wealth of initiatives taken from different levels in the school system as a whole. The schools promote an alignment of instructional methods, content, and assessments and foster collaborative efforts to raise students' achievement levels and reduce barriers to educational equity. Notably, these services are helpful not only for immigrant-origin students but also for other at-risk youth (Suárez-Orozco, Martin, et al., 2013).

CONCLUSION

Multiple studies have documented the varieties of immigrant student optimism, academic engagement, and faith in schools and in the future. For immigrant children and youth, schools have great potential as the "sites of possibilities" (Fine & Jaffe-Walter, 2007) for systematic, intimate, and long-term immersion in the new culture and society. Nevertheless, by enacting current policies and practices noxious to their needs, schools are in too many cases conferring disadvantage, perpetuating parental disempowerment, and revealing a studied indifference to authentically and successfully engaging their newest future citizens (Allen & Reich, 2013). We know how to do better. As societies, we must demonstrate the will and the care to do so.

NOTES

1. Defined as "fear or hatred of strangers or foreigners" (*Merriam-Webster's Collegiate Dictionary,* 11th ed.).

2. We thank the National Science Foundation, the W. T. Grant Foundation, and the Spencer Foundation.

3. We thank C. Suárez-Orozco's coauthors and co-investigators on this project—as well as a National Science Foundation's PIRE grant that made this research possible.

REFERENCES

Agbenyega, S., & Jiggetts, J. (1999). Minority children and their over-representation in special education. *Education, 119*(4), 619–632.

Alegría, M., Mulvaney-Day, N., Torres, M., Polo, A., Zhun, C., & Canino, G. (2007). Prevalence of psychiatric disorders across Latino subgroups in the United States. *American Journal of Public Health, 97,* 68–75.

Allen, D., & Reich, R. (2013). Introduction. In D. Allen & R. Reich (Eds.), *Education, justice, and society.* Chicago, IL: University of Chicago Press.

American Psychological Association (APA). (2010). *Resilience and recovery after war: Refugee children and families in the United States.* Report of the APA Task Force on the Psychosocial Effects of War on Children and Families Who Are Refugees from Armed Conflict Residing in the United States. Washington, DC: Author. Retrieved from www.apa.org/pi/families/refugees.aspx

American Psychological Association (APA). (2012). *Crossroads: The psychology of immigration in the new century.* Report of the APA Presidential Task Force on Immigration. Washington, DC: Author.

Amnesty International. (1998). From San Diego to Brownsville: Human rights violations on the USA–Mexico border [Press release]. Retrieved from https://www.amnesty.org/download/Documents/152000/amr510331998en.pdf

August, D., & Hakuta, K. (Eds.). (1997). *Improving schooling for language-minority children: A research agenda.* Washington, DC: National Academies Press.

August, D., & Shanahan, T. (2006). Synthesis: Instruction and professional development. In D. August & T. Shanahan (Eds.), *Developing literacy in second-language learners: Report of the National Literacy Panel on Language-Minority Children and Youth* (pp. 321–335). Mahwah, NJ: Lawrence Erlbaum.

Banks, J. A., & Banks, C.A.M. (Eds.). (2016). *Multicultural education: Issues and perspectives* (9th ed.). Hoboken, NJ: Wiley.

Batalova, J., Fix, M., & Murray, J. (2007). *Measures of change: The demography and literacy of adolescent English learners.* Washington, DC: Migration Policy Institute.

Bean, F. D., & Lowell, B. L. (2007). Unauthorized migration. In M. Waters & R. Ueda (Eds.),

The new Americans: A guide to immigration since 1965 (pp. 70–81). Cambridge, MA: Harvard University Press.

Berry, J. W., Phinney, J. S., Sam, D. L., & Vedder, P. (Eds.). (2006). *Immigrant youth in cultural transition: Acculturation, identity, and adaptation across national contexts.* Mahwah, NJ: Lawrence Erlbaum.

Birman, D., & Chan, W. Y. (2008). *Screening and assessing immigrant and refugee youth in school-based mental health programs* (Issue Brief No. 1). Washington, DC: Center for Health and Health Care in Schools.

Bourdieu, P., & Passeron, J. (1977). *Reproduction in education, society and culture.* Beverly Hills, CA: Sage.

Bronfenbrenner, E., & Morris, P. (1998). The ecology of developmental processes. In W. Damon & R. M. Lerner (Eds.), *Handbook of child psychology* (pp. 993–1028). New York, NY: Wiley.

Callahan, R. M. (2005). Tracking and high school English learners: Limiting opportunity to learn. *American Educational Research Journal, 42*(2), 305–328.

Callahan, R. M., & Gándara, P. C. (2004). On nobody's agenda: Improving English language learners' access to higher education. In M. Sadowski (Ed.), *Teaching immigrant and second-language students: Strategies for success* (pp. 107–127). Cambridge, MA: Harvard Education Press.

Callahan, R. M., &. Gándara, P. C. (Eds.). (2014). *The bilingual advantage: Language, literacy and the US labor market.* Bristol, United Kingdom: Multilingual Matters.

Callahan, R. M., Wilkinson, L., Muller, C., & Frisco, M. (2009). ESL placement and schools: Effects on immigrant achievement. *Educational Policy, 23*(2), 355–384.

Capps, R., Castañeda, R., Chaudry, A., & Santos, R. (2007). *The impact of immigration raids on America's children.* Washington, DC: The Urban Institute.

Capps, R., Fix, M., Murray, J., Ost, J., Passel, J. S., & Herwantoro, S. (2005). *The new demography of America's schools: Immigration and the No Child Left Behind Act.* Washington, DC: The Urban Institute. Retrieved from files.eric.ed.gov/fulltext/ED490924.pdf

Carhill, A., Suárez-Orozco, C., & Páez, M. (2008). Explaining English language proficiency among adolescent immigrant students. *American Educational Research Journal, 79*(4), 1155–1179.

Carter, A., Lawrence, M., & Morse, A. (2011). *2011 Immigration-related laws, bills, and resolutions in the states: Jan. 1–March 31, 2011.* Washington, DC: National Conference of State Legislatures. Retrieved from www.ncsl.org/default.aspx?tabid=13114

Castro, D. C., Páez, M. M., Dickinson, D. K., & Frede, E. (2011). Promoting language and literacy in young dual language learners: Research, practice, and policy. *Child Development Perspectives, 5*(1), 15–21.

Chavez, L. (2008). *The Latino threat: Constructing immigrants, citizens, and the nation.* Palo Alto, CA: Stanford University Press.

Christensen, G., & Stanat, P. (2007). *Language policies and practices for helping immigrants and second-generation students succeed* [Policy brief]. Washington, DC: Migration Policy Institute.

Collier, V. P. (1995). Acquiring a second language for school. *Directions in Language and Education, 1*(4): 1–14.

Cummins, J. (1991). Language development and academic learning. In L. M. Malavé & G. Duquette (Eds.), *Language, culture, and cognition.* (pp. 161–175). Clevedon, United Kingdom: Multilingual Matters.

Cummins, J. (2000). *Language, power, and pedagogy: Bilingual children in the crossfire.* Clevedon, United Kingdom: Multilingual Matters.

Delgado-Gaitan, C. (2004). *Involving Latino families in schools: Raising student achievement through home–school partnerships.* Thousand Oaks, CA: Corwin Press.

Delpit, L. (2006). *Other people's children: Cultural conflict in the classroom.* New York, NY: New Press.

Eccles, J. S., Midgley, C., Buchanan, C. M., Wigfield, A., Reuman, D., & MacIver, D. (1993). Development during adolescence: The impact of stage/environment fit. *American Psychologist, 48*(2), 90–101.

Escamilla, K., Mahon, E., Riley-Bernal, H., & Rutledge, D. (2003). High-stakes testing, Latinos, and English language learners: Lessons from Colorado. *Bilingual Research Journal, 27*(1), 25–49.

Falicov, C. J. (1998). *Latino families in therapy: A guide to multicultural practice.* New York, NY: Guilford Press.

Faulstich-Orellana, M. (2001). The work kids do: Mexican and Central American immigrant children's contribution to households and schools in California. *Harvard Educational Review, 71*(3) 366–89.

Fine, M., & Jaffe-Walter, R. (2007). Swimming: On oxygen, resistance and possibility for immigrant youth under siege. *Anthropology & Education Quarterly, 38*(1), 76–96.

Fuligni, A. (2001). A comparative longitudinal approach among children of immigrant families. *Harvard Educational Review, 71*(3), 566–578.

Gándara, P., & Contreras, F. (2009). *The Latino education crisis: The consequences of failed policies.* Cambridge, MA: Harvard University Press.

García Coll, C., & Magnuson, K. (1997). The psychological experience of immigration: A developmental perspective. In A. Booth, A. C. Crouter, & N. Landale (Eds.), *Immigration and the family* (pp. 91–132). Mahwah, NJ: Lawrence Erlbaum.

García Coll, C., & Marks, A. K. (2009). *Immigrant stories: Ethnicity and academics in middle childhood.* New York, NY: Oxford University Press.

García Coll, C., & Marks, A. K. (Eds.). (2011). *The immigrant paradox in children and adolescents: Is becoming American a developmental risk?* Washington, DC: American Psychological Association Press.

Gibson, M. (1988). *Assimilation without accommodation: Sikh immigrants in an American high school.* Ithaca, NY: Cornell University Press.

Hagelskamp, C., Suárez-Orozco, C., & Hughes, D. (2010). Migrating to opportunities: How family migration motivations shape academic trajectories among newcomer immigrant youth. *Journal of Social Issues, 66* (4) 717–739.

Hakuta, K., Butler, Y. G., & Witt, D. (2000). *How long does it take English learners to attain proficiency?* (Policy Report 2000-1). University of California Linguistic Minority Research Institute. Retrieved from http://escholarship.org/uc/item/13w7m06g#page-2. *Adolescence, 40,* 503–512.

Hanson, G. H. (2010). *The economics and policy of illegal immigration in the United States.* Washington, DC: Migration Policy Institute.

Hernández, D. J., Denton, N. A., & Macartney, S. E., (2007). *Children in immigrant families—the U.S. and 50 States: National origins, language, and early education* (Research Brief, Publication No. 2007-11). Albany, NY: Child Trends and The Center for Social and Demographic Analysis (SUNY–Albany).

Hernández, D. J., & Napierala, J. S. (2012). *Children in immigrant families: Essential to*

America's future (FCD Child and Youth Well-being Index Policy Brief). New York, NY: Foundation for Child Development. Retrieved from http://fcd-us.org/sites/default/files/FINAL%20Children%20in%20Immigrant%20Families%20(2)_0.pdf

Jia, G., & Aaronson, D. (2003). A longitudinal study of Chinese children and adolescents learning English in the United States. *Applied Psycholinguistics, 24,* 131–161.

Kanstrom, D. (2010) *Deportation nation: Outsiders in American history.* Cambridge, MA: Harvard University Press.

Kao, G., & Tienda, M. (1995). Optimism and achievement: The educational performance of immigrant youth. *Social Science Quarterly, 76* (1), 1–19.

Kasinitz, P., Mollenkopf, J., Waters, M. C., & Holdaway, J. (2008). *Inheriting the city: The children of immigrants come of age.* New York, NY: Russell Sage Foundation.

Kieffer, M. J., Lesaux, N. K., Rivera, M., & Francis, D. J. (2009). Accommodations for English language learners taking large-scale assessments: A meta-analysis on effectiveness and validity. *Review of Educational Research, 79*(3), 1168–1201.

Krogstad, J. M., & Fry, J. (2014). Public school enrollment disparities exist 60 years after historic desegregation ruling. *Pew Research Center.* Retrieved from: pewrsr.ch/Tc6RHV

Leadership Conference on Civil Rights Education Fund. (2009). *Confronting the new faces of hate: Hate crimes in America, 2009.* Washington, DC: Author. Retrieved from www.civilrights.org/publications/hatecrimes/

Levitt, P., & Schiller, N. G. (2004). Conceptualizing simultaneity: A transnational social field perspective on society. *International Migration Review, 38*(3), 1002–1039.

Li, G. (2004). Family literacy: Learning from an Asian immigrant family. In F. Boyd, C. Brock, & M. Rozendal (Eds.), *Multicultural and multilingual literacy and language practices* (pp. 304–322). New York, NY: Guilford Press.

López, G. (2001). The value of hard work: Lessons on parental involvement from an (im)migrant household. *Harvard Education Review, 41*(3), 416–437.

Lucas, T. (1997). *Into, through, and beyond secondary school: Critical transitions for immigrant youths.* Washington, DC: Center for Applied Linguistics.

Lustig, S. L., Kia-Keating, M., Knight, W. G., Geltman, P., Ellis, H., Kinzie, J. D., . . . Saxe, G. N. (2004). Review of child and adolescent refugee mental health. *Journal of American Academy of Child and Adolescent Psychiatry, 43*(1), 24–36.

Luthar, S. S. (1999). *Poverty and children's adjustment.* Thousand Oaks, CA: Sage.

Marks, A. K., Seaboyer, L., & García Coll, C. (2015). The academic achievement of U.S. immigrant children and adolescents. In C. Suárez-Orozco, M. Abo-Zena, & A. K. Marks (Eds.), *Transitions: The development of children of immigrants* (pp. 259–275). New York, NY: NYU Press.

Massey, D. S. (Ed.). (2010). *New faces in new places: The changing geography of American immigration.* New York, NY: Russell Sage Foundation.

Massey, D. S., & Denton, N. A. (1993). *American apartheid: Segregation and the making of the underclass.* Cambridge, MA: Harvard University Press.

Masten, A. S., & Narayan, A. J. (2012). Child development in the context of disaster, war, and terrorism: Pathways of risk and resilience. *Annual Review of Psychology, 63*(1), 227–257.

Mather, M. (2009). *Children in immigrant families chart new path.* Washington, DC: Population Reference Bureau. Retrieved from www.prb.org/Publications/Reports/2009/childreninimmigrantfamilies.aspx

Mendoza, F. S., Joyce, J. R., & Burgos. A. E. (2007). Health of children in immigrant families. In J. E. Lansford, K. Deater-Deckard, & M. H. Bornstein (Eds.), *Immigrant families in contemporary society* (pp. 30–50). New York, NY: Guilford Press.

Menjívar, C. (2006). Liminal legality: Salvadoran and Guatemalan immigrants' lives in the United States. *American Journal of Sociology, 111*, 999–1037.

Menken, K. (2008). *English language learners left behind: Standardized testing as language policy.* Clevedon, United Kingdom: Multilingual Matters.

Milner, H. R. (2013). Analyzing poverty, learning, and teaching through a critical race theory lens. *Review of Research in Education, 37*(1), 1–53.

Motomura, H. (2008). Immigration outside the law. *Columbia Law Review, 108*(8), 2037–2097.

National Center for Education Statistics (NCES). (2000). High school dropouts by race/ethnicity and recency of migration (NCES 2001-602). *Education Statistics Quarterly, 2*, 25–27.

Nieto, S. (2010). *The light in their eyes: Creating multicultural learning communities* (10th anniversary ed.). New York, NY: Teachers College Press.

Olsen, L. (1999). *Igniting change for immigrant students: Portraits of three high schools.* Oakland, CA: California Tomorrow.

Olsen, L. (2014). *Meeting the unique needs of long-term English language learners.* Washington, DC: National Education Association.

Orfield, G. (2002). Commentary. In M. M. Suárez-Orozco & M. M. Paez (Eds.), *Latinos: Remaking America* (pp. 389–397). Berkeley: University of California Press.

Orfield, G., & Lee, C. (2006). *Racial transformation and the changing nature of segregation.* Cambridge, MA: The Civil Rights Project at Harvard University.

Padilla, A., Lindholm, K., Chen, A., Duran, R., Hakuta, K., Lambert, W., & Tucker, R. (1991). The English-only movement: Myth, reality, and implications for psychology. *American Psychologist, 46*(2), 120–30.

Passel, J. S. (2006). *Size and characteristics of the unauthorized migrant population in the U.S.* Washington, DC: Pew Hispanic Center.

Perreira, K. M., Harris, K. M., & Lee, D. (2006). Making it in America: High school completion by immigrant and native youth. *Demography, 43*, 511–536.

Pew Research Center, Hispanic Trends. (2013). *A nation of immigrants: A portrait of the 40 million, including 11 million unauthorized.* Washington, DC: Pew Research Center.

Pianta, R. C. (1999). *Enhancing relationships between children and teachers.* Washington, DC: American Psychological Association.

Portes, A., & Rumbaut, R. G. (2006). *Immigrant America: A portrait.* Berkeley: University of California Press.

Portes, A., & Zhou, M. (1993). The new second generation: Segmented assimilation and its variants. *Annals of the American Academy of Political and Social Science, 530*(1), 74–96.

Preston, J. (2011, June 4). Immigrants are focus of harsh bill in Alabama. *New York Times,* p. A10.

Ream, R. K. (2005). Toward understanding how social capital mediates the impact of mobility on Mexican American achievement. *Social Forces, 84*(1), 201–224.

Rhodes, R. L., Ochoa, S. H., & Ortiz, S. O. (2005). *Assessing culturally and linguistically diverse students: A practical guide.* New York, NY: Guilford Press.

Roffman, J., Suárez-Orozco, C., & Rhodes, J. (2003). Facilitating positive development in immigrant youth: The role of mentors and community organizations. In D. Perkins, L. M. Borden, J. G. Keith, & F. A. Villaruel (Eds.), *Positive youth development: Creating a positive tomorrow.* Brockton, MA: Kluwer Academic Press.

Roy, L., & Roxas, K. (2011). Whose deficit is this anyhow? Exploring counter-stories of Somali Bantu refugees' experiences in "doing school." *Harvard Educational Review, 81*(3), 521–542.

Rueda, R., August, D., & Goldenberg, C. (2006). The sociocultural context in which children acquire literacy. In D. August & T. Shanaham (Eds.), *Developing literacy in second-language learners: Report of the National Literacy Panel on language-minority children and youth* (pp. 319–340). Mahwah, NJ: Lawrence Erlbaum.

Ruíz-de-Velasco, J., Fix, M., & Clewell, B. C. (2001). *Overlooked and underserved: Immigrant students in U.S. secondary schools.* Washington, DC: The Urban Institute.

Ryan, R. M., Stiller, J., & Lynch, J. H. (1994). Representations of relationships to teachers, parents, and friends as predictors of academic motivation and self-esteem. *Journal of Early Adolescence, 14*(2), 226–249.

Sirin, S. R., & Fine, M. (2008). *Muslim American youth: Understanding hyphenated identities through multiple methods.* New York, NY: New York University Press.

Sirin, S. R., & Rogers-Sirin, L. (2005). Components of school engagement among African American adolescents. *Applied Developmental Science, 9*(10), 5–13.

Solano-Flores, G. (2008). Who is given tests in what language by whom, when, and where? The need for probabilistic views of language in the testing of English language learners. *Education Researcher, 37*(4), 189–99.

Solórzano, R. W. (2008). High stakes testing: Issues, implications, and remedies for English language learners. *Review of Educational Research, 78*(2), 260–329.

Stanton-Salazar, R. D., & Dornbusch, S. M. (1995). Social capital and the reproduction of inequality: Information networks among Mexican-origin high school students. *Sociology of Education, 68*(2), 116–135.

Suárez-Orozco, C., Abo-Zena, M., & Marks, A. K. (Eds.). (2015). *Transitions: The development of children of immigrants.* New York, NY: New York University Press.

Suárez-Orozco, C., Martin, M., Alexandersson, M., Dance, J. L., & Lunneblad, J. (2013). Promising practices: Preparing children of immigrants in New York and Sweden. In R. Alba & J. Holdaway (Eds.). *The children of immigrants at school: A comparative look at integration in the United States and Western Europe* (pp. 204–251). New York, NY: New York University Press.

Suárez-Orozco, C., Rhodes, J., & Milburn, M. (2009). Unraveling the immigrant paradox: Academic engagement and disengagement among recently arrived immigrant youth. *Youth and Society, 41*(2), 151–185.

Suárez-Orozco, C., & Suárez-Orozco, M. M. (1995). *Transformations: Immigration, family life, and achievement motivation among Latino adolescents.* Palo Alto, CA: Stanford University Press.

Suárez-Orozco, C., & Suárez-Orozco, M. (2001). *Children of immigration.* Cambridge, MA: Harvard University Press.

Suárez-Orozco, C., Suárez-Orozco, M. M., & Todorova, I. (2008). *Learning a new land: Immigrant students in American society.* Cambridge, MA: Harvard University Press.

Suárez-Orozco, C., Todorova, I., & Louie, J. (2002). Making up for lost time: The experience of separation and reunification among immigrant families. *Family Process, 41*(4), 625–643.

Suárez-Orozco, C., Yoshikawa, H., Teranishi, R., & Suárez-Orozco, M. M. (2011). Growing up in the shadows: The developmental implications of unauthorized status. *Harvard Educational Review, 81*(3), 438–472.

Suárez-Orozco, M., & Suárez-Orozco, C. (2013). Taking perspective: Context, culture, and history. *New directions for child and adolescent development, 2013*(141), 9–23.

Sugarman, J., & Howard, E. R. (2001). *Development and maintenance of two-way immersion programs: Advice from practitioners* (Practitioner Brief #2). Santa Cruz: University of California, Center for Research on Education, Diversity and Excellence.

Thomas, W. P., & Collier, V. P. (2002). *A national study of school effectiveness for language minority students' long-term academic achievement*. Berkeley: University of California, Berkeley Center for Research on Education, Diversity and Excellence.

United Nations Development Programme. (2009). *Human development report 2009: Overcoming barriers: Human mobility and development*. New York, NY: United Nations Development Programme.

Walqui, A. (2000). *Access and engagement: Program design and instructional approaches for immigrant students in secondary school*. Brooklyn, NY: Delta Publishing Group.

Weinstein, R. S. (2002). *Reaching higher*. Cambridge, MA: Harvard University Press.

Yin, R. K. (2003). *Case study research: Design and methods* (3rd ed.). Thousand Oaks, CA: Sage.

Yoshikawa, H. (2011). *Immigrants raising citizens: Undocumented parents and their children*. New York, NY: Russell Sage Foundation.

CHAPTER 5

Narratives of Success of Ethiopian Immigrants

Implications for Civic Education

Miriam Ben-Peretz and Tali Aderet-German

More people live as immigrants outside their country of origin today than at any time in history (United Nations General Assembly, 2012). Immigrants experience many problems integrating into and attaining citizenship in their host societies. A number of contextual factors and personal characteristics help immigrants overcome the difficulties of immigration and become effective citizens in their new nations. Berry, Phinney, Sam, and Vedder (2006) state that young immigrants live between cultures—their cultures of origin and the cultures of their new nations. Enabling immigrants to retain strong ties to both cultures by fostering a multicultural approach has enormous potential for the academic and social success of immigrant youth (Berry et al., 2006). Schools can help immigrant students attain the knowledge and skills needed to become effective citizens as well as retain important aspects of their home and community cultures (Banks, 2008).

After a brief discussion of definitions of major terms such as *multiculturalism, multicultural education, citizenship, effective citizens,* and *modes of civic education,* we describe our study of the narratives of successful young adult Ethiopian immigrants in Israel. We identify five distinctive themes in the data from the narratives that have implications for civic education: (1) racism, discrimination, and skin color; (2) support; (3) dual cultural identity; (4) sense of mission; and (5) personal autonomy. These themes appeared in all of the interviews with different levels of intensity. This chapter describes the implications of these five themes for the civic education of immigrants as well as for all students.

STUDENTS IN DEMOGRAPHICALLY CHANGED SOCIETIES

In the following section, we present several major concepts that are important for our discussion. The first is *multiculturalism,* which is the status that describes the nature of student populations in this new world of demographically changed societies. We will describe the relationship between multiculturalism and civic education. Different types of citizens will be described, as well as their implications for civic education.

Multiculturalism and Multicultural Education

Multiculturalism describes the polyethnic composition of a society. Policymakers use this concept to describe a specific type of policy regarding cultural diversity. It is also a psychological concept related to political ideology, which refers to the acceptance and support of the culturally heterogeneous population of a society (Van de Vijver, Breugelmans, & Schalk-Soekar, 2008). This comprehensive definition of multiculturalism provides a basis for examining societies today in a world of changing demographics and migration. Israel can be viewed as an example of multiculturalism from a demographic point of view because it is made up of a variety of ethnic, national, religious, and ideological communities. The Ethiopian Israeli community is an example of this diversity.

Multiculturalism characterizes the social and political realities of the interaction between a minority group and a dominant society— in our case, Ethiopian Jews and the Israeli culture. Conceptualizing Israeli culture is very complicated because of its heterogeneous society of immigrants from many cultures and a native population of myriad ethnic and religious identities. In this chapter we describe how policymakers adopted specific types of policies about the cultural diversity of Israel and the political ideology that underlies these policies. We also show how these theoretical concepts are exemplified in the lives of Ethiopian immigrants in Israel. They state in their own words the meaning of living in a multicultural society.

Multicultural education recognizes "the right and need of citizens to maintain commitments both to their cultural communities and to the national civic culture" (Banks, 2013). That means that the national civic culture should reflect the diversity of the various communities that constitute the nation-state. Multicultural education might be viewed from several perspectives. One perspective concerns value conflicts in schools between the values of immigrant minority groups and those of the dominant society. Another perspective of multicultural education concerns "intercultural" training (Albert & Triandis, 1985). This approach suggests a shift from goals of assimilation to an approach of mutual education of all cultural groups. Sleeter and Grant (1987) examine several approaches to multicultural education. We adopt their definition of the multicultural education approach, which advocates reforming the school program for all students to make it reflect diversity, thus promoting cultural pluralism and social equality.

Civic Education of Immigrant Students

We start with several definitions of *citizenship*. Citizenship is a complex and multidimensional concept. According to Ichilov (2013), it "consists of legal, cultural,

social and political elements, and provides citizens with defined rights and obligations, a sense of identity, and social bonds. The classical definition of citizenship
rests on the assertion that citizenship involves a balance or fusion between rights
and obligations" (p. 11). Marshall (1964) stated that citizenship is a status express-
ing a capacity or competence to be a member of society. He described a historical
typology of citizenship, composed of civil, political, and social elements. *Civil citizenship* included individual freedoms such as freedom of speech and faith. *Political citizenship* consisted of the right to vote and participate in public decisions.
Social citizenship included the right to security and welfare and to share in the
"social heritage and to live the life of a civilized being according to the standards
prevailing in society" (Marshall, 1950/1992, p. 8).

Banks (2008) extended Marshall's typology of citizenship and developed a typology of differentiating levels of citizenship. It begins with the basic level, *legal
citizenship*, which does not require any active participation, and concludes with
the highest level, *transformative citizenship*, which involves actions that promote
social justice and challenge existing discriminatory laws or conventions. Other
conceptions of citizenship also emphasize the role of active participation designed
to change society; for example, Miller (2000) identified three models of citizenship:

1. The first, or liberal, model understands citizenship as a set of rights and
   obligations giving each citizen an equal status in the community. In this
   model the citizen as a right-holder is mostly passive, reduced to voting in
   order to defend these rights.
2. The second model views the citizen as a consumer of public services entitled to consumer rights. This is an individualistic understanding of citizenship, viewing the citizen as a claimant and therefore lacking the need
   for communal activities as part of citizenship.
3. The third model views the citizen as "someone who is actively involved in
   shaping the way his or her community functions" (p. 28). This mode of
   citizenship involves public responsibility and "a sense that what you are
   doing is for the good of the public as a whole, not merely one sectional
   interest" (p. 28).

Miller (2000) emphasizes that "to be a citizen in the fullest sense you must
in some way be actively involved in shaping the way that your community develops, whether this is through political activity in the strict sense or through public
involvement of a political kind" (p. 34). This definition of what it means to be a
citizen concurs with Dudley and Gitelson's (2002) claim that "citizenship requires
active participation and engagement in politics. This kind of political engagement
most surely requires a stronger knowledge base than simply the citizen-as-voter"
(p. 178).

Active participation is expressed, as well, in Banks' (2008) concept of transformative citizenship. Transformative citizens feel a deep belonging to the soci-

ety they wish to transform. Sacks (2000) highlights the close connection between giving and belonging in society. The feeling of belonging can be related to the idea of active participation in society at large, as well as in your own community. Immigrants who have a sense of belonging and contribute to their community have the potential for being recognized in society as effective citizens. The term *effective citizens* includes both the notion of belonging to your community and your society, being a citizen, as well as playing an active, recognized, and valued role in the everyday life and development of the society at large. Our study of Ethiopian immigrants in Israel explores the way they view their role as citizens in their new society.

Ways of Educating Effective Citizens

Sacks (2000) presents an interesting view of citizenship education, stating that the best way to educate citizens who have a sense of belonging to the society they live in is to engage them in meaningful active participation in their society. This idea might be most important for the civic education of immigrants. Sacks uses the following metaphor for the relationship between immigrants and their receiving countries: "A house in which I take refuge is one where I am a guest. A house I help build is one that I can call mine" (p. 62).

Immigrant students live in a dual world—both in their own community and in the general society. Immigrant students are likely to suffer from a sense of social alienation in the receiving culture, as expressed in their rejection of complete assimilation because they are afraid to distance themselves from their home culture. On the other hand, they do wish to become active and effective in their present society. Education systems should recognize this aspect of educating immigrant children and find ways to overcome the difficulties caused by this two-sided existential reality linked to migration.

Tate (2000) suggests several "big ideas" for civic education, among them helping young people shape their identities through involvement and participation in carrying out duties as well as seeking rights. Clarke (2000) also views active participation as an important part of citizenship, stating, "Part of the process of education for citizenship is the need to develop in all young people a sense of belonging, and the skills and motivation to want and be able to make a difference to their own lives and the lives of their communities. That is the only way in which we can build an inclusive society" (p. 85).

We view the model proposed by Cohen (2013) as most appropriate for planning civic education because it emphasizes the role of participation in society. We learned from our study that immigrants might emphasize their role in their own community. Consequently, we conceive of the civic education of immigrant students as related to this dual nature of their experience, emphasizing both knowledge of their own home culture as well as knowledge of the dominant society. Cohen's model includes three phases:

1. The building of foundational knowledge—the knowledge needed to recognize government structures and modes of governing, as well as historical changes in civic regulations, such as understanding the idea of "separation of powers" (a disciplined conception of civic education)
2. The demonstration of an active mode of citizenship—translating knowledge of the discipline into actions (a participatory conception of civic education)
3. The development of a critical stance—encouraging thoughtful, active citizens who may have a critical stance toward the disciplinary knowledge they acquired and the social reality of inequality (a critical conception of civic education) (p. 188)

Cohen (2013) argues that all phases should be part of civic education and states, "All students should have equitable access to the knowledge, values and dispositions that are crucial for any democratic citizen" (p. 5). These phases are congruent with other models in the literature. Banks's (2008) typology of levels of citizenship, from the basic level of legal citizenship up to the highest level transformative citizenship, has direct implications for civic education. In order to learn to implement legal citizenship, the first phase of Cohen's model—foundational knowledge—is required. We view the basis for transformative citizenship called for by Banks as a synthesis of the participatory and critical conceptions of civic education in Cohen's model (phases 2 and 3).

This model of educating immigrant students has to overcome some of the challenges of everyday life in schools. According to Banks (2008), immigrant students are often perceived as the "Other" and marginalized in schools. This situation might cause these students to develop weak attachments to the nation-state in which they live (Banks, 2015). Moreover, Banks claims that in multicultural education systems several issues continue to be unresolved, such as achievement gaps between minority and majority groups and the language rights of immigrant students. Most ethnic minority groups, especially new immigrants, might experience discrimination both in schools and the wider society. Civic education in a multicultural society has to grapple with this situation and find ways to provide immigrant students with a kind of transformative citizenship that includes both the demonstration of an active mode of citizenship—namely participatory citizenship—as well as the development of a critical stance that promotes a rejection of inequality. The analysis of the nature of civic education, especially for immigrant students, leads us to the presentation of a current example of the education of immigrant students in Israel and their road to integration into Israeli society. Narratives of the integration of Ethiopian immigrants into Israeli society might reveal components of civic education that can be effective for other immigrant populations and multicultural societies.

THE ROAD TO SUCCESS: NARRATIVES OF SUCCESSFUL ETHIOPIAN IMMIGRANTS IN ISRAEL

The basic premise of our study, "The Road to Success: Narratives of Successful Ethiopian Immigrants in Israel," was that immigrants can excel and become highly successful in the receiving countries, not as exceptions to the rule but as a common goal for all students, regardless of their ethnic backgrounds (Ladson-Billings, 2012). Our study focused on Ethiopian immigrants who face all the difficulties entailed by moving to a new culture and amplified by their different skin color. Narratives of successful young adult Ethiopian immigrants have the potential to uncover the link between their experiences in the process of education and their becoming effective citizens in a new country, and yields implications for civic education for immigrants as well as for all students.

Israel has been coping with significant demographic changes as a result of an influx of a large percentage of immigrants since 1990. Of a population of approximately 8 million, approximately 18% are immigrants from the former Soviet Union, most of whom immigrated to Israel during the 1990s. In addition, during the past two decades, about 125,000 immigrants arrived from Ethiopia; our study focuses on this population. These immigrants come mainly from rural areas and are different culturally and socioeconomically from the majority of the Israeli population. Their educational experiences vary widely from the culture and norms of Israeli classrooms. A large-scale research study by Levin, Shohamy, and Spolasky (2003) compared the academic achievement of Israeli native students and immigrant students from Ethiopia and the Soviet Union. The researchers found that the academic status of students of Ethiopian origin is especially low in both Hebrew and mathematics at all grade levels. The low academic status of Ethiopian students is also reflected in the small percentage of them who matriculate in higher education. Moreover, only 53% were found to aspire to higher education compared to 84% among nonimmigrant students (Kahan-Strawezynski, Amiel, Levi, Konstantinov, 2012).

A CLOSER LOOK AT THE ETHIOPIAN IMMIGRANT POPULATION

The Ethiopian immigrants to Israel have had adjustment challenges since they started immigrating to Israel in the early 1990s. Some of these challenges arose because of the transition from an oral, traditional, non-Western culture to a modern literate culture. Ethiopian families speak their first language at home (Amharic or Tigris) while learning Hebrew, so their children, who were born in Israel, are exposed to bilingualism from birth. Furthermore, they experience difficulties related to unfamiliar religious rituals, employment, a different status for women, and a new physical climate (Stavans, Olshtain, & Goldzweig, 2009).

Our study consisted of interviews with nine adult Ethiopian immigrants who have excelled in various professional domains, such as theatre and arts, business and social organizations, politics, and engineering. Participants were recruited through personal contacts in educational institutions and immigrant organizations. Criteria for inclusion in the study were as follows: young Ethiopian adults—from both genders—who had attained high educational, professional, or societal status in a variety of occupations, between the ages of 30 to 45. In order to maintain the anonymity of participants—and because of the relatively small population of the Ethiopian community in Israel—we will not present a detailed account of the participants' demographics. The study participants consisted of four men and five women, ages 35 to 42. All of the participants were born in Ethiopia and migrated to Israel at different ages—some were very young and some had graduated from high school. The participants were educated in Israeli boarding schools and higher education institutes and were counseled and supported by social workers and other professionals.

We adopted a blended approach to narrative analysis using both autobiographical "big stories" (Clandinin & Connelly, 2000) as well as "small stories" (Bamberg, 2010) elicited in interaction with the participants. This approach is similar to Bloom's (1985) study of the development of talent in exceptionally accomplished young adults through retrospective interviews. In Bloom's study, semi-structured interactive interviews were held with the participants, which encouraged the individual to tell his or her own story.

Examining the Interviews

The first stage of the data collection consisted of in-depth narrative interviews with the participants in which they described their perceptions of the processes and circumstances that helped them in their personal histories. Participants were asked to describe their individual stories of immigration and their route to professional and personal achievement. The interviews were conducted one-on-one, took 1 to 3 hours, and were semi-structured. They were scheduled at a mutually convenient time and place and were audio-recorded with the participants' consent. The audio-recorded interviews were transcribed verbatim. The interviews consisted of a big opening question, "Tell me about the story of your education: Where did you study, when, for how long, what were your goals?" as well as probing questions during the interview to clarify the responses of participants, including asking for examples of concrete experiences concerning the role of home, school, and any other factors regarded as relevant for achieving success. Fieldnotes were taken during and after the interview. At research team meetings the interview process and findings were highlighted and discussed.

Recurrent themes and categories were identified in the texts transcribed from the interviews (Ryan & Bernard, 2003). Our data analysis procedure started with each team member analyzing the transcriptions and identifying big ideas conveyed in the text. Ryan and Bernard (2003) suggest reading the text over and over. On the first reading, major themes can be quickly marked; in the next stage, less obvious themes can be uncovered. Following Ryan and Bernard's suggestion, our research team focused on similarities and differences, making systematic comparisons across units of data to identify categories that constituted each big idea. Repetition is one of the easiest ways to identify themes through topics that reoccur throughout the text; "the more the same concept occurs in a text the more likely it is a theme" (Ryan & Bernard, 2003, p. 89). These themes were compared with concepts in the literature on the civic education of immigrants.

Using Concept Mapping to Uncover Perceptions

In the second stage of the data collection, concept maps were created by four of the nine participants from the first stage of the data collection, using the Concept Structuring Analysis Task (ConSAT) interview. Mahler and Brandfeld (1995) found that concept maps were an effective tool for uncovering attitudes because they reveal the complexity of views and perceptions. The ConSAT interview described by Mahler and Brandfeld (1995) was used in our study to expand our understandings of the participants' narratives of their journey to success.

Based on the themes identified in the first phase of our study, our research team identified a set of 15 terms with which the participants constructed concept maps. The interview protocol consisted of the following stages:

1. Each participant was asked to explain each of the terms and their link to the participant's "success story."
2. The participant placed the cards on a large page so that the spatial arrangement reflected the relations among the terms (e.g., in groups).
3. The participant could add terms that she or he felt were missing (the terms in gray ovals in Figure 5.1), or disregard concepts she or he felt were not relevant.
4. The participant was asked to categorize the various terms and to give titles to each group that was identified. The groups were numbered by the interviewer.
5. The participant was asked to identify significant relationships among terms or groups of terms, or between terms and groups.
6. The participant was asked to characterize in his or her own words the links noted in Stage 5. Each link was numbered.
7. The interviewee was asked to assign a name to the entire map.

Each concept map was converted to a digitized version (see Figure 5.1). The terms the participants added are in gray ovals. The phrases the participants chose to describe the significant links they identified between the terms and groups are numbered in the digitized version and detailed in Table 5.1.

The maps were analyzed by content and structural analysis (Simon& Levin, 2012). The structural analysis is based on dimensions of the maps' spatial structure: central ideas and processes; consolidation; unlinked concepts; nuclear con-

Figure 5.1. Mark's Concept Map

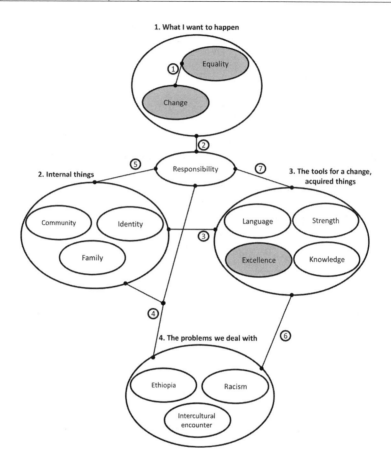

cepts (terms with multiple links); and terms added or removed (see also Simon & Levin, 2012). The content analysis of the maps focused on the interviewees' concept definitions, group titles, and phrases that described the links between nodes. The objective of this type of analysis was to examine the main ideas conveyed by the text and to observe which themes were not part of the interviewees' perception (Ryan & Bernard, 2003). Rather than generalizing to all Ethiopian immigrants in Israel, we are interested in developing analytical lenses and practical understandings of immigrant youth's experiences that might hinder or support their process of becoming effective citizens.

Table 5.1. The Links Between Terms or Groups of Terms in Mark's Concept Map

Link Number on Concept Map	Terms/Groups of Terms Linked	Phrase Linking the Terms/Groups of Terms
1	Equality–Change	In order to create equality a change must occur
2	What I want to happen–The tools for a change, acquired things	The tools to create a change and to change people's minds, even if it is without responsibility, it will make a change
3	Internal things–The tools for a change, acquired things	Two different groups, that in order to achieve what you want, you need both
4	Responsibility–Internal things–The problems we deal with	Group 4 is another stimulant to create identity and responsibility for family and community

ETHIOPIAN IMMIGRANT PERCEPTIONS: FIVE THEMES FOR CIVIC EDUCATION

The narratives of the nine young successful Ethiopian immigrants in Israel revealed perceptions related to obstacles they faced as well as factors that supported them in their path to becoming effective citizens. We present several themes that were uncovered by analyzing their narratives. We describe each theme with examples of statements the participants made in the interviews. When we analyzed the transcripts of the first-stage narrative interviews, several recurrent themes were identified. We elaborate on five distinctive themes that have implications for civic education for immigrant students: racism, discrimination and skin color; support; dual cultural identity; sense of mission; and personal autonomy. These themes appeared in all of the interviews with different intensity.

The concept maps constructed via the ConSAT interview revealed the different relations between the themes. For each participant the acculturation and integration processes were experienced differently—therefore each map structure reflects an individual's unique background. However, all four maps testify to the importance and centrality of the concepts "sense of mission" or "responsibility" to the interviewees' personal narratives. We conclude the findings with an example of one of the conceptual maps created by a participant. This concept map is presented and analyzed, providing insights into the participant's views concerning the connections among the themes. Presenting findings from both modes of inquiry enriches our understanding and provides insights into the meaning of the different themes in the lives of the study participants.

Racism, Discrimination, and Skin Color

All the participants had to deal with racism. Their skin color necessitated developing strategies to overcome open and subtle discrimination. One of the participants, Tammy, described the obstacles she met: "I felt that every time, every place I came to, I needed to break the glass with my face and after it broke and I was left with a scar, only then I got a chance." Tammy also said that people are used to meeting Ethiopians living on the margin of society: "It is sometimes so difficult for people that I'm Ethiopian and successful that they talk to me in English because it is convenient for them to think I'm someone from the United States who succeeded." Patricia mentioned that when she first arrived in Israel and started going to kindergarten, the kids treated her differently because of her skin color. They asked her, "Do you want us to paint you in white color so you'll look like us?" Mark described how people rejected Ethiopians in every area: "People don't want Ethiopians to live next door to them, they don't want their kids to study in the same class with Ethiopians." Dealing with racism made it harder for the study participants to find their way and place in their new society. They had to overcome these prejudices in order to succeed. "Racism, discrimination, and skin color" are the kinds of experience that are part of the reality of immigrants of color and constitute a major phenomenon that has to be studied in order to combat and overcome it.

Support

The interviewees described the presence of one or more persons who were important in giving them hope and confidence and in supporting their academic and professional trajectory. Participants emphasized that support from their surroundings was an important factor for their success. Nathan explained that "the boarding school is your home, it doesn't matter it's like a family." Adam expressed gratitude to a teacher who inspired him: "This teacher suggested that I participate in an exhibition. I said, 'Now you have gone too far' and she said 'you must.' This teacher encouraged me and it helped me to fulfill what I had inside." The participants in our study—like many of the Ethiopian immigrants in Israel—were placed at boarding schools in order to assist their integration into the Israeli society and to ease the financial burden on their families. The participants found their boarding school experiences positive and rewarding. Polly described her experience:

> When I heard about the religious boarding school in Jerusalem, I didn't think it meant not seeing my home. Because of the living conditions, so I decided to go for it. . . . Because there I really could get a wide support of as-

sistance in lessons . . . and the extracurricular activities there filled my afternoons much more . . . it gave me much more than academic capabilities.

It seems to us that in the context of civic education it is extremely important to relate not only to the negative sides of societal processes, but to show the positive elements that inspire hope and motivation that enable students to become active civic participants.

Dual Cultural Identity

Identity formation is essential in the transition of immigrants from one culture to another. The integration strategy mentioned above (Berry & Sabatier, 2010) was found to be dominant in the personal narratives. The study's participants perceived their identity as being composed of two subidentities: Ethiopians and new Israeli citizens. This dichotomy led to different views on the way these two identities could be integrated and acted upon. Some participants felt the need for a separation between these two identities, usually giving priority to the new Israeli identity by separating themselves temporarily from the immigrant community and characteristics. Macie, for example, distanced herself from her Ethiopian identity: "As a teenager I really didn't want to get close to the Ethiopian community." After John finished his study at the Hebrew school (called ULPAN) when he first arrived, he grew distant from everything he knew. He said, "Since I finished that part of the ULPAN, I detached myself from anything related to the community." Nathan also felt separated from Ethiopian culture: "In boarding school, I really loved folk dancing and Israeli old songs. Until I was 17 or 18 I never listened to Amharic music and of course we never talked in Amharic between us in boarding school, only in Hebrew." John understood very early that he sounded different from the other children: "When I was in 2nd grade I realized not everyone talked that way, everyone recognizes me for my accent, so I changed it to an Israeli accent."

Other participants managed to integrate their two identities and found a way to benefit from both. Patricia said, "On the one hand, I'm Israeli, and on the other hand, I don't forget and I know that the only reason I got where I am today is because I'm Ethiopian." Nathan mentioned that he eventually understood why it is important "to feel good about your heritage, not to deny it. You can also choose which part of your heritage to embrace and which to drop." As an adult, Macie did not want to lose her Ethiopian identity: "You understand that being Israeli and erasing your identity is not the solution." Macie states that her daughter "is Ethiopian [and] needs to know about her roots, the same way she needs to know about her German roots. She is this and this and this and this, and it is OK, and she doesn't need to choose right now." It seems that the participants in our study present evidence that acculturation is a transactional process that allows for change and development. Moreover, analysis of the narratives indicates that the participants are aware of the active identity choices they made.

Sense of Mission

The participants' acute sense of mission was an intriguing personal characteristic revealed in the narratives. *Sense of mission* means commitment to carry out activities for the Israeli community, and particularly the participants' own Ethiopian community. The term *sense of mission* is different from the phenomenon that immigrants might choose to perform activities for their communities. A sense of mission concerns the inner feeling of accountability, not necessarily accompanied by relevant actions. Some of the participants chose their career and workplace as a way to act upon their sense of mission, and to help the Ethiopian immigrant community with the difficulties they experience adapting to Israeli society. Mark worked in a nonprofit organization helping Ethiopian immigrants because "people should find a way into appropriate workplaces . . . and we try to influence and help them open the door." Adam wrote a play that depicts the journey that most of the immigrants made from Ethiopia to Israel. He stated, "I feel fulfillment when I see children who were ashamed of their culture, and now are proud . . . this is a mission for me, and not only a way to make a living."

Several of the study participants were political activists. Patricia chose this path since she felt that "it became my responsibility because it is such a weakened community." Macie felt ambivalent about the role she was given to represent the Ethiopian community. Nevertheless, she said that she took responsibility because she understood that Israeli society felt that her actions influenced other Ethiopian immigrants. Other participants' sense of mission extended beyond advancing the immigrant community to changing the receiving society for the better. Nathan emphasized this approach by stating, "I still have the chance to fix the rotten world you leave behind." He referred to the universal aspect of the immigrants' community relationship with the receiving society: "I don't go there to represent the Ethiopian people. I go to represent my attitude, which says we need to live here in coexistence, we should have a dialog, we need civil rights." There is a close connection between giving and belonging to society. We view the sense of mission identified in the narratives of the participants as representing an expression of the desire for strong integration into Israeli society. The participants' sense of mission might be understood as part of their active participation as effective citizens.

Personal Autonomy

All the narratives emphasized a turning point when the participants transformed themselves from passive subjects to active decision-makers in their life stories. These autonomous actions seemed to change the participants' paths and exemplified their independent and self-reliant approach to the difficulties they encountered. Nathan exhibited great independence as a young boy of 13 when he decided to leave Ethiopia without his parents. He stated, "I came to my parents and told [them] that I am running away to Sudan." This active pursuit of solutions to difficult situations is also exemplified in the way he dealt with discrimination in boarding school. Nathan felt discriminated against by a teacher and described how he handled the situation:

> He [the teacher] takes me in the room and then I turn over the table and I tell him, "Listen now, what you've done with my grade you won't do again to anyone here!" And really from that moment on in the boarding school they didn't [reduce grades] to anyone, I don't know if they added [points] that's their issue. But to reduce [points] they didn't.

Adam explained how he and a group of older student immigrants showed initiative and asked the social worker if they could move to a different facility to study Hebrew because they could not study properly in the first environment. He said, "We asked to leave because we couldn't study. We started to study half days [in the new place] because it helped us learn Hebrew and . . . [to get accepted into] university." Several other participants had similar stories about decisions that were not easy but were important for their future. Macie decided to leave a boarding school she liked: "I told myself that if I want to concentrate on schoolwork and learn, I have to move, even though I had fun." Patricia analyzed her roots in her political career and emphasized the difference between her actions and other immigrants' actions when they experienced injustice. She said, "The difference is that while everyone was silent then I, at the age of 20, went to protest and found another mission and I've done everything, but everything, to not sit quiet . . . and I couldn't understand why others are sitting and others don't do what I do." It seems that these self-directed actions by the participants helped them to advance their personal and professional development.

Using a Concept Map to Identify Themes

We will be relating the themes described above to our analyses of the salient features of civic education for immigrant students as well as for all students. In the following section we present one of the concept maps created in the second stage of the study. It complements the insights gained on the themes "sense of mission" and "personal autonomy" found in the narrative interviews, and exemplifies their significance in the participants' perceptions. It is important to note that we chose the concept "responsibility" to represent the participants' "personal autonomy" in the ConSAT interview initial set of concepts because a pilot interview indicated that "personal autonomy" was unclear and too complex.

Figure 5.1 is a digitized version of the concept map Mark created. The concept map Mark created emphasizes his view of the importance of action to change society. Mark added terms that stress his perception on the need for change ("change" and "equality") and linked them to the group of terms he titled as "The tools for change, acquired things" (group 3). The term "responsibility" is a "nuclear concept" as it has multiple links to the other groups in the map. Mark does not use the term "sense of mission" in his map; yet placing the term "responsibility" at the focal point of his map may be interpreted as an illustration of his feelings of duty to actively changing society. This concurs with the understandings we gained from Mark's narrative interview concerning his deep sense of mission and his activities to better Israeli society. Mark chose his career and workplace as a way to act upon his sense of mission, and to aid the Ethiopian immigrant community in their difficulties in adapting to Israel. His map exemplifies how his sense of mission extended beyond advancing the immigrant community to changing Israel for the better.

REALIZING THE POTENTIAL OF IMMIGRANT STUDENTS

The narratives in this study present the processes that led young Ethiopian immigrants to become effective and engaged citizens of their new country. The following discussion elaborates on the implications of this study for civic education. The education and development of immigrants not only determine their integration into the receiving countries, but also have far-reaching implications for the host society and its economy and well-being (Suárez-Orozco & Suárez-Orozco, 2001). The major issue of our study was how to realize the potential of immigrant youth as students and members of society (Masten, Liebkind, & Hernandez, 2012). We decided to focus on the narratives of success in order to gain insights into the factors that enabled immigrant students to overcome crucial difficulties and reach high achievement despite severe obstacles.

Our study participants told their stories with satisfaction and pain. The pain was expressed in the prevalent themes of racism, discrimination, and dual cultural identity. Because of their skin color, discrimination was an ongoing experience for the study participants that did not cease over time. The first meeting of the Ethiopian Jews with racial discrimination based on skin color was when they arrived in Israel. In Ethiopia they considered themselves qeyy, a term best translated as "reddish-brown" like all the Ethiopians of the north (Kaplan, 1999). In Israel they became "Black," and met for the first time a poisonous combination of the classic racism of White people against Blacks and a religious xenophobia professed by the religious establishment that doubted the authenticity of their Jewishness. Despite the harsh experiences of our study participants, their narratives indicated that they did reach successful integration into Israeli culture without losing their affiliation with their Ethiopian–Jewish culture. The participants' narratives demonstrated the importance of support by the educational system and other factors that deal with immigrants—such as social workers—to their integration and success. Attempting to construct a framework for civic education, we started by formulating several questions: What themes originating in the narratives of participants in our study have implications for civic education? Based on both the literature and our findings, what is a relevant civic education for immigrants? and How can civic education be integrated into the overall school experience?

IMPLICATIONS FOR CIVIC EDUCATION

Dual Cultural Identity

Berry and colleagues (2006) developed a bidimensional model of acculturation and successful integration related to both heritage and host cultures. Maintaining one's own cultural identity while valuing the culture of the larger host society leads to an integration option—which according to Berry is preferred. Research on ethnic identity, immigration, and well-being indicates that the combination of a strong ethnic identity with a strong national host-country identity promotes the best adaptation of immigrants (Phinney, Horenczyk, Liebkind, & Vedder, 2001). A study of immigration adaptation in Canada by Sayegh and Lasry (1993) indicates that when "immigrants identify with both the heritage and host cultures [it is] without being a detriment to their full participation in the host society" (p. 107). Van der Zee (2006) states, "Seeking interactions in the new culture, but also maintaining aspects of the old culture is called integration. . . . Research has clearly shown that, in terms of well-being, integration is associated with more favorable outcomes than assimilation" (pp. 179–180).

Israel has moved from a "melting pot" approach to immigration in the early years of the nation to a more open acceptance of immigrants keeping their cultural identity while functioning in mainstream Israeli society. Our study indicates that the successful Ethiopian immigrants who participated in our study maintained dual cultural identities. While accepting Israeli cultural norms and modes of behavior—the Hebrew language, modes of dress, and use of free time—they also maintained pride in their culture of origin. Constructing dual identity in Israel is very complex because Israel is an extremely heterogeneous society that consists of immigrants from many different nations and cultures that have varying ethnic and religious identities. Despite this complexity, it seems that it is possible to imagine an Israeli common receiving culture. It is interesting to know that Kashua (2015)—an Israeli Arab author—described the difficulties that Arab citizens face trying to be recognized as "Israelis" and to "feel at home" in their dual identity as Muslim Arabs and Israelis. Lapid (2005) a well-known Israeli author and politician, wrote about the qualities and characteristics of the Israeli citizen. It is this "Israeli identity" that becomes part of the dual identity of immigrants. Citizenship education theorists such as Banks (2008) recognize and legitimize cultural and group identities as important identities in multicultural democratic societies.

Because of the large demographic transitions, the situation of multiple identities is common in many nations. In order to promote both a recognition of differences as well as a sense of commonality, a way to conduct civic education in multicultural nations might be to start with learning about the different cultures and ethnic groups within the society and then proceed to an understanding of the importance of a common vision for society and how to construct and contribute to it.

Word of Warning—The Paradox of Integration

Our participants exemplify "the paradox of integration" (ten Teije, Coenders, & Verkuyten, 2013). These highly successful immigrants perceive deep discrimination against their own group. They speak about racism and open discrimination and worry about the reaction of mainstream Israelis. On the one hand, the participants did achieve integration according to the definition given by Berry et al. (2006), namely, connection to both origin and absorption cultures. On the other hand, the paradox of integration raises great problems in Israel. Presently, Ethiopian youth are demonstrating militantly against perceived discrimination, claiming that, despite their educational level and service to society, they are not accepted as equals. Ward and Kennedy (1992) argued that if dual identification does not lead to positive evaluation by the majority group, immigrants can be expected to experience psychological distress, a low level of life satisfaction, and even militant rejection of the receiving society. The narratives of highly successful Ethiopian immigrants present a warning in this respect. Civic education can respond to this issue by emphasizing that differences should not have hierarchical implications and by providing students with a comprehensive view of the richness of diversity. Studying the history of various cultures might be one way of integrating these issues into the curriculum.

Personal Autonomy and Integration in Society

Another important theme revealed in this study concerns the sense of autonomy and being active in decision-making about one's education and future. Immigrant students as well as adults often find themselves in situations that are determined by others, like parents, principals, teachers, social workers, and policymakers. The successful young Ethiopian adults in our study emphasized their independence and role in shaping their lives. Autonomy and decision-making can yield a sense of accomplishment that can lead to competencies in immigrants. Kagitcibasi (2012) argues that the ability to act as an autonomous self promotes "proficiency for 'sociocultural adjustment,' that is, success in school, work, and social integration in general" (p. 282).

A sense of autonomy in decision-making is perceived as contributing to successful integration in society. The model described by Moradi and Risco (2006) might explain the relationship between autonomy and decision-making and successful integration. Their model examines the relationship of personal control with self-esteem and reduction of psychological distress. A sense of personal control was associated positively with high self-esteem and negatively with psychological distress. Moreover, personal control/environmental mastery was observed as a mediator of the influence of perceived discrimination on the outcome variables of self-esteem and psychological distress. They write, "Sense of personal control partially mediated the link of perceived discrimination events to psychological distress" (p. 418). Thus we might understand that a sense of personal control promotes the ability of immigrants to overcome discrimination and other negative experiences by raising their self-esteem and reducing psychological distress. Moradi and Risco's study indicated that "U.S. acculturation was related to lower distress, to the extent that it was linked with greater sense of personal control" (p. 418). The overall pattern of different relations between perceived discrimination, personal control, and distress is critical for understanding their role in the integration of immigrants.

Our study participants seemed to be fully aware of the contribution of taking control of their own development for their future success. They did not talk about failure, but rather about success, avoiding being defensive or using the hardship they encountered as an excuse for failure. We view the theme of "personal autonomy" as especially important for civic education—expecting citizens to be active decision-makers in their own lives as well as playing an active role in their society. Providing students with opportunities for decision-making in choices of activism might strengthen their self-identity as autonomous individuals. Schimmel (2003) argues that involving students in collaborative rule-making in schools will help prepare them to be responsible active citizens. In civic education personal autonomy might be promoted in a variety of ways. Students could be planners of their own learning, decide on the kinds of their reading materials, or conduct small inquiries into social issues. Students should be taught about the options they have to influence their society and encouraged to take action on issues that are significant to them. For example, students can study about the preservation of the environment and plan actions to foster preservation by writing letters to the authorities or volunteering for ecological activities. Civic education should not be limited to learning about civic organization and modes of government, but should include practical expressions of ways that students can influence their society.

Sense of Mission and Community Participation

The successful young Ethiopian immigrants in our study expressed an acute sense of mission—high motivation for volunteering and social action. Involvement in volunteer work and social participation is described in the literature concerning immigrants' integration in receiving societies. Rochelle and Shardlow (2012) examined factors affecting involvement in voluntary work and social participation among the Chinese in the United Kingdom. They concluded that a better understanding of the motivation and practices of British Chinese in social participation and voluntary activities might lead to more culturally inclusive involvement of immigrants. Guo (2014)—viewing immigrants as active citizens—studied the volunteering experiences of Chinese immigrants in Vancouver, British Columbia. Guo's study indicated that when Chinese immigrants volunteered, they learned language, skills, and knowledge that were needed by new citizens for their integration into Canadian society.

In Israel, Jaffe and Sasson (2014) studied first-generation immigrant adolescents' motives for volunteering. They compared the motives of first-generation immigrants and native adolescents who volunteer. They found that first-generation immigrants were more motivated to volunteer than native adolescents. First-generation immigrant adolescents perceived volunteerism as an integrative action for social participation. Volunteerism helped them express their focus on the new community. The sense of mission accompanied by appropriate actions, as expressed by participants in our study, resembles the term *participatory communal citizenship* described and analyzed by Knight and Watson (2014, p. 542). In a study of African immigrant youth and young adults, Knight and Watson focused on the influence of families and schooling on participatory communal citizenship expressed, for instance, in political awareness or community service. The researchers view service to the community as an indication of positive integration. Relevant approaches to citizenship include active participation in community affairs (Banks, 2008; Marshall, 1950/1992; Miller, 2000; Sacks, 2000). Fostering personal autonomy and a sense of mission can become central components of civic education in our globalized world. Such a framework would be relevant for diverse sectors in nation-states, including newcomers and native members of society.

WHAT IS A RELEVANT CIVIC EDUCATION FOR IMMIGRANTS?

Cohen (2013) described a theoretical model for planning civic education based on his empirical examination of civic education in schools. This model includes three phases: (1) one centered on acquiring knowledge; (2) the second concerned with active citizenship; and the (3) third focused on developing a critical view as a citizen. The three-phase model of civic education reflects the ideas suggested by Tate (2000) and Clarke (2000) that concern the active role of citizens in their society. We suggest the following interaction among the different phases in Cohen's model. Phase 2, engagement in an active mode of citizenship based on a participatory conception of civic education, is proposed as the starting phase. Examples of this phase are engaging students in shared activities in their communities, for example, in the realm of action to improve the environment. Active participation in communication with political figures concerning acute societal problems is another mode of involving students in participatory citizenship. Phase 2 would become intimately linked, on the one hand, with Phase 1, namely, acquiring the necessary knowledge for carrying out Phase 2, and on the other hand, with developing a critical stance as called for in Phase 3. Acquired knowledge and a critical stance would feedback into participatory active citizenship (see Figure 5.2).

Starting with Phase 2, participatory civic activities are based on a philosophical pedagogical approach that views experience as the foundation of acquired knowledge. Dewey (1938/1998) argues that all genuine education comes about through experience. He stated, "I take it that the fundamental unity of the newer philosophy is found in the idea that there is an intimate and necessary relation between the process of actual experience and education" (p. 20). Dewey paraphrases

Figure 5.2. The Relationship Between the Three Phases of Civic Education

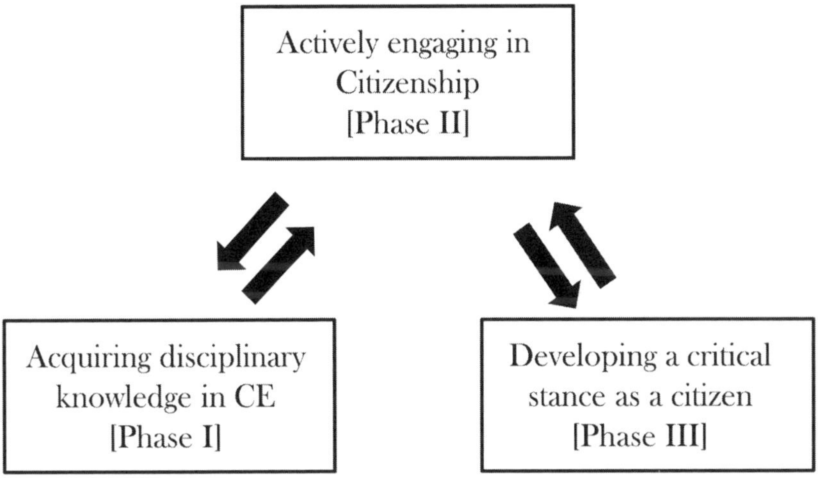

Actively engaging in
Citizenship
[Phase II]

Acquiring disciplinary
knowledge in CE
[Phase I]

Developing a critical
stance as a citizen
[Phase III]

Lincoln's saying about democracy and speaks of "education of, by and for experience" (p. 29). Emphasizing civic education for action and through actions concerns both norms of behaviors (Phase 2) and disciplinary knowledge (Phase 1).

Professional education in all practical domains utilizes the need for experience in the process of education, usually at some point in the curriculum. An interesting example of starting with experience is the Canadian McMaster University School of Medicine. This school is acknowledged to be a world leader in innovative learning and testing systems. Learning is based on clinical experience, a case-based learning. This educational model is known as "problem-based Learning" and was introduced at McMaster in 1969, and since then has been adopted by many medical schools in different regions in the world (Lee & Kwan, 1997). Problem-based learning (PBL) is an acknowledged productive mode of teaching and learning. Starting civic education with activities in the community can be turned into PBL that is close to the teaching-learning process exemplified by the McMaster School of Medicine.

"I hear and I forget, I see and remember, I do and I understand." This Chinese proverb states a similar educational approach. We suggest that civic education adopt a comparable process of learning, starting with concrete experiences in participatory activities in the community and turning to the theoretical frameworks of citizenship, as required by the practical experiences. Thus, in an experience of involvement in environmental issues, students can learn about relevant laws and where and how they are promoted, as well as about the role of local institutions in comparison with the central government system like parliament or ministries.

The participatory phase is linked, as well, with Phase 3, developing a critical stance. Through involvement in concrete aspects of citizenship, students become exposed to problems and critical issues of equity, socioeconomic levels, and power relationships. Thus they are provided with opportunities to develop a critical stance toward existing situations and a desire to improve and overcome some of the problems of society. The combination of the three phases discussed above might become part of the transformative civic education recommended by Banks (2008):

> Transformative citizenship education helps students to develop decision-making and social action skills that are needed to identify problems within society, acquire knowledge related to their home and community cultures and languages, identify and clarify their values, and to take thoughtful individual or collective civic action that will improve their local communities, nation-states, and the world. (p. 135)

Transformative civic education is pivotal for immigrants as well as native students and might advance the creation of a bridge for these two student groups. Community action is a two-way process—it serves the need of the community while simultaneously promoting the individual growth of the participants, as well as the development of citizens committed to action.

HOW CAN CIVIC EDUCATION BE INTEGRATED IN THE SCHOOL CURRICULUM?

We believe that participatory engagement of students in their community should be part of the experience of students in all school grades, whether immigrants or natives in their community. Examples of activities at the elementary grade level are assisting adults in collecting books for senior citizens' homes, or cleaning school grounds, parks, or beaches. Such experiences might foster their sense of mission and responsibility toward their peers and their environment. Another education strategy might include providing students from an early age with opportunities to exercise personal autonomy and to be involved in decision-making. An example might be providing students with choices of curricular subjects and activities in math, geography, and history, and allowing freedom of choice while demanding commitment to individual decisions. Through such activities the sense of personal autonomy, important for citizens, might develop. At later stages in school life the necessary disciplinary knowledge required for effective citizenship will be acquired in relationship to the active experiences of students. Sacks (2000) encouraged societies to accept immigrants through their involvement, not only as guests in their new home, but also as active participants in its building and maintenance. Engaging immigrant students in civic activities as part of civic education in school might contribute to their sense of belonging and being "builders" who are valued by their fellow citizens.

REFERENCES

Albert, R. D., & Triandis, H. C. (1985). Intercultural education for multicultural societies. *International Journal of Intercultural Relations, 9,* 319–337.

Bamberg, M. (2010). Who am I? Narration and its contribution to self and identity. *Theory and Psychology Journal, 21*(1), 1–22.

Banks, J. A. (2008). Diversity, group identity, and citizenship education in a global age. *Educational Researcher, 37*(3), 129–139.

Banks, J. A. (2013). Citizenship education and migration. In I. Ness (Ed.), *The encyclopedia of global human migration.* Hoboken, NJ: Blackwell. doi: 10.1002/9781444351071.wbeghm137

Banks, J. A. (2015). Failed citizenship, civic engagement, and education. *Kappa Delta Pi Record, 51*(4), 151–154.

Berry, J. W., Phinney, J. S., Sam, D. L., & Vedder, P. (2006). Immigrant youth: Acculturation, identity, and adaptation. *Applied Psychology, 55*(3), 303–332.

Berry, J. W., & Sabatier, C. (2010). Acculturation, discrimination, and adaptation among second generation immigrant youth in Montreal and Paris. *International Journal of Intercultural Relations, 34*(3), 191–207.

Bloom, B. S. (1985). *Developing talent in young people.* New York, NY: Ballentine Books.

Clandinin, D. J., & Connelly, F. M. (2000). *Narrative inquiry: Experience and story in qualitative research.* San Francisco, CA: Josey-Bass

Clarke, C. (2000). Creating listening schools. In N. Pearce & J. Hallgarten (Eds.), *Tomorrow's citizens: Critical debates in citizenship and education* (pp. 84–89). London, United Kingdom: Institute for Public Policy Research.

Cohen, A. (2013). *Conceptions of citizenship and civic education: Lessons from three Israeli civics classrooms* (Unpublished doctoral dissertation). Columbia University, New York, NY.

Dewey, J. (1998). *Experience and education* (60th anniversary ed.). West Lafayette, IN: Kappa Delta Pi. (Original work published 1938)

Dudley, R. L., & Gitelson, A. R. (2002). Political literacy, civic education, and civic engagement: A return to political socialization? *Applied Developmental Science, 6*(4), 175–182.

Guo, S. (2014). Immigrants as active citizens: Exploring the volunteering experience of Chinese immigrants in Vancouver. *Globalisation, Societies and Education, 12*(1), 51–70.

Ichilov, O. (2013). Patterns of citizenship in a changing world. In O. Ichilov (Ed.), *Citizenship and citizenship education in a changing world* (pp. 11–27). London, United Kingdom: Routledge.

Jaffe, E., & Sasson, U. (2014). First generation immigrant adolescents' motives to volunteer. *Modern Management Science & Engineering, 2*(1), 10–18.

Kagitcibasi, C. (2012). Autonomous-related self and competence. In A. S. Masten, K. Liebkind, & D. J. Hernandez (Eds.), *Realizing the potential of immigrant youth* (pp. 281–306). New York, NY: Cambridge University Press.

Kahan-Strawezynski, P., Amiel, S., Levi, D., & Konstantinov, V. (2012). *Bney Noar Yotsey Ethiopia Ve'yotsey Brit Ha'moatsot Le'she'avar: Olim Ve'bney Olim—Dimyon Ve'shony [First and second generations of immigrant youth from Ethiopia and the Former Soviet Union—Similarities and differences].* Jerusalem, Israel: Myers-JDC-Brookdale Institute.

Kaplan, S. (1999). Can the Ethiopian change his skin? The Beta Israel (Ethiopian Jews) and racial discourse. *African Affairs, 98*(393), 535–550.

Kashua, S. (2015*). Ben Haaretz [Son of the land].* Jerusalem, Israel: Keter Publishing House.

Knight, M. G., & Watson, V. W. (2014). Toward participatory communal citizenship rendering visible the civic teaching, learning, and actions of African immigrant youth and young adults. *American Educational Research Journal, 51*(3), 539–566.

Ladson-Billings, G. (2012). Through a glass darkly: The persistence of race in education research and scholarship. *Educational Researcher, 41*(4), 115–120.

Lapid, Y. (2005). *Omdim Be-tur [Standing in a column].* Tel Aviv, Israel: Yedioth Ahronoth Books.

Lee, R. M. K. W., & Kwan, C. Y. (1997). The use of problem-based learning in medical education. *Journal of Medical Education, 1*(2), 149–157.

Levin, T., Shohamy, E., & Spolasky, D. (2003). *Heysegey Talmidim Olim [Educational achievement of immigrant students].* Unpublished research report submitted to the Ministry of Education. Tel Aviv University, School of Education, Tel Aviv, Israel.

Mahler, S., & Brandfeld, A. (1995). Potential Le'Hasifat Emdot Hagalum Be'Mipuy Musagim: Ha'Sichsuch Ha'Yehudi Aravi [The potential for uncovering attitudes in concept mapping: The Jewish-Arab conflict]. *Hachinuch Ve'Svivo, 17,* 131–148.

Marshall, T. H. (1964). *Class, citizenship, and social development: Essays of T. H. Marshall.* Westport, CT: Greenwood Press.

Marshall, T. H. (1992). Citizenship and social class. In T. H. Marshall & T. Bottomore, *Citizenship and social class* (pp. 8–17). London, United Kingdom: Pluto Press. (Original work published 1950)

Masten, A. S., Liebkind, K., & Hernandez, D. J. (2012). Introduction. In A. S. Masten, K. Liebkind, & D. J. Hernandez (Eds.), *Realizing the potential of immigrant youth* (pp. 1–13). New York, NY: Cambridge University Press.

Miller, D. (2000). Citizenship: What does it mean and why is it important? In N. Pearce & J. Hallgarten (Eds.), *Tomorrow's citizens: Critical debates in citizenship and education* (pp. 26–35). London, United Kingdom: Institute for Public Policy Research.

Moradi, B., & Risco, C. (2006). Perceived discrimination experiences and mental health of Latino/a American persons. *Journal of Counseling Psychology, 53,* 411–421.

Phinney, J. S., Horenczyk, G., Liebkind, K., & Vedder, P. (2001). Ethnic identity, immigration, and well-being: An interactional perspective. *Journal of Social Issues, 57*(3), 493–510.

Rochelle, T. L., & Shardlow, S. M. (2012). Involvement in volunteer work and social participation among UK Chinese. *International Journal of Intercultural Relations, 36*(5), 728–736.

Ryan, G. W., & Bernard, H. R. (2003). Techniques to identify themes. *Field Methods, 15*(1), 85–109.

Sacks, J. (2000). The Judaic vision of citizenship education. In N. Pearce & J. Hallgarten (Eds.), *Tomorrow's citizens: Critical debates in citizenship and education* (pp. 55–63). London, United Kingdom: Institute for Public Policy Research.

Sayegh, L., & Lasry, J. C. (1993). Immigrants' adaptation in Canada: Assimilation, acculturation, and orthogonal cultural identification. *Canadian Psychology/Psychologie Canadienne, 34*(1), 98–109.

Schimmel, D. M. (2003). Collaborative rule-making and citizenship education: An antidote to the undemocratic hidden curriculum. *American Secondary Education, 31*(3), 16–35.

Simon, D., & Levin, T. (2012). Uncovering differences in the conceptual views of expert and novice teachers through concept maps produced by sconsat interviews. In A. J. Cañas, J. D. Novak, & J. Vanhear (Eds.), *Concept maps: Theory, methodology, technology: Pro-*

ceedings of the fifth international conference on concept mapping (vol. 2, pp. 430–437). Msida, Malta: University of Malta. Retreived from cmc.ihmc.us/cmc/CMCProceedings.html

Sleeter, C., & Grant, C. (1987). An analysis of multicultural education in the United States. *Harvard Educational Review, 57*(4), 421–445.

Stavans, A., Olshtain, E., & Goldzweig, G. (2009). Parental perceptions of children's literacy and bilingualism: The case of Ethiopian immigrants in Israel. *Journal of Multilingual and Multicultural Development, 30*(2), 111–126.

Suárez-Orozco, C., & Suárez-Orozco, M. M. (2001). *Children of immigration.* Cambridge, MA: Harvard University Press.

Tate, N. (2000). Citizenship education in a liberal democracy. In N. Pearce & J. Hallgarten (Eds.), *Tomorrow's citizens: Critical debates in citizenship and education* (pp. 64–73). London, United Kingdom: Institute for Public Policy Research.

ten Teije, I., Coenders, M., & Verkuyten, M. (2013). The paradox of integration: Immigrants and their attitude toward the native population. *Social Psychology, 44*(4), 278–288.

United Nations General Assembly. (2012). *International migration and development: Report of the Secretary-General* (67th session, 3 August 2012) A/67/254. Retrieved from www.un.org/en/ga/search/view_doc.asp?symbol=A/67/254

Van de Vijver, F. J. R., Breugelmans, S. M., & Schalk-Soekar, S. R. (2008). Multiculturalism: Construct validity and stability. *International Journal of Intercultural Relations, 32*(2), 93–104.

Van der Zee, K. I. (2006). Ethnic identity and solidarity with functional groups. In S. Lindenberg, D. Fetchenhauer, A. Flache, & A. P. Buunk (Eds.), *Solidarity and prosocial behavior: An integration of sociological and psychological perspectives* (pp. 175–190). New York, NY: Springer.

Ward, C., & Kennedy, A. (1992). Locus of control, mood disturbance, and social difficulty during cross-cultural transitions. *International Journal of Intercultural Relations, 16*(2), 175–194.

CHAPTER 6

Ethnonational Politics of Citizenship Education in Israel and the Counterknowledge of Palestinian Teachers

Ayman K. Agbaria

Despite the growing international attention given to citizenship education, Quaynor (2012) notes that "few reviews of civic education scholarship include research from post-conflict societies" (p. 33). Addressing this lacuna, this chapter provides a review of the Israeli case, focusing on how the politics of identity in Israel has been shaping the field of citizenship education. Specifically, it highlights the recent changes in the citizenship education curriculum in Israel and contextualizes these changes within the religionized and nationalistic Israeli political culture. In addition, it examines Israeli Palestinian teachers' resistance pedagogies and counterhegemonic attempts to challenge the hardline nationalist agenda of the right in Israel.

Ethnonationalism is distinguished from regular nationalism by its perception of the nation not in terms of citizenry but in terms of ethnicity, which is often based on descent from shared ancestors. In this sense, membership in the nation-state is conditioned upon belonging to a specific ethnic community that is perceived to be entitled to absolute authority over the state's affairs (Travis, 2013). Travis (2013) states that ethnonationalism signifies a form of extremism of national values or politics that results in violence directed toward other national identities. Religious ethnonationalism is a more specific form of ethnonationalism that is distinguished by being based on a transcendent set of ideals and norms that gives ethnonational values, politics, and identities a seal of sanctity and inevitability. It is an all-explaining ideology that imbues national identities with zeal, absolutism, and ahistorical justifications in the name of an imagined collectivity that is often conceived of as superior, sacred, pure, and with a longstanding historic mission. Among national minorities, it is worth observing that ethnonationalist movements often develop contentious identity politics in the service of the minority's interests of equality and recognition that are perceived as not being well-catered to under the present political arrangements (Haklai, 2011).

This chapter focuses on the Palestinian minority in Israel that consists of the people who remained within the boundaries of the newly created State of Israel after the war of 1948 and its aftermath. In 2015 this minority constituted about 20.7% (approximately 1.73 million people) of the total population of Israel (Central Bureau of Statistics, 2015). This chapter argues that both the recent changes in citizenship education and the attempts to counteract the indoctrination of the curriculum in favor of moralizing and justifying an exclusive definition of the state as a Jewish state that is above and beyond any democratic deliberation reflect both the ethnonational turn in the political paths followed by both the State of Israel and, in response, the Palestinian minority within it.

On the one hand, the changes reflect a zealous adherence to the politics of the extreme right that has become more consensual in Israel, and has been persistent in maintaining Israeli citizenship as differential and hierarchal vis-à vis various ethnic groups in Israel. Specifically, the politics of the extreme right has downplayed the differences between what is considered as political and what is considered as religious, between Israeli politics and intra-Jewish politics, and between the interests of state and those of the Jewish majority. This condition in which the state lacks autonomy from the Jewish majority keeps the boundaries of exclusion impermeable and sustains the inequalities and subordination experienced by the Palestinian Arab citizens of Israel. On the other hand, the attempts to resist these neo-Zionist politics—be it by civil society organizations or the citizenship education teachers on whom this chapter focuses—are part and parcel of the Palestinian minority's endeavor to decolonize its education system at times in which the central government's capacity to constrain minority organizations and set narrow boundaries for contestation has diminished appreciably. These attempts have become more parochial, proliferated, and vociferous in seeking to challenge the Jewish hegemony over the material and cognitive resources of the state and in demanding concessions of more power-sharing, recognition, and equality.

UNDERSTANDING CITIZENSHIP

Citizenship is a conflated and complex concept. It can be perceived as a formal and legal status endowed with specific rights and duties; as an identity marker of belonging to certain cultural, ethnic, and even socioeconomic groups; as a stipulation of a range of expected civic virtues; and as a framework of various forms of participation in the political system (Heater, 2004).

A major question in citizenship education is how to define and educate toward "good citizenship" (Westheimer & Kahne, 2004). Galston (2001) reminds us that "good citizens are made, not born. The question is how, by whom, to what end?" (p. 217). Indeed, this question is the focus of extensive debate. The normative aspect of this debate concerns the question of what good citizenship is, while the deliberative aspect pertains to the question of how to educate for good citizenship. The literature offers various answers to each question, but answers that are yet inherently intertwined.

Nevertheless, there is growing agreement on the competencies necessary for an engaged and effective citizen, competencies that Althof and Berkowitz (2006) describe as follows:

> (a) civic and political knowledge (such as concepts of democracy, understanding the structure and mechanics of political decision-making and legislation, citizens' rights and duties, current political issues and problems); (b) intellectual skills (e.g., the ability to understand, analyse and check the reliability of information about government and public policy issues); (c) social and participatory skills (e.g., the ability to reason, argue and express own views in political discussions; conflict solution skills; knowing how to influence policies and decisions by petitioning and lobbying, build coalitions and cooperate with partner organisations); and (d) certain values, attitudes and "dispositions" with a motivational power (e.g., interest in social and political affairs, a sense of responsibility, tolerance and recognition of own prejudices; appreciation of values on which democratic societies are founded like democracy, social justice and human rights). (p. 503)

What is notable about this list is that the role of citizenship education is now broader than its historical designated role in the process of nation-state building, which is basically to contribute to the formation of a common identity and the inculcation of patriotism and loyalty to the nation. The agenda of citizenship education now underscores a "broad-based promotion of socially useful qualities," and is now far more complex and multilayered than "civics" education, which refers generally speaking to the "provision of information about formal public institutions" (Davies & Issitt, 2005, p. 389). This agenda places more emphasis on developing an "autonomous" citizen who is not only essentially law-abiding and public-spirited, but also questioning and critical (Galston, 2001). Put differently, citizenship education should aspire to cultivate a maximal citizen, not a minimal one (McLaughlin, 1992).

In the same vein, Westheimer and Kahne (2004) argue that citizenship education is not only about being well-mannered, responsible, and law-abiding citizens who are politically active and engaged in their communities as individuals; it is also about cultivating critical citizens who are cooperative, motivated, and committed to social change and justice. This "maximal" citizen has been referred to as a "deep citizen" (Clarke, 1996), a "critical-democratic citizen" (Veugelers, 2007), and a "transformative citizen" (Banks, 2008). Notwithstanding the differences between these conceptualizations, I believe that Banks's (2008) description is indeed sufficient to understand what type of citizen is required: A citizen who can "take action to promote social justice even when their actions violate, challenge, or dismantle existing laws, conventions, or structures" (p. 136). To achieve this ideal, scholars have suggested multidimensional models of citizenship education that are more holistic in attempting to link structural and personal dimensions and are more critical and active (see these models in Johnson & Morris, 2010).

In the background of the advocacy for these critical and maximal conceptualizations of citizenship education was a sense of crisis about the levels of engagement or disengagement among young citizens in Western countries and a strong belief that the crisis can be countered with effective citizenship education. In this regard, Hughes, Print, and Sears (2010) observed that most countries have adopted models of citizenship that are committed "to a largely civic republican conception of citizenship; and . . . constructivist approaches to teaching and learning as best practice in citizenship education" (p. 295). Fulfilling these requirements, according to Johnson and Morris (2010), requires "limiting the validity of ethno-nationalistic forms of identity," and advancing "forms of citizenship based on the promotion of a common set of shared values (e.g., tolerance, human rights and democracy), which prepare young people to live together in diverse societies and which reject the divisive nature of national identities" (p. 78).

One should bear in mind that "how we think about the formation of democratic citizens," according to Galston (2001), "depends on the specific conception of democracy we embrace." In line with this argument, one could argue the depth and scope of citizenship education depends on the dominant "educational regime" (pp. 217–218). Manzer (2003) states that an "educational regime" is "a stable ordering of political principles and public authority for the governance of education . . . instituted on a core of political ideas that may derive from a dominant political ideology but more often will be created from conflict and compromise among the proponents of opposing doctrinal positions" (pp. 3–4).

These educational regimes seem to be prejudiced and repressive against colonized minorities, Indigenous peoples, and homeland groups, especially in divided societies and periods of political transitions. In postcolonial contexts, for example, the colonial state produces an educational regime that confines the colonized populations into repressive subject positions and thereby limits, shapes, or even denies their possible expressions of identity (Subedi & Daza, 2008). It does so by engineering a selective, uniform, and hegemonic narrative of its collective memory, especially in school subjects such as history, civics, geography, and literature. For the purposes of this chapter, the term *colonial* is understood as "imposed and dominating" rather than simply "foreign or alien" (Simmons & Dei, 2012).

In citizenship education these colonizing regimes—using McLaughlin's (1992) theorization of citizenship as a continuum of maximal and minimal conceptions of identity, virtues, political involvement, and societal prerequisites—confer on the colonized population a minimal view of identity that is "seen merely in formal, legal, juridical terms," while denying them the possibility of a maximal identity, which would provide the citizen with a "consciousness of him or herself as a member of a living community with shared democratic culture involving obligations and responsibilities as well as rights" (p. 236).

Therefore, under colonizing educational regimes, ethnic and cultural identities are subjected to social injustices in terms of their representation and recognition in the educational field and the school curricula in particular. Fraser (2000) conceived misrecognition of cultural identities as a social injustice that may involve the following: cultural domination (being subjected to patterns of interpretation and communication that are associated with another culture and are alien and/or hostile to one's own); nonrecognition (being rendered invisible by means of authoritative representational, communicative, and interpretative practices); and disrespect (being routinely maligned or disparaged in stereotypic public cultural representations and/or in everyday life situations).

However, when "only specific groups' knowledge becomes official knowledge" (Apple, 1993, p. 65), and dominant groups mask their collective power by promulgating their worldview as if it were universally shared by all, counterdiscourses (Terdiman, 1985) emerge to challenge the terms, images, and language of the "official knowledge" through which sociopolitical identities are deployed and recognized. In other words, by confronting the official hegemonic memory with various versions of "counter-memory" (Foucault, 1977, p. 160), subordinated groups question their oppression, and misrecognized groups attempt to resist dominance, invert their inferior status, and affirm the value of their previously undermined identity (Simmons & Dei, 2012). With counterdiscourses, misrecognized groups attempt not only to resist dominance, but also to cultivate their own societal culture in ways that will eventually be officially endorsed by the state (Kymlicka, 1995). Writing on the topic of resistance, Said (1993) explained that resistance mobilizes political forces toward "restoration of community, assertion of identity, [and the] emergence of new cultural practices" (p. 218). Unsurprisingly, as the process of oppression is never all-encompassing, practices of misrecognition and unrecognition are always resisted in a variety of sites, including schools, to reclaim the authenticity of the Indigenous identity and knowledge, amplify its voice, and empower its agency for social change.

ETHNIC TRENDS IN POLITICS AND EDUCATION

Yiftachel (2006) conceptualizes the political regime in Israel as an ethnocracy rather than a democracy, which implies that the boundaries of its citizenry are determined by belonging to the Jewish group rather than adhering to universal criteria of civic membership. Conversely, Smooha (2002) argues that Israel is an ethnic democracy and as such it should be distinguished from liberal and multicultural democracies. An *ethnic democracy* is a distinct type of democracy, according to Smooha, insofar as it still fulfills the procedural definition of democracy—rule by majority vote—and respects the individual rights of its citizens. At the center of this debate is the relationship between the Jewish and democratic characteristics of the state, which are seen as either conflictual or compatible principles.

According to Shafir and Peled (2002), Israeli citizenship is differential, hierarchical, and in service of the political interests of the Jewish majority. This majority is constituted as a gated ethnonational polity, which excludes Arab citizens. Arab citizens are treated as an aggregate of individuals entitled to selective individual liberal rights, but deprived of collective rights of self-definition or collective claims over the nature and distribution of the public good in Israel. In this regard, the Palestinian minority is an example of what Kymlicka (1995) classifies as national minorities whose minority status was acquired involuntarily and often unwillingly. It is worth remembering that following the *Nakba*—the Palestinian term (meaning "catastrophe") for the 1948 war and its aftermath—Palestinians who remained within the boundaries of the newly created State of Israel became a national minority.

Notwithstanding other historical developments, it seems that the rise of the right and the decline of the left since the 1970s is of particular relevance to the recent developments in citizenship education in Israel. Mustafa and Ghanem (2010) argue that the extreme right has been empowered and has consolidated its control over Israeli politics. The political agenda of the right seeks to redefine the Israeli consensus on the exclusive ethnocentric nature of the state in line with the right-wing perception that subordinates democracy not only to the Jewish nature of the state, but also to the settlers' political interest in advancing the Judaizing of historic Palestine and expanding further the colonialization process in the West Bank region.

Ram (2000) conceptualizes these politics as ethnic neo-nationalism (neo-Zionism) that seeks to place more emphasis on the national–religious character of the state, while reducing its democratic character to a mere formality and ritual. In contrast to classical Zionism—which might be considered as an expression of modern nationalism and which defined the state of Israel as the home of the Jewish people—neo-Zionism wishes to define Israel overtly not only as a Jewish homeland but as a Jewish state, a definition that trumps its formal democratic characteristics.

In the last decade, several examples have been indicative of the ultra-ethnonationalistic trend that has been taking hold of Israeli politics in the field of education. Azoulay and Ophir (2013) write:

> Civil habitus in Israel has been thoroughly nationalized. . . . The Israeli educational system denies young citizens elementary historical and geopolitical knowledge, nurtures forgetting and ignorance, and disseminates falsehoods. Whole chapters in the history and culture of the Jews that do not coincide with the Zionist meta-narrative are excluded from school curricula. The narrative of the founding of the State of Israel does not, for example, include the Nakba—the expulsion of the Palestinians, making them refugees. . . . The Green Line has been erased from maps and from Israelis' consciousness, and the scope of jurisdiction in which Israel's law applies is unknown to the public. . . . The common dominator of all these forms of denying knowledge and nurturing ignorance is the effort to separate the citizenry (the civil nation) from the ethnic nation, drawing the image of the nation along the precepts of the Zionist narrative and blurring difference between recruiting citizens for the government, the state, and the nation. The state apparatuses in Israel proper nationalize citizenship and systematically impair the development of civil habitus. (pp. 229–230)

Although the majority of schoolchildren in Israel are enrolled in the state education system, it does not provide any form of common education. Jewish and Arab schoolchildren, as well as secular and religious Jews, attend different schools. Consequently, the bilingual integrated Palestinian-Jewish schools (Bekerman, 2005), generally speaking, do not represent a real challenge to the hegemony of the official state education system. Still, a common feature of the Israeli education system is its commitment to function as a main carrier of the Zionist historiography, while disregarding the Palestinian narrative. Specifically, the study of history and civics in Israel is rendered with a full commitment to uphold the Jewishness of the state and its national ethos. Despite the fact that Arab schools teach in Arabic, the literature (Agbaria, 2013) is consistent in observing the absence of recognition of the Palestinian collective identity in the school curricula and textbooks, which are void of any substantial engagement with Palestinian history and culture.

Unsurprisingly, the curricula for the subjects of history and civics have become fertile ground for political conflict in which the regulative and normative powers of the state collide with the counterforce of Arab civil society organizations (Agbaria, 2013). During the past two decades, as these organizations have been deeply involved in empowering the Palestinian minority vis-à-vis the state (Jamal, 2007), they have likewise become more proactive in mobilizing politics of recognition initiatives in education (Agbaria, 2013).

Against the state's efforts to render the hegemonic Israeli narrative as canonical and shared by all ethnic and cultural groups in Israel, these organizations proposed many counter and "insurgent discourses" to contest "the given symbols of authority" (Bhabha, 2004, p. 277). A recent example of the attempts to resist the state's attempts to impose its "official knowledge" (Apple, 1993) is the initiative entitled the Arab Pedagogic Council. This civil society initiative was launched under the auspices of the National Committee for Arab Mayors and the Supreme Follow-Up Committee for Palestinian Arabs in Israel. The initiative demanded group-based rights, particularly institutional self-rule in the field of education. Additionally, the initiative issued a founding document, "The Educational and Pedagogical Aims of the Arab Minority in Israel," published in Arabic and Hebrew (see Agbaria, 2013). The document specified ten goals for the Palestinian education system as an alternative to the goals of the Ministry of Education. These goals included:

> To deepen the Arab-Palestinian identity as a national identity, taking pride in its culture, and maintaining constant and effective contact with its Arab and Islamic roots. This identity will be based on solidarity among members of the Palestinian people, on the strengthening of the Palestinian memory and narrative, on holding firmly to the historic and political rights of the Palestinian people and on cultural, religious, and social pluralism. (Agbaria, 2013, p. 687)

Another example occurred when the Ministry of Education (2003) imposed the curriculum of "100 Concepts in Heritage, Zionism, and Democracy," according to which Arab students were expected to study and be tested on the history of Zionism in a sort of "light-Zionism" for Arabs. In response to this program, Palestinian civil society organizations in Israel developed an alternative curriculum entitled "Identity and Belonging: The Basic Concepts Project for Arab Pupils." Ghanem (2006) asserts that this project is an act of resistance to "save the younger generation from the loss of national identity and from their negative assimilation into Israeli society . . . [and] to counter curricula aimed at the colonialist eradication of identity" (p. 3). For more about these programs, see Agbaria, Mustafa, and Jabareen (2014).

The two examples described above illustrate the resisting collective action of the Palestinian civil society, which became more prominent upon concluding that the relationship between allocation of resources and political recognition is categorically interdependent. It likewise became more persistent in employing strategies of politics of contention to demand both recognition of the Palestinian minority's indigenous status in Israel and a number of collective rights in the cultural, religious, and educational realms (Jamal, 2007).

REORIENTING CITIZENSHIP EDUCATION

Hughes et al. (2010) argue that, "the field of education generally, and citizenship education in particular, seems especially vulnerable to flights of rhetoric from politicians and policymakers without commensurate action" (p. 293). The citizenship education curriculum and textbook in Israel are good examples of how citizenship has been transformed into an arena for a heated public debate. More specifically, there has been an active debate in recent years between those who endorse citizenship education that promotes democracy and liberal values at the expense of Israel as a Jewish state and those who advocate nationalistic citizenship that emphasizes the state's Jewish identity, thus undermining minority concerns and representation (Pinson, 2007a, 2007b).

In the last decade, several examples have been indicative of the recent ultranationalistic trend that has been taking hold of Israeli politics. Lebel (2007), for example, points to the reformation of the Israeli politics of national memory to emphasize the nationalist ethos of Revisionist Zionism and to include representations of extremist underground groups, such as the Irgun Tzvai Leumi (or Etzel, for short) and the Lohamei Herut Yisrael (Lehi), who were responsible for some of the most infamous massacres of Palestinians during the Nakba, in the national pantheon of the official Israeli national narrative, including in education.

More recently, in light of the normative inclination toward the hardline Zionist ethos and practices, the Ministry of Education's (2009) strategic plan, entitled "The Government of Israel Believes in Education," stated as a major goal "to strengthen education for Zionist, Jewish, democratic, and social values" (p. 7). Specifically, the policy statement stipulated obligatory tours to Jerusalem, "the eternal capital of Israel and the Jewish people," hands-on learning programs intended to strengthen the sense of belonging to the Jewish people and the Land of Israel (Ministry of Education, 2009, p. 8), what the statement termed "Our fathers' heritage program." Moreover, this official statement also introduced under these goals tours to the Jewish settlements in the Palestinian city of Hebron in the West Bank. In the same year, 2009, the Ministry of Education regulations removed the term *Nakba* from the curricula and textbooks used in Arab schools and took the unusual step of collecting all copies of an 11th- and 12th-grade history textbook, *Nationalism: Building a State in the Middle East*, which presented the Palestinian claim that there had been ethnic cleansing in 1948. In 2010, the Ministry of Education banned a textbook entitled *Learning the Historical Narrative of the Other*, which presented both the Israeli and the Palestinian narratives (see more on these developments in Agbaria et al., 2014).

As for citizenship education, the Institute for Zionist Strategies, a right-wing think-tank institute established in 2005 to counter leftist and liberal trends in Israel, issued a seminal report authored by Yitzhak Gaiger (2010) that claimed that citizenship education is not patriotic enough, as it is heavily influenced by post-Zionist, postmodernist, and critical conceptions of citizenship. Specifically, the report recommended updating the curriculum and textbook of the Ministry of Education itself, which is entitled *To Be Citizens in Israel: A Jewish and Democratic State* (Ministry of Education, 2000). This textbook was described by Pinson (2007a) as reflecting an ethnocentric curriculum that glorifies the concept of a Jewish state and marginalizes the ideal of Israel as a state for all its citizens. Nevertheless, this curriculum was perceived by hardliners as too liberal.

Consequently, in 2010 Dr. Zvi Zameret, Chairman of the Pedagogical Secretariat of the Ministry of Education, who was appointed by Gideon Sa'ar, then Minister of Education from the Likud party (the major right-wing party in Israel), instructed the curriculum committee to revise the curriculum as a basis for rewriting the official textbook. Zameret objected to the textbook for being "too critical of the state." He was particularly disturbed by a sentence that appeared in the textbook and read: "Since its establishment, the State of Israel has engaged in a policy of discrimination against its Arab citizens" (Kashti, 2010). To facilitate the revisions, the chairman of the civics curriculum committee, Professor Yedidia Stern, was replaced by Professor Asher Cohen, who is affiliated with the Institute for Zionist Strategies. Professor Cohen told *Haaretz* that his appointment was part of an ideological move (Shtull-Trauring, 2013). Seemingly, this move included appointing Dr. Aviad Bakshi, who is also affiliated with the Institute for Zionist Strategies, as the scientific advisor for the Ministry of Education's updated chapters. In response to these personnel changes, all the Arab members of the committee resigned and the Education Ministry fired the civics studies coordinator who was attacked by the right (Nesher, 2012).

Pinson (2013) closely examined eight revised chapters and concluded that the changes in these chapters reflect a clear shift from the attempt to mitigate and balance the conflict between the Jewish and democratic characteristics of the state toward strong adherence to the ethnonationalist ethos that prioritizes the Jewish characteristics of the state, while amplifying a neo-Zionist narrative that perceives the Jewishness of the state as permanent and beyond democratic contestation. In doing so, a new introductory chapter of historical background reviewing the creation of the State of Israel from the Balfour Declaration to the establishment of the state was added, emphasizing the international recognition of the right of the Jews to a nation-state and the Arab refusal of partition in 1947. Most important, the revised chapters persistently downplay theoretical approaches that associate nationality and citizenry in the modern nation-state, and promote almost exclusively an ethnonational approach that encourages the students to imagine the "nation" as an ethnocultural community that is distinct from the citizenry of the state, and presents justifications for the Jewish nation-state based on the majority's cultural preference. This approach to nationalism is advocated as the most appropriate for the Israeli case and the most legitimate, although when "nation" is imagined in this way, nationalism can be internally as well as externally exclusive, for it can define some fellow citizens as outsiders to, perhaps even enemies of, the nation. Pinson points out how the place of the Palestinian citizens of Israel is undermined by portraying them as an aggregated group and individuals while denying their narrative and collective identity.

The revised chapters provide justifications that the model of a Jewish ethnocultural state is the preferred political model for Israel. In doing so, they downplay Israel's character as both a Jewish and a democratic state, for the most part, presenting Israel as a Jewish state, and as such, its Jewishness precedes its definition as a democratic state. As for minorities, the book denies their right to influence the general identity of the state, although their right to their own culture in their communities is recognized. More specifically, information about the Palestinian minority is often presented disconnected from the sociopolitical context in which this minority still suffers discrimination, racism, marginalization, and inequality—concepts that are hardly mentioned in the new chapters. Pinson (2013) observed that the book adopts a discourse accepted up to the 1980s that viewed Arab citizens as a collection of religio-cultural or language groups, not an ethnic minority.

When it comes to the state religious education system, Barak (2014) argued that this system is structured to promote the religious Zionism ideology, which dictates hardline right-wing positions in a wide variety of issues. According to the State Education Law of 1953, this system enjoys administrative and pedagogical autonomy, especially when it comes to the content of its Jewish education curricula. Yet it was not until 1998 that the law was amended to state that the state religious education system is educating the spirit of religious Zionism (Barak, 2014). In 2008 the Ministry of Education explained what this spirit specifically means—stating that the religious Zionist viewpoint "sees the revival of the Jewish people in its land and the establishment of the State of Israel as the beginning of redemption" (Barak, 2014, p. 5). Since the late 1990s, and especially after the withdrawal of Israel from Gaza in 2005, the state religious education system has been witnessing a process of radicalization, in which the state's authority is increasingly challenged and debated vis-à-vis Halakhic laws, which are perceived as equally important as, and at times as superseding, the laws of the state (Hellinger, 2013; Saragossi, 2013).

More recently, the Religious Education Administration has supervised and supported a mandatory social studies curriculum in elementary state religious schools that includes a section on the "Love of the Land and the Temple." This section completely ignores the religious meaning of the Temple Mount (for Muslims: Haram al-Sharif) and does not refer to the existence of Al-Aqsa Mosque therein. "I'm afraid that this heavy emphasis on a yearning for the Temple and concrete study of the work of the Temple could spur rather good students to think about other practical actions," Ariel Picard, a research fellow at the Shalom Hartman Institute in Jerusalem, said to *Haaretz*. He added, "It's enough for one student to decide that it's worth blowing up mosques to advance the building of the [Third] Temple" (quoted in Kashti, 2015d).

One can provide many examples that taken together demonstrate a significant escalation in the religious nationalist assault on the public education system under the leadership of the current Minister of Education, Naftali Bennett, who is also the head of the staunchly nationalist Habayit Hayehudi party. For example, Israel's religious Jews not only get more school funds per student than other sectors (Dattel, 2014), but also more funds for projects and extracurricular activities. Kashti (2015c) reports that in 2014, NIS 56 million were invested in activities in Jewish education, while only NIS 5–6 million were invested in education for strengthening democracy. In 2015 the Ministry of Education banned Dorit Rabinyan's novel *Borderlife*, a love story that chronicles the relationship between an Israeli woman and a Palestinian man, and removed it from the list of reading material for students studying for their matriculation exams (Kashti, 2015b). Among the reasons stated by the Education Ministry's officials for the disqualification of the book is the need to maintain "the identity and the heritage of students in every sector," and the belief that "intimate relations between Jews and non-Jews threaten the separate identity."

THE COUNTERKNOWLEDGE OF PALESTINIAN TEACHERS IN CITIZENSHIP EDUCATION

For misrecognized groups, the remedy for the denial of the expression of their societal culture in the public sphere lies with official, yet meaningful, equality and recognition. To achieve this goal, minorities often apply various strategies of identity politics in which "identity is constituted within, not outside of, discourse, [and is] produced in specific historical and institutional sites within specific discursive formations and practices" (Hall, 1996, p. 4). Perceived as located within socially situated, yet contested "regimes of representation" (Hall, 1990, p. 225), identities become the political target of the politics of recognition.

The identity politics of recognition are always dynamic and dialogic, especially when they suggest counterdiscourses of reasserted collective memories and identities. These counterdiscourses correspond intertextually with the official discourses, as they concurrently relate to similar historical and political events, figures, and institutions and imbue them with rival meanings. In postcolonial contexts in particular, counterdiscourses are not independent of the colonial relationship and do not emerge in isolation from the dominant discourse, but result from a re-centering of marginalized discourses. Hall (1990) explains this point by stating that the reifications of culture that occur through the creation and dispersal of visual images, texts, and language become "resources of resistance and identity, with which to confront the fragmented and pathological ways in which experience [of the colonized] has been reconstructed within the dominant regimes of . . . representation" (p. 225).

Against the efforts to render the hegemonic Israeli narrative as canonical and shared by all ethnic and cultural groups in Israel, "insurgent discourses" emerged to counter and contest the authority of this narrative (Bhabha, 2004, p. 277). These counter- and anticolonial discourses have become more prominent as the Palestinian civil society in Israel has become more proactive in linking civic equality to national recognition, placing more emphasis on the indigenous status of the Palestinian minority in Israel to justify demands for collective rights (Jamal, 2007). Haklai (2011) states that Palestinian political mobilization in Israel has moved from the politics of inequality and grievance to the politics of recognition and belonging, becoming more ethno-nationalist and vociferous.

In the last decade I have been studying the counterknowledge produced by Palestinian civil society organizations, especially in education (e.g., Agbaria, 2013; Agbaria et al., 2014). Dr. Hallei Pinson has also conducted some of the most seminal studies in citizenship education in Israel (e.g., Pinson, 2007a, 2007b, 2008). In an attempt to understand how Arab and Jewish teachers understand their profession as citizenship educators, what civic ideals they embrace, what pedagogies they use, and what challenges they face, Dr. Pinson and I initiated a joint research project in which we interviewed Arab and Jewish teachers and conducted focus groups. I will provide insights from this study (Agbaria, 2016) focusing on how Palestinian teachers counter the official knowledge introduced into the curriculum by manipulating its content and providing an alternative historical narrative. I will argue that Palestinian teachers produce counterknowledge by applying five major strategies.

The first strategy is providing an alternative narrative of the historical events surrounding the founding of Israel and the Palestinian Nakba. With this strategy, teachers provide supplementary materials and resources to their students that present the Palestinian perspective. Teachers also introduce their students to other accounts and interpretations of the historical trajectory of the Palestinian minority in Israel, while emphasizing specific events that have influenced the collective identity and memory of this minority. For example, they deliberate with their students on the meaning and implications of Land Day (observed annually on March 30 by Palestinians in Israel to commemorate the events of that date in 1976, when six Palestinian Israeli citizens were killed as they protested against the Israeli government's plan to expropriate thousands of acres) and the Events of October 2000 (when 12 Palestinian Israeli citizens were killed by Israeli police).

Contentious as it might be, this strategy supports the Israeli citizenship framework because it enables Arab teachers to accept the democracy, despite its being partial and selective in protecting their rights, but resist the Jewishness of the state, as stipulated in the curriculum. Teachers encourage their students to know in depth the democratic characteristics of the Israeli political regime and the possibilities it offers for political influence. Specifically, they describe the Israeli legal system as, to a large extent, a fair system capable of protecting individual rights. Moreover, when it comes to the narrative of discrimination and racism regarding the harsh conditions of violence, poverty, unemployment, and poor infrastructure in the Arab communities in Israel, they provide a very contextualized Israeli narrative that is anchored in the specifics of Israeli laws and regulations and the particularities of the Israeli political system. In this supplemental social narrative of the roots, causes, and evolution of the improvised socioeconomic and political status of the Palestinian minority in Israel, teachers persistently confront the Jewishness of the state with its democratic claims. The status of the minority is explained as "democratic failures," as shortcomings of the democratic system in Israel that stem from the Jewishness of the state, which is conceived as inherently undemocratic.

The second strategy, which is tightly connected to the previous strategy, relies on focusing citizenship education on studying current events, as these are reported in the media and as they are experienced by the students in their local communities. In doing so, the teachers shift citizenship education from teaching lessons from the past to teaching present insights, from history to current events, and from citizenship as an ideology to citizenship as a practice. Of course, this shift helps the teachers to downplay the Zionist narrative and to help the students to juxtapose its morality against the current events of discrimination and racism that Arabs experience in Israel. The emphasis on current events also helps teachers fit into the Israeli citizenship framework and show their students that they are, after all, Israeli citizens who should learn to obey the law, participate in Israeli politics, protect their rights and liberties under Israeli laws and regulations, and struggle for equality and recognition as individuals and as members of the Palestinian minority in Israel. Indeed, an Israeli Palestinian identity is constructed through teaching citizenship education, by providing an alternative Palestinian historical narrative, and by teaching students about the rules of Israeli politics.

The third strategy is "teaching for the test" that transforms citizenship knowledge into information about citizenship. With this strategy, teachers instruct the content of the curriculum because it is "obligatory material" and is needed to succeed in the Bagrut, the Israeli matriculation exam, without which their students cannot be accepted into the higher education system. Palestinian teachers approach citizenship education instrumentally, teaching it as material for the test, but not for life or commitment to responsible future citizenry. They place an emphasis on achieving high grades that will eventually facilitate their students' socioeconomic mobility. They rationalize teaching about the Jewishness of the state by arguing that it is required for the Bagrut exam and that the students are not required to internalize or adopt the narrative of the textbook. Students are taught to differentiate between their personal opinions, something that they should keep to themselves and within the boundaries of classroom talk, and the content that they are expected to deliver in the test. Hence, teachers enable the students to express their opinions with regard to the marginalization and discrimination against Arabs in Israel, yet they are consistent in conveying the message that students should learn how to provide "correct" answers that do not instigate antagonism and that are in line with the official knowledge of the textbook, especially when it comes to the Jewishness of the state.

The teachers avoid positioning themselves as suspicious collaborators with the state of Israel and as individuals who have no problem conveying a de-Palestinianizing content. On the contrary, as they place emphasis on the meritocracy of the subject (high grades means better chances of admission to competitive departments in the universities) and as they emphasize the importance of learning legal rights and how to use these as a means of protection from the state's discrimination, they preserve their integrity and position themselves as caring educators. They provide their students with practical tools for navigating their mobility and career paths in Israel, by knowing more about how Israeli authorities work and govern, and learning what individual rights are protected under the law against discrimination. For the teachers, the emphasis on the academic achievement of their students and equipping them with needed information on their rights is perceived as contributing to building a new Arab elite that is committed to its collective identity, has increased opportunities for elevating its socioeconomic conditions, and is keenly aware of its rights.

The fourth strategy is creating an alternative sphere of belonging in which the students' community replaces the state. With this strategy, they demand rights from the state and confine their duties within the boundaries of local communities. The teachers position the local community of the students—be it a town, a village, or a neighborhood—as the main arena in which they are expected to exercise civic verities and demonstrate civic involvement. In this sphere, students are encouraged to learn about the history of their local communities and connect that information to the Palestinian collective narrative. Most important, teachers encourage their students to ponder the violence, poverty, unemployment, and poor living conditions and infrastructure in their local communities. Students deliberate on the causes of these conditions and are encouraged to act locally. The teachers do not blame only the Israeli authorities for the impoverished socioeconomic status of Palestinians, but also the Arab leadership for their ineffective work in the Parliament and in the local municipalities, and they encourage their students to be critical and involved vis-à-vis local matters and politics. The remedy prescribed by teachers against the students' chaotic and vandalized reality is exercising more involvement in community work and cultivating values of discipline, responsibility, and care for the shared public sphere's property.

The fifth strategy is teaching legal education: knowledge about and for rights. Teachers place a heavy emphasis on demanding and protecting rights as a way of ensuring socioeconomic mobility and political activism away from the state's persecution and discrimination. Teachers educate their students about their rights under Israeli law and how they can protect them in case they are violated. They also encourage students to demand the rights to which they are entitled in theory and under Israeli and international law, in light of current rights violations reported in the media and Israeli policies and measures, especially when it comes to issues of land confiscation, demolition of houses whose owners failed to obtain building permissions, and humiliating security measures at Israeli checkpoints and the airport. Teachers encourage their students to ponder what rights were violated and how they can protect them.

With these strategies, Palestinian teachers are resisting the goals of the Israeli education system "to instill feelings of self-disparagement and inferiority in Arab youth; to denationalize them, and particularly to de-Palestinize them; and to teach them to glorify the history, culture, and achievements of the Jewish majority" (Mari, 1978, p. 37). These strategies also expose the fragility of the double marginality of the Palestinians in Israel by juxtaposing the rival meanings of being part of both Israel and the Palestinian people. Rabinowitz (2001) describes this political status of being marginalized by the Jewish majority on one side, and the majority of non-Israeli Palestinians on the other, as a "trapped minority." In exposing the complexity of belonging to a "trapped minority," the teachers help their students to realize that the struggle of the Palestinian minority in Israel is not only over the material resources of the state, but also over the symbolic ones. In doing so, they express a "critical approach" to citizenship education that does not refrain from exposing "asymmetries in power" and "relationships between the individual's behavior in society and structures of social injustice" (DeJaeghere & Tudball, 2007, pp. 48–49).

CONCLUSION

The Ministry of Education in Israel publishes a monthly pamphlet entitled "Director General Directives," which states its regulations and policies. One of these official documents, published in 2014, specified that "it is important to clarify and emphasize the significant differentiation between education for political, social and civic awareness and involvement, which is allowed and even desired, and education for specific political-partisan perception, which is unacceptable and prohibited by law" (Ministry of Education, 2014). Michaeli (2014) argues that this document, indeed, an earlier version of it, is indicative of the Ministry of Education's policy to keep Israeli education distanced from ideological indoctrination. He states that since the 1980s, the Ministry of Education has struggled to preserve political education as sterile and as objective as possible, on the one hand, and yet, on the other hand, has allowed privatizing political education through civil society and business organizations, which are mobilized by economic and political interests.

Given the various examples described in the previous sections of this chapter, I am skeptical about the neutrality of the state and the ability to escape the right-wing spirit that dominates current Israeli politics. This skepticism is further strengthened by the results of a recent survey that indicated that nearly half of secular Jewish students and Arab students are not interested in having any contact with each other (Kashti, 2015e). Moreover, another survey showed that "roughly one half of the Jewish respondents agreed with the statement that Jews should enjoy more rights than non-Jews" (Herman, Heller, Atmor & Lebel, 2013, p. 106).

Kashti (2014) believes that when young people shout "Death to Arabs," this indicates the success of the educational system rather than its failure. It is an education system that is based on separation and isolation, Kashti (2015a) concluded, while reporting a story that illustrates how low the values of integration and coexistence are on the priority list of the Ministry of Education. In August 2015, about 15 organizations engaged in improving relations between youngsters from different segments of society asked the Ministry of Education to double its funds to NIS 3 million ($763,000). To prove how insignificant this budget is, Kashti (2015a) pointed out that the Education Ministry allocated NIS 12 million for its press budget.

While many countries, as a result of globalization and the growing ethnic, racial, and linguistic diversity within nation-states, have been "advancing forms of citizenship based on the promotion of a common set of shared values (e.g., tolerance, human rights, and democracy), which prepare young people to live together in diverse societies and which reject the divisive nature of national identities" (Johnson & Morris, 2010, p. 78), the Israeli agenda is far different. In Israel, the politics of the right have been shaping citizenship education to be more particularistic and nationalistic.

To a great extent, one can argue that Israel promotes a conservative communitarian concept of citizenship that places a heavy emphasis on the Jewish religion, tradition, national identity, and consensus. Conservative communitarianism is further distinguished by its commitment to a strong group identity, social cohesion, and its perception of participation as a civic responsibility (Delanty, 2000). It fosters an ethnonational political discourse (Shafir & Peled, 2002) that ultimately shifts citizenship education from a state-centered and rights-centered discourse to a nation-centric education, which aims to instill among its students a monolithic ethnonational identity and a sense of patriotism.

As for the Palestinian teachers of citizenship education, they conceptualize Israeli citizenship in relation to their local sociopolitical context as members of the Palestinian minority and of specific communities and localities. Their conceptualization is framed by the "whereness" of the citizenship, as perceived and practiced by citizenship educators. Palestinian teachers in Israel are, on the one hand, aware of the state's discrimination against their communities and their harsh socioeconomic living conditions. On the other hand, they are also attentive to the possibilities for individual socioeconomic mobility and for the partial protection the legal system provides against discrimination and for individual rights.

Consequently, the mission of these teachers is twofold: to educate for awareness of discrimination and for success in the matriculation exam in civics, which is obligatory for the higher education system's entrance requirements. These are complementary tasks, knowing how to cope better with discrimination's obstacles facilitates a smoother and "smarter" mobility, while individual success will eventually produce stronger elites that are capable of improving the status of Palestinian society in Israel. Success and excellence are strategies for coping with discrimination and marginalization; these are part and parcel of neoliberal ethics—civic republicanism—which include leadership, responsibility, self-discipline, public spirit, law-abidingness, sincerity, and community involvement, all of which are perceived as necessary for the cultivation of the citizen's good character.

These teachers conceptualize citizenship as an existence strategy, and as a practice that is relational and contingent on the local context in which it appears. They articulate a citizenship that is eclectic and hybrid, which posits the local community as the main sphere for belonging and civic action. On the one hand, the local community is perceived as conservative, impoverished, and violent, yet it is also seen as the major site in which citizenship education can be relevant for exercising responsibility and belonging and for materializing the good character of students. The state is conceived as discriminating and excluding, and as such it is the sphere where contentious politics have to be maintained to demand equality and recognition, yet with no sense of solidarity or commitment, as in the community sphere. Indeed, the community is often advocated as a replacement for the state, from which teachers feel alienated and incapable of achieving effective influence and tangible changes—as an alternate sphere for civic action and responsibility. Local citizenship is advocated as a viable alternative to state-centered citizenship, not only to resist the state's discrimination and to assume responsibility, but also as a vehicle for social change. In their local communities students can practice struggle for their citizenship rights for better living conditions, and they can struggle for better solidarity. Teachers value law-related education—education that focuses on knowing and adhering to laws and regulations—as a means of coping with discrimination and of restoring conformity and public order in their fragmented and violent communities. Under aggressive individualism and in a reality in which violence, poverty, and humiliation are dominant, the law is perceived as a refuge. The law is used to resist discrimination and chaos.

Remarkably, Palestinian teachers of citizenship education in Israel did not avoid the exploration of controversial issues in the classroom, including topics related to the Palestinian-Israeli conflict, and inequality and discrimination based on nationality. Although they performed their professional duties under pressure to cover the material needed for the matriculation exam in civics, they were persistent in highlighting the national identity of their students, as Arabs and Palestinians. However, it seems that they were less successful in promoting a more active and participatory citizenship education. The weak emphasis placed on participatory methods and civic engagement may be explained by the lack of professional training in this field, and by the absence of a strong school ethos in the Arab education system that encourages deliberation, community involvement, and critical thinking.

REFERENCES

Agbaria, A. K. (2013). Arab civil society and education in Israel: The Arab pedagogical council as a contentious performance to achieve national recognition. *Race Ethnicity and Education, 18*(5), 675–695.

Agbaria, A. K. (2016). The 'right' education in Israel: Segregation, religious ethnonationalism, and depoliticized professionalism. *Critical Studies in Education*, 1–17. doi: 10.1080/17508487.2016.1185642

Agbaria, A. K., Mustafa, M., & Jabareen, Y. T. (2014). "In your face" democracy: Education for belonging and its challenges in Israel. *British Educational Research Journal, 41*(1), 143–175.

Althof, W., & Berkowitz, M. W. (2006). Moral education and character education: Their relationship and roles in citizenship education. *Journal of Moral Education, 35*(4), 495–518.

Apple, M. W. (1993). *Official knowledge: Democratic education in a conservative age.* New York, NY: Routledge.

Azoulay, A., & Ophir, A. (2013). *The one-state condition: Occupation and democracy in Israel/Palestine.* Stanford, CA: Stanford University Press.

Banks, J. A. (2008). Diversity, group identity, and citizenship education in a global age. *Educational Researcher, 37*(3), 129–139.

Barak, M. (2014). *Chinuch politi b'yisrael [Political education in Israel]*. Jerusalem, Israel: Molad, the Center for the Renewal of Israeli Democracy.

Bekerman, Z. (2005). Complex contexts and ideologies: Bilingual education in conflict-ridden areas. *Journal of Language Identity and Education, 4*(1), 1–20.

Bhabha, H. K. (2004). *The location of culture.* New York, NY: Routledge.

Central Bureau of Statistics. (2015). *67th Independence Day—8.3 million residents in the State of Israel* [Press release]. Retrieved from www.cbs.gov.il/reader/newhodaot/hodaa_template.html?hodaa=201511099

Clarke, P. B. (1996). *Deep citizenship.* London, England: Pluto Press.

Dattel, L. (2014, December 8). Israel's religious Jews get more school funds than other sectors. *Haaretz.* Retrieved from www.haaretz.com/business/.premium-1.630529

Davies, I., & Issitt, J. (2005). Reflections on citizenship education in Australia, Canada and England. *Comparative Education, 41*(4), 389–410.

DeJaeghere, J. G., & Tudball, L. (2007). Looking back, looking forward: Critical citizenship as a way ahead for civics and citizenship education in Australia. *Citizenship teaching and learning, 3*(2), 40–57.

Delanty, G. (2000). *Citizenship in a global age: Society, culture, politics.* Buckingham, United Kingdom: Open University Press.

Foucault, M. (1977). *Language, counter-memory, practice: Selected essays and interviews.* New York, NY: Cornell University Press.

Fraser, N. (2000, May–June). Rethinking recognition: Overcoming displacement and reification in cultural politics. *New Left Review, 3*, 107–120.

Gaiger, Y. (2010). *Position paper concerning civics education.* Retrieved from www.izsvideo. org/videos/full/CivicPaper.pdf

Galston, W. A. (2001). Political knowledge, political engagement, and civic education. *Annual Review of Political Science, 4*(1), 217–234.

Ghanem, A. (2006). "Identity and belonging": A pioneering project, which must be the starting point for an alternative, comprehensive educational plan. *Adalah's Newsletter, 27*, July-August. Retrieved from www.adalah.org/newsletter/eng/jul-aug06/ar2.pdf

Haklai, O. (2011). *Palestinian ethnonationalism in Israel.* Philadelphia, PA: University of Pennsylvania Press.

Hall, S. (1990). Cultural identity and diaspora. In J. Rutherford (Ed.), *Identity: Community, culture, difference* (pp. 222–237). London, United Kingdom: Lawrence & Wishart.

Hall, S. (1996). Introduction: Who needs identity? In S. Hall & P. du Gay (Eds.), *Questions of cultural identity* (pp. 1–17). London, United Kingdom: Sage.

Heater, D. (2004). *Citizenship: The civic ideal in world history, politics and education.* Manchester, United Kingdom: Manchester University Press.

Hellinger, M. (2013). Chinuch ezrachi democrati b'tziyonut hadatit b're'ie etgari hatkufa [Democratic civic education within religious Zionism in context of current challenges]. In D. Avnon (Ed.), *Chinuch ezrachi b'yisrael [Civic education in Israel]* (pp. 236–275). Tel Aviv, Israel: Am Oved.

Herman, T., Heller, E., Atmor, N., & Lebel, Y. (2013). *Madad hademocratia ha'yisraelit [The Israeli democracy index].* Jerusalem, Israel: The Israel Democracy Institute.

Hughes, A. S., Print, M., & Sears, A. (2010). Curriculum capacity and citizenship education: A comparative analysis of four democracies. *Compare: A Journal of Comparative and International Education, 40*(3), 293–309.

Jamal, A. (2007). Strategies of minority struggle for equality in ethnic states: Arab politics in Israel. *Citizenship Studies, 11*(3), 263–282.

Johnson, L., & Morris, P. (2010). Towards a framework for critical citizenship education. *Curriculum Journal, 21*(1), 77–96.

Kashti, O. (2010, August 29). Education ministry revising textbook for being too critical of Israel. *Haaretz.* Retrieved from http://www.haaretz.com/education-ministry-revising-textbook-for-being-too-critical-of-israel-1.310751

Kashti, O. (2014, August 20). Blame Israel's schools for the racism. *Haaretz.* Retrieved from www.haaretz.com/opinion/.premium-1.611395

Kashti, O. (2015a, September 1). Education in Israel is based on separation. *Haaretz.* Retrieved from www.haaretz.com/news/israel/.premium-1.673866

Kashti, O. (2015b, December 31). Israel bans novel on Arab-Jewish romance from schools for "threatening Jewish identity." *Hararetz.* Retrieved from www.haaretz.com/israel-news/.premium-1.694620

Kashti, O. (2015c, January 17). Jewish and democratic—Yet ten times more the funding for the Jewish. *Haaretz.* Retrieved from www.haaretz.co.il/news/education/.premium-1.2540775

Kashti, O. (2015d, November 1). Religious public schools teach children to "long for the third temple." *Hararetz.* Retrieved from www.haaretz.com/israel-news/.premium-1.683333

Kashti, O. (2015e, January 2). Study: Half of Israel's Jewish, Arab pupils want no contact with each other. *Haaretz.* Retrieved from www.haaretz.com/news/israel/.premium-1.635019

Kymlicka, W. (1995). *Multicultural citizenship: A liberal theory of minority rights.* Oxford, United Kingdom: Oxford University Press.

Lebel, U. (2007). *Haderech el ha'panteon: Etzel, lehi ugvulot hazikaron haleumi hayisraeli [The road to the pantheon: Etzel, Lehi, and the borders of Israeli national memory].* Jerusalem, Israel: Magnes Press.

Manzer, R. (2003). *Educational regimes and Anglo-American democracy.* Toronto, Canada: University of Toronto Press.

Mari, S. (1978). *Arab education in Israel.* Syracuse, NY: Syracuse University Press.

McLaughlin, T. H. (1992). Citizenship, diversity and education: A philosophical perspective. *Journal of Moral Education, 21*(3), 235–250.

Michaeli, N. (2014). Mavo: Chinuch b'ma'arechet hachinuch hayisraelit upolitika [Introduction: Education and politics in the Israeli education]. In N. Michaeli (Ed.), *Ken b'beit sifreinu: Ma'amarim al chinuch politi [Yes in our school: Articles on political education]* (pp. 9–29). Bnei Brak, Israel: Hakibbutz Hameuchad.

Ministry of Education. (2000). *L'hiyot ezrachim b'yisrael: Medina yehudit demokratit [To be citizens in Israel: A Jewish and democratic state].* Jerusalem, Israel: Ministry of Education.

Ministry of Education. (2003). *100 musagim bemoreshet, tziyonut v'demcratia [100 concepts of heritage, Zionism, and democracy].* Retrieved from lib.cet.ac.il/pages/articleitem.asp?item=7

Ministry of Education. (2009). *Memshelet Israel mamina bechinhuch [The government of Israel believes in education].* Retrieved from meyda.education.gov.il/files/Owl/Hebrew/SarHachinuch/Education_presentation_final_opt.pdf

Ministry of Education. (2014). *Chozer mankal (9.2-2) [Director General directive (9.2-2)].* Retrieved from cms.education.gov.il/EducationCMS/Applications/Mankal/EtsMedorim/9/9-2/HoraotKeva/K-2014-1-1-9-2-2.htm

Mustafa, M., & Ghanem, A. A. (2010). The empowering of the Israeli extreme right in the 18th Knesset elections. *Mediterranean Politics, 15*(1), 25–44.

Nesher, T. (2012, August 6). Israel Education Ministry fires civics studies coordinator attacked by right. *Haaretz.* Retrieved from www.haaretz.com/print-edition/news/israel-education-ministry-fires-civics-studies-coordinator-attacked-by-right-1.456182

Pinson, H. (2007a). At the boundaries of citizenship: Palestinian Israeli citizens and the civic education curriculum. *Oxford Review of Education, 33*(3), 331–348.

Pinson, H. (2007b). Inclusive curriculum? Challenges to the role of civic education in a Jewish and democratic state. *Curriculum Inquiry, 37*(4), 351–382.

Pinson, H. (2008). The excluded citizenship identity: Palestinian/Arab Israeli young people negotiating their political identities. *British Journal of Sociology of Education, 29*(2), 201–212.

Pinson, H. (2013). *M'mdenah yehodeat v'demokratit l'mdenah yehodeat nekodah [From a Jewish and democratic state to a Jewish state period].* Retrieved from www.acri.org.il/he/wp-content/uploads/2013/12/Pinson-Report.pdf

Quaynor, L. J. (2012). Citizenship education in post-conflict contexts: A review of the literature. *Education, Citizenship and Social Justice, 7*(1), 33–57.

Rabinowitz, D. (2001). The Palestinian citizens of Israel: The concept of trapped minority and the discourse of transnationalism in anthropology. *Ethnic and Racial Studies, 24*(1), 64–85.

Ram, U. (2000). National, ethnic or civic? Contesting paradigms of memory, identity and culture in Israel. *Studies in Philosophy and Education, 19*(5–6), 405–422.

Said, E. (1993). *Culture and imperialism.* New York, NY: Knopf.

Saragossi, S. (2013). Bein kochot meshicha menugadim: Hachinuch hammlachti sati ben halacha l'demokratiah [Between opposing pulling forces: The state religious education between Halakhic law and democracy]. In D. Avnon (Ed.), *Chinuch ezrachi b'yisrael* [*Civic education in Israel*] (pp. 202–235). Tel Aviv, Israel: Am Oved.

Shafir, G., & Peled, Y. (2002). *Being Israeli: The dynamics of multiple citizenship*. (Vol. 16). Cambridge, United Kingdom: Cambridge University Press.

Shtull-Trauring, A. (2013, June 13). Professor Asher Cohen to head civics panel at education ministry. *Haaretz*. Retrieved from www.haaretz.com/print-edition/news/professor-asher-cohen-to-head-civics-panel-at-education-ministry-1.367342

Simmons, M., & Dei, G. (2012). Reframing anti-colonial theory for the diasporic context. *Postcolonial Directions in Education*, *1*(1), 67–99.

Smooha, S. (2002). The model of ethnic democracy: Israel as a Jewish and democratic state. *Nations and Nationalism 8*(4), 475–503

Subedi, B., & Daza, S. L. (2008). The possibilities of postcolonial praxis in education. *Race Ethnicity and Education*, *11*(1), 1–10.

Terdiman, R. (1985). *Discourse/counter-discourse: The theory and practice of symbolic resistance in nineteenth-century France*. Ithaca, NY: Cornell University Press.

Travis, H. (2013). *Ethnonationalism, genocide, and the United Nations: Exploring the causes of mass killing since 1945*. New York, NY: Routledge.

Veugelers, W. (2007). Creating critical democratic citizenship education: Empowering humanity and democracy in Dutch education. *Compare: A Journal of Comparative and International Education*, *37*(1), 105–119.

Westheimer, J., & Kahne, J. (2004). What kind of citizen? The politics of educating for democracy, *American Educational Research Journal*, *41*(2), 237–269.

Yiftachel, O. (2006). *Ethnocracy: Land and identity politics in Israel/Palestine*. Philadelphia, PA: University of Pennsylvania Press.

Part III

GLOBAL MIGRATION AND DIVERSITY: IMPLICATIONS FOR PRACTICE

CHAPTER 7

The Changing Role of Citizenship Education in a Globalizing Society

Gregory White and John P. Myers

Increasing globalization calls for a new approach to citizenship education that takes into consideration the local, national, and global aspects of citizenship and identity. Although new programs of citizenship education are emerging in response to this need, much more needs to be accomplished in order to address the complex ways that these levels are intertwined. The goal of this chapter is to examine the changing role of citizenship education as nations struggle to balance social cohesion and cultural sustainability while also preparing youth for citizenship activities in an increasingly global, diverse, and interconnected world. The chapter begins with a review of globalizing trends that are having an impact on citizenship and national identity, including the formation of more diverse and transnational societies, the spread of universal human and cultural rights, and the expansion of globally interconnected markets. Next, the chapter examines how these trends relate to key areas of citizenship education, and further explores implications for practice in formal and informal settings. The chapter concludes with a typology of emergent approaches to citizenship education that have developed in response to the question of how educators attend to the needs of local and national citizenship while also instilling a more global and transnational understanding of interconnectedness.

A GLOBALIZING WORLD

Several worldwide processes are leading to changing conceptions of citizenship and national identity and reorienting social, economic, and political institutions toward global logics (Sassen, 2006). These processes include increasing flows of labor and migration, spreading ideational forms, expanding global economic markets, and improving technologies that are easing barriers to communication and travel. These changes are leading to (1) the formation of more diverse societies, networked diasporas, and enduring transnational communities; (2) increased recognition of human and cultural rights; and (3) the emergence of globally interconnected economies as well as multilevel institutional and political arrangements

(Castles, 2004; Lee, 2002; Sassen, 2006; Soysal, 1996). In addition, the cultural ideas of educational institutions themselves are seen as reinforcing a globalized, cosmopolitan perspective and reducing the influence of nationalism (Baker, 2014). These societal changes have profoundly shaped the ways that citizenship is exercised with new political practices, actors, and settings that are less bound to the nation-state.

INCREASING MIGRATION, DIVERSITY, AND RECOGNITION OF CULTURAL AND HUMAN RIGHTS

International migration is not a new phenomenon; however, its reach took a more globalized character with European expansion beginning in the 16th century, including the great transatlantic migrations of the late 19th and early 20th centuries. After World War II, widespread migration picked up again, with large increases after the 1980s. What makes migration "globalized" is that it increasingly involves all regions of the world, is driven by demographic and economic inequalities within and among nations, and is facilitated by advances in cross-national telecommunications and transportation (Castles & Miller, 2009; Martin & Zurcher, 2008).

According to the most recent figures available, there were 244 million international migrants in 2015, a figure forecast to increase to over 400 million by 2050 (Martin, 2013; United Nations, 2016). The United States serves as home to the largest number of immigrants—nearly a fifth of the worldwide total (United Nations, 2016)—as well as a large number of immigrant and ethnic minority children in its schools. When combined with other students from diverse backgrounds, these students now make up a new majority of all children in attendance (Krogstad & Fry, 2014).

The complex and interrelated factors influencing family migration include those that are economic (e.g., differential wage-earning opportunities and labor recruitment practices) as well as those that are social and cultural (e.g., ideational factors, family reunification processes, and other social network chains). Migration can also be caused by refugees escaping political upheaval and ethnic violence (Castles & Miller, 2009; Martin & Zurcher, 2008; and Suárez-Orozco & Suárez-Orozco, 2009).

Increasing migratory flows, as well as changing political boundaries, raise important questions regarding the role of citizenship and national identity. Among these are the relationship between citizenship and ethnocultural identity, and whether citizenship is framed individually (regardless of background) or based on ethnicity or other group characteristics (Banks, 2008; Brubaker, 1996; Tilly, 1996). Several theories address how immigrants are integrated into society, both from the perspective of assimilation as well as from the perspective of multiculturalism and ethnic retention. More recent theories focus on transnationalism, and the changing reality that immigrants may no longer be leaving the past behind, but instead are forging and maintaining multinational ties.

Assimilation involves the integration to a shared cultural life by different immigrant groups, although scholars differ as to what extent this is a one-way process or a bidirectional one between immigrants and their new community (Hirschman, Kasinitz, & DeWind, 1999; Park & Burgess, 1921). A stage in the development of a higher degree of assimilation is acculturation, a process in which an immigrant group adopts the cultural patterns of the native population, including the acquisition of language (Alba & Nee, 1999; Gordon, 1964).

Assimilation is often contrasted with multiculturalism, which poses the question whether cultural pluralism can coexist within a society with a dominant majority group (Banks, 2004, 2008; Glazer & Moynihan, 1970; Hirschman, Kasinitz, & DeWind, 1999; Zhou, 1999), or if a lack of assimilation will lead to social fragmentation and failed citizenship (Banks, 2015; Hirschman et al., 1999; Schlesinger, 1991). To be successful, multiculturalism must balance unity and diversity in ways that are mutually supportive (Banks, 2004; Kymlicka, 2004). In order for a citizenship attachment to take place, however, citizens need to feel a sense of belonging and connection to the national community that affirms their cultural identity (Banks, 2004; Ladson-Billings, 2004). In addition, identity is often dialectical, and is reactive to social experiences, including social movement participation and overcoming barriers and experiences of discrimination (Hirschman et al., 1999; Rumbaut, 1999). Maintaining a strong ethnic identity can also facilitate the development of social capital, a resource through which individuals can draw strength from a supportive network of groups and institutions in order to maintain or advance their social position in a society (Bourdieu, 1986; Massey, 1999).

Banks (2008) sees multiculturalism as an expansion of T. H. Marshall's (1950/1992) classic conceptualization of citizenship as "a status bestowed on those who are full members of a community" (p. 18). In Marshall's view, citizenship is generally composed of civil, political, and social rights that have accumulated over the past two centuries. Banks (2008) advocates the addition of cultural citizenship as a fourth component of citizenship to preserve the ability for an individual or group to retain its language and cultural rights. Tilly (1996) similarly takes a relational and cultural view of citizenship that "locates identities in connections among individuals and groups" (p. 5). The United Nations Universal Declaration of Human Rights also encourages more humanistic definitions of citizenship that lead to respect for cultural rights and the development of multiculturalism in its emphasis on protecting individual as well as group identities and rights (Lee, 2002).

The issue of transnationalism poses a special challenge for the preparation of democratic citizens as transnational networks can result in durable social, cultural, political, and economic relationships between nations and interfere with social cohesion, given the level of commitment that a particular group can exhibit with any one society (Castles & Miller, 2009). Several trends are responsible for the increased development of transnational relationships and diasporic communities, including formalized mechanisms (such as dual citizenship and temporary work visas) as well as nonformalized mechanisms (partially sanctioned labor participation of undocumented workers, globalized professional networks, and transnational civil society activities organized around humanitarian and political concerns). In addition, advances in communication technologies along with ease of travel are leading to a form of immigration that maintains ties and remittances to households in countries of origin, and the development of global classes (Sassen, 2006). These transnational networks formed by migration can sustain important cultural ties and resemble what Appadurai (1996) describes as diasporic public spheres. Facilitated by advances in communications, members of the diaspora are held together through the preservation of cultural ideas in art, literature, activism, and common interest institutions. As a potential downside, however, transnational relationships can lead to divided loyalties and an inability to fully invest in one's geographic community and future given the need to split attention and remittances (Castles & Miller, 2009; Kasinitz, Mollenkopf, Waters, & Holdaway, 2008).

Expanded migration, deepened transnational relationships, and an increased value placed on multicultural diversity and human rights raise important issues for the teaching of citizenship education. These include the extent to which these practices focus on a nation-centered model of assimilation and narrow conceptions of social and political cohesion, or on more pluralistic/flexible models that also affirm cultural and global identities. Since the late 1800s in immigrant-receiving democracies such as the United States, universal common schools have emphasized the development of knowledge and patriotic values among a diverse student body in order to promote effective citizenship (Fuhrman & Lazerson, 2005). The past several decades have also seen the emergence of multicultural education practices that emphasize ethnic retention and valuing difference while at the same time creating shared meanings (Banks, 2004, 2008).

Although instruction varies, the 19th-century model of civic education as indoctrination (as seen in such nations as France, Germany, and United States) now includes attention to issues of diversity and a valorization of multiculturalism (Ramirez, Bromley, & Russell, 2009; Schwille & Amadeo, 2002). This paradigm shift can be characterized as a movement from exclusion to inclusion, with current debates now focused on variations of the inclusion model, including cosmopolitanism, multiculturalism, and emphasis on universal human rights (Ramirez, 2006). Central to this shift is an increase in coverage of human rights, global environmental concerns, and international perspectives in social science textbooks cross-nationally, as well as the elevation of the individual as an agentic actor responsible for upholding these rights (Bromley, Meyer, & Ramirez, 2011a, 2011b; Meyer, Bromley, & Ramirez, 2010).

WORLDWIDE ECONOMIC EXPANSION AND INTERCONNECTED MARKETS

Globalized processes can be both grounded in the nation-state and simultaneously influenced by other structures and dynamics such as globally interconnected markets. These can lead to novel assemblages that reconfigure public and private spheres with increased power and norm-making ability exercised by global economic and institutional actors (Sassen, 2006). These new formations have spurred temporary migration of executives and low-wage workers motivated by economic concerns, whether for financial gain or overcoming financial struggle (Sassen, 2006), as well as increased globally interconnected workplaces bringing diverse constituencies together through advances in communication (Levy & Murnane, 2004).

To prepare students for this globalizing, interconnected economy, there has also been an increased focus on educational practices that emphasize academic achievement (in areas other than civics) and development of skills such as intercultural communication (Callahan & Muller, 2013; *Partnership for 21st Century Learning*, 2016). Beginning in the early 20th century, a noticeable shift occurred with schools aiming to develop the necessary skills to prepare a future workforce (Fuhrman & Lazerson, 2005). More recently, an increased focus on testing and accountability, international comparisons, and a focus on STEM (science, technology, engineering, and mathematics) as strategies to ensure economic competitiveness has crowded out civic education and other non-STEM related functions of schooling (Callahan & Muller, 2013; Mintrop, 2002; National Academy of Sciences, National Academy of Engineering, and Institute of Medicine, 2010).

The changing aims of education systems as supporting economic ends combined with increasingly interconnected global workplaces has led to a growing emphasis on college and career readiness skills for success (sometimes known as 21st-century skills). As a result, part of the terrain of civic education now includes emphasis on preparing students with cross-cultural communication and problem-solving skills to more effectively collaborate and compete in a globalized society (Partnership for 21st Century Learning, 2016). These include: cognitive skills (critical thinking/problem solving), interpersonal skills (complex and cross-cultural communication/social skills), collaborative teamwork skills, advanced technology skills, and intrapersonal skills (responsibility and self-management skills) (National Research Council, 2011; Suárez-Orozco & Suárez-Orozco, 2009). Over time, Baker (2014) sees that increased levels of educational attainment will continue to increase demand for these skills because a more highly educated workforce will in turn continue to construct and transform institutions in ways that value more complex cognitive and other workplace skills in a reinforcing and expanding cycle.

Finally, even though these skills are pushed as part of a focus on economic and life preparation, there could be an indirect effect on political and social movement citizenship. In particular, Gutmann (2005) sees the benefits of critical thinking and interpersonal skills for political citizenship as "includ[ing] the ability to argue and appreciate, understand and criticize, persuade and collectively decide in a way that is mutually respectable" (p. 358). To fully engage in these types of activities, however, it is important for students to learn diverse perspectives, discern social justice issues, and deliberate and make reflective decisions that promote social justice and the recognition of group differences (Banks, 2004, 2008). These same skills can be used in a reflective study of global citizenship, including a comparative study of different types of government systems as well as the investigation of experiences of ethnicity and economic inequality across nations (Parker, 2014).

DO WE NEED A NEW CIVIC EDUCATION?

Globalization poses new challenges for citizenship education. While more traditional concepts focus on the development of civic knowledge, skills, and dispositions for effective democratic citizenship and community engagement within nations (Gould, 2011), the trends discussed in the previous section point to the need for a new citizenship education that would apply these skills in a broader global context. Hahn (2008) offers a description of the multilevel nature of preparing youth for various forms of citizenship, and states that "broadly conceived, civic or citizenship education includes all the ways in which young people come to think of themselves as citizens of local and cultural communities, the nation and global society" (p. 263). Such practices should also balance "cultural, national, and global identifications and attachments [that] are complex, interactive, and contextual" (Banks, 2004, p. 7). In addition, new citizenship education practices should also strengthen a sense of connection to the civics curriculum and address persistent civic education opportunity gaps for immigrant and other disadvantaged groups of students (Callahan & Muller, 2013; Kahne & Middaugh, 2008; Levinson, 2012; National Center for Education Statistics, 2014; Niemi & Junn, 1998; Torney-Purta, Barber, & Wilkenfeld, 2007).

However, despite the importance of a broader conceptualization of citizenship education, there are two concerns that need to be raised. First, what is globalized in a cross-culturally oriented curriculum may run the risk of reflecting the perspective of dominant groups (Ritzer, 2008). In addition, a one-size-fits-all civics curriculum based on developing cross-national shared meanings and preparing skills for a globalized workforce runs the risk of resembling what Ritzer (2007a) characterizes as "the globalization of nothing." Here *nothing* refers to empty forms largely devoid of distinctive (local) content making them easier to export (Ritzer, 2007a, 2008).

To avoid these pitfalls, an alternative conception of civic education that would include both global and local foci can be found in the sociological concept of *glocalization* emerging from theories of cultural hybridization and relational social processes (Ramirez, 2006; Ritzer, 2008; Robertson, 1992). Robertson (1992, 1995) is credited with popularizing the term *glocalization* in sociology, drawing on a Japanese concept of *dochakuka* used in agriculture and business (local adaptation of the global). In this view, the local and global can co-occur as an interplay of the particular and universal, heterogeneous and homogeneous, with an emphasis on locality as a site of diversity (Robertson, 1995). The idea of glocalization was further extended by Ritzer (2008) as the "interpenetration of the global and local resulting in unique outcomes in different geographic areas" with "local individuals and groups as important and creative agents" (p. 461). In addition, studies of globalized processes should examine the dialectical relationship between local and global levels (Ritzer, 2007b). Finally, glocalization relates to Beck's (2002) concept of rooted cosmopolitanism as opposed to viewing cosmopolitans and locals as distinct identities.

CITIZENSHIP EDUCATION IN A GLOBAL AGE

New Directions

Understanding the influence of globalization on citizenship education requires a broader rethinking of the field's purposes for current school and classroom practices. In order to prepare youth for the challenges of a globalizing world, educators need to consider glocalized practices that take into account that citizenship is no longer solely defined by the nation, that national borders are more permeable, and that there is a greater diversity of settings in which politics and social change occur. In this section we attempt to map the ways in which globalizing changes impact students' civic selves, the curriculum, and teaching citizenship in formal and informal settings.

The influence of globalization on citizenship education is most profound, in our view, in three key areas: (1) civic identities and values, (2) social issues, and (3) political participation. The first of these considers the ways in which diverse students' experiences and subjectivities have changed and what this means for schooling. The second highlights what a globalization paradigm suggests for what a citizen needs to know about an increasingly diverse and multicultural world. The third examines how globalization changes the nature of youth participation in political/social movement activities. We believe these three areas are an essential starting point to inform new directions for the practice of citizenship education in light of globalization.

Civic Identities and Values

Due to the fact that globalization has fostered new and multiple ways to identify as a citizen, citizenship education must confront the mismatch between the curriculum's master narrative and diverse students' experiences of belonging and allegiance in a globalizing world. Youth are pulled between bonds to a cultural group and universal frameworks such as human rights and global responsibilities, a tension captured in the notion of cosmopolitan multiculturalism as navigating back and forth between the global and local (Donald, 2007; see also Kymlicka, 1998). C. Suárez-Orozco (2004) asserts that hybrid identities are commonplace among youth as they more easily hold loyalties to different cultural and national communities at the same time, yet often they are not full members of either. The challenge of holding multiple identities creates "identity trouble" (Caldas-Couthard & Iedema, 2010, p. 1) for many young people as they attempt to negotiate the kind of public person and citizen they want to be in the world (Abu El-Haj, 2007; Myers & Zaman, 2009; Rippberger & Staudt, 2003).

In addition, students are now more likely to have transnational loyalties and hybrid identities that confront complex issues of becoming and being certain types of citizens. As Willinsky (1998) asked, "Where is here?" becomes a central question for the identities of young people as they make choices about the kind of citizen they want to be. Consequently, the case has been made for a transformative form of citizenship education that helps students construct and understand complex cultural, national, and global identities (Banks, 2008). This issue is much more involved in a global age than it was in the past when national identity provided the sole purview of civic identity.

Students' multiple, overlapping cultural identities, perspectives, and allegiances (Ladson-Billings, 2004) shape the beliefs they bring to the classroom, which influence how they make sense of the curriculum (Myers & Zaman, 2009). The influx of immigrant students likewise brings unique challenges, as well as cross-cultural strengths, to schools' efforts to counter and minimize the socioeconomic and other discriminatory challenges that these students may face (Suárez-Orozco & Suárez-Orozco, 2009). These youth are pulled toward diverse and contradictory allegiances and ways of being a citizen that conflict with social norms and taken-for-granted beliefs about moral responsibility to others, the meaning of patriotism, and the goal of civic participation (Myers, McBride, & Anderson, 2015). Identity is salient because it is a window to the ways that youth make sense of their role in the world by recognizing their "possible selves" as an ongoing process that is situated and evolving over the long term.

In classroom settings, civic identities are constructed discursively within relations of power as students and teachers negotiate, contest, and assign ways of being a good citizen. As an example, Abu El-Haj's (2007) work with Palestinian American youths' experiences in school focused on the multiple, sometimes conflicting roles they experienced when confronting everyday school events such as pledging allegiance and interacting with peers who sometimes viewed them as not fully American. These experiences shaped the students' beliefs about U.S. citizenship and democracy, creating resistance to existing school practices in the short term, and ultimately, an uncertain path toward their own sense of citizenship. Abu El-Haj (2007) argues that citizenship education needs to address the transnational affiliations that youth increasingly hold:

> For an increasing number of young people, transnationalism shapes their identities, political sensibilities, and capacity to participate both in this society and on a global stage. . . . Rather than viewing multiple national affiliations as a threat to social incorporation, we might consider transnational communities as an important source of new visions of identity and belonging, and as a resource for engaging with alternate perspectives on local and global issues. (p. 311)

Scholars have documented the tenuous quality of youth civic identities that are developed by globalization, zeroing in on the contradictory nature of the form of citizenship available to them within the traditional narrative of nationalism conveyed in schools. In a study of current events discussion in world history classrooms, Myers, McBride, and Anderson (2015) found that the participating students held different beliefs about the meaning of citizenship and contested what moral responsibility to distant people means in a globalizing world. The students did not create a fixed category of "the good citizen," but instead enacted and performed multiple versions as they navigated the often unsteady relationship between their national identity and a global self. Their identities were fluid as they explored and sometimes tried on identity positions that allowed them to reexamine their own beliefs. Collectively, the students presented a complex and dynamic portrait of good citizenship.

Social Issues

The process of globalization has changed what citizens need to know about human cultures and the world. This shift requires a curriculum that enhances students' understanding of the world as a system in which public issues cannot be managed by singular actors or nations alone. Although globalization is one of the most significant concepts for the 21st century, K–12 students rarely study it with a degree of sophistication that it deserves compared with other essential big ideas (e.g., democracy) until they reach the university level. The K–12 curriculum is structured around traditional disciplines that have been resistant to a variety of reform efforts to globalize the curriculum. Despite some advances, global issues remain largely without a place in the curriculum in K–12 schooling.

Globalizing the curriculum has been most successful at the university level where global studies have flourished since the 1990s (Stearns, 2009). Nederveen Pieterse (2013) commented on the growth of these programs: "Global studies have been spreading because global relations and problems require a global approach, a need that is felt by social forces, international organizations, governments and corporations the world over" (p. 500). These programs are based on the premise that nations are no longer the primary international actors but that they coexist in a world driven by transnational processes and new epistemological and philosophical understandings.

These innovations at the higher education level illustrate the potential of globalizing the K–12 civics curriculum, particularly in terms of preparing youth to engage significant public issues of the time. Scholars argue that it is important for students to develop the ability to think critically, learn diverse perspectives, discern social justice issues, and to deliberate and make reflective decisions that promote social justice and the recognition of group differences (Banks, 2004, 2008). However, such innovative schools and programs are not typically part of the public school curriculum and therefore unavailable to the majority of young people.

The emergence of global-themed schools, especially charter schools, have made global studies a focus of whole-school reform. Although such schools are not widespread, they have become increasingly sought after in large urban centers where they compete with International Baccalaureate schools to prepare primarily affluent students for life in the 21st century and in the global workplace. Like other curriculum reform in public education, these schools have a range of ideological purposes and practices that fall loosely under the idea of global studies (Parker, 2011). The Ross School is one worthwhile example that is pushing the limits of the traditional formula of schooling; it is committed to preparing students for engaged global citizenship (Suárez-Orozco & Sattin-Bajaj, 2010). The school aims to convey "what it means to be a child, and then a citizen, of the world" (p. 7) by teaching a holistic understanding of academic disciplines that are supported with experiences such as international service learning to foster civic engagement and study trips that examine global issues firsthand.

Within schools, the adaptation of world history as a core course is also a significant development for addressing a global dimension in the curriculum. World history is the primary course that uses a global perspective to make sense of controversial public and contemporary issues that are a mainstay of citizenship education. World history contributes to a citizenship of the 21st century by fostering inquiry into global issues and providing an understanding of the world as an interconnected system. Unfortunately, it is not always the case that these goals are accomplished. Yet a major criticism of world history is that the course pays too little attention to the significant global issues of the modern period that are expected to matter in the near future, as Stearns (2007) points out:

> Too often, major developments over the past century are slighted, simply for want of time; or they are presented breathlessly, through factual surveys that fail to highlight major changes and continuities and so fail to help students really use the world history available to them to help grasp the world around them. Too often, talented and diligent leaders in the world history movement devote passionate intensity to the question of where to begin the course, but save little or no energy for the (even more important) question of how to end it effectively. (para. 17)

Studying global issues such as cultural diversity, the environment, and human rights as core topics in world history rather than as add-ons at the end of the year would provide students with a more complete education for the 21st century.

Discussion of controversial public issues is a longstanding best practice for citizenship education. However, global issues are epistemologically distinct from controversial issues concerning national public policy (e.g., Hess, 2009). Although global issues are identical in the sense that they foster an understanding of competing political views, develop decision-making abilities, and make reasoned arguments, they are also fundamentally different in at least three ways:

1. *Complex patterns of interdependencies:* Global issues by their nature include a larger territorial context, a greater diversity of actors, and a fuller

account of the issue (even if not literally "global" in reach). The patterns that attempt to describe the relationships between actors and issues are decidedly complex and have required new, often interdisciplinary, paradigms for understanding the world. For example, world-systems analysis has been adopted in a variety of social science disciplines and world history to understand how the world works.

2. ***Different understanding of the "public":*** The "public" in public issues is generally used to denote a particular "us," as Americans. Thus public policy refers to those issues significant within the U.S. national context. When the scale of the public is extended to potentially include the entire world and all people, then distant others cannot be viewed as "foreign" or "out *there*" or as minor actors in an American world. In addition, global issues require that we ask how actors across the world frame the same problem and what is "American" about the way we think about it and the assumptions we hold.

3. ***Distinct theoretical frameworks:*** Differences 1 and 2 signal the need for distinct theories that are used to understand global issues. These are wide-ranging and still emergent, providing diverse and sometimes conflicting paradigms for understanding globalizing processes. For example, transnationalism points to the process of movement and flows across and despite borders. Hybridization also describes the ways that these flows are renegotiated to be given local meanings.

In addition to the incorporation of changes to the world history course, another approach is to globalize other courses that are historically bounded by the nation. Globalizing the existing history and civics curriculum involves reframing national narratives by placing events and themes within a global narrative. Today, many key historical themes, such as human rights, immigration, diasporas, and ethnicity and race, do not fit within the self-contained history of a single nation. Bender (2006) observed that "America's interconnections and interdependencies beyond its borders are rarely captured in these courses, and the revised curriculum reinforces the very split between America and the world that contemporary citizenship must overcome" (p. 6). Conversely, history education has for centuries been the core subject area for transmitting national citizenship. In recent years, efforts have been made to revise the U.S. history survey course to include the impact of globalization in a way that helps students understand its role in global context without casting the nation aside: "not to dismiss national history but to propose a different mode for it, one that . . . better serves us as citizens of the nation and the world" (Bender, 2006, p. 8). Reichard and Dickson's (2008) book, *America on the World Stage: A Global Approach to U.S. History*, was written to provide such a reframing of U.S. history for secondary Advanced Placement and general history courses based on the belief that "if we are to succeed in preparing today's young Americans for life as global citizens, it is important to help them understand how the United States has always been part of world history" (p. x).

This initiative stems from the Organization of American Historians' *La Pietra Report* (Bender, 2000), which argues for a fundamental reframing of U.S. history to incorporate globalization. For example, Chapter 10 of *America on the World Stage* by Kevin Gaines reorients the U.S. civil rights movement as part of worldwide freedom movements:

> Viewing the black freedom movement within the context of decolonization and African national liberation movements goes beyond acknowledging the origins of the movement's tactic of nonviolent direct action in the Gandhian philosophy of Satyagraha. . . . Such a global reframing highlights the tension between the U.S. conception of civil rights reforms, understood in terms of color blindness, or formal civil and political equality, and an evolving postwar international discourse of human rights. (Gaines, 2008, p. 192)

Political Participation

The emergence of global civil society is a political outcome of globalization that involves new, nonstate actors interacting in a "multi-centric" and "polymorphous world" (Mittelman, 2005, pp. 20–21). Globalization has also expanded the number of settings and issues for citizens to engage with, potentially offering new avenues to counteract warnings of the "disturbing trends related to youth civic engagement" (Gibson & Levine, 2003, p. 5). For example, the global justice movement concerns itself with the actual effects of globalization on people and seeks to democratize the institutions and state actors involved. Importantly, the debate over whether youth are portrayed as disengaged from politics or adopting new forms of engagement depends on one's model of the ideal citizen (Wells, 2010).

Citizenship education programs, to the extent that they aim to foster active citizenship, need to consider the ways that youth are interested in activities concerning a range of political issues. Traditional civics courses have focused on the "structures and functions" of national government and formal politics, especially voting, paying little attention to social movements operating outside of, and often in opposition to, institutions (Davies & Issitt, 2005; Myers, 2007). In addition, youth are increasingly alienated from the formal political system and view politicians suspiciously, which further channels them toward more familiar settings to enact change (Lawless & Fox, 2015). Yet research has shown that young people are interested in social movements such as the environment and human rights. Despite an overall decline in civic engagement, participation in social movements is the one setting that has grown in recent years (Galston, 2007). The growth of membership in social movement and political pressure groups amounts to "a widening of the avenues of political expression" or even, for some, to a "radical alternative narrative of democratic participation" (Driver, Hensby, & Sibthorpe, 2012, p. 159-160). As a result, we agree with Cohen, Kahne, Bowyer, Middaugh, and Rogowski (2012, p. 36) that "rather than viewing interest-driven practices as distractions or a waste of time, those seeking to promote youth engagement, be they youth organizations, schools, or other concerned parties, must recognize their value and potential."

International research has also documented that youth across nations are more interested in participating in social movement politics that address issues of human rights and the environment than in voting (Torney-Purta, Lehmann, Oswald, & Schulz, 2001). Although engagement in global social movements may not persist, it remains an important topic of interest in the civic education research literature. In particular, Flanagan (2009) highlights the new role of social movement issues and settings that are now important to youth:

> Increasingly political issues transcend the borders of states and many new forms of youth activism reflect this transnational reality. Both the causes (e.g., workers' rights in sweatshops) and the methods (networking with IT) are transnational in their reach. Activists focus on justice in labor, environmental, and procedural practices and underscore the lack of accountability of new multi-national entities (the WTO, G8, or World Bank) to the people affected by their policies. Organizations such as the World Social Forum provide alternative images of a world other than the one these multi-national entities portend. (p. 298)

As a new medium of participation, information communication technologies (ICT) facilitate youths' understanding of and involvement in global issues. A key research finding in this field is that being part of an online community encourages political activism through new opportunities for political discussion, expression, and exposure to different viewpoints (Cohen et al., 2012). Affinity networks have enabled greater participation for young people to access political action that is related to their identities and personal interests (Ito et al., 2015). Organizations such as TakingITGlobal (www.takingitglobal.org), UNESCO's Associated Schools Project (www.unesco.org/new/en/education/networks/global-networks/aspnet), Voices of Youth (www.unicef.org/voy), Facing the Future (www.facingthefuture.org), and the Global Nomads Group (www.gng.org), to name a few, have been successful in mobilizing youth across the world to engage with global issues that matter to them, both through online networks and in projects undertaken in school classrooms.

TYPOLOGY OF CITIZENSHIP EDUCATION PROGRAMS INFORMED BY GLOBALIZATION

We have discussed three key areas in which globalization impacts citizenship education and the implications that these have for the curriculum and teaching citizenship in formal and informal settings. These areas of impact are civic identities and values, social issues, and political participation. Institutions and nongovernmental organizations (NGOs) have developed innovative programs that address these areas and are available to teachers across the world. We understand these

Table 7.1. Typology of Citizenship Education Programs Informed by Globalization

		CIVIC PURPOSES	
		Political Enlightenment	Political Engagement
CIVIC VALUES	Culturally Specific Values	1. Cross-cultural sensitivity	2. Glocal service
	Universal Values	3. International understanding	4. Global justice

programs of citizenship informed by globalization to be a burgeoning worldwide education reform effort. These organizations and their educational programs are shaping the discourse of citizenship education and driving the redefinition of the way that civic identities are taken up by young people. Yet, despite their shared focus on the impact of globalization for citizenship education, these programs differ in substantive ways in terms of pedagogy, curriculum, and their conceptualization of global citizenship. No single program addresses all of the three areas of impact nor do they address these issues in the same way.

Building on the three areas outlined previously, we provide a typology of citizenship education programs along two axes: (1) civic purposes and (2) civic values. For civic purposes, we use political engagement and political enlightenment for the two poles of the continuum to represent two fundamental goals of citizenship education. For civic values, the continuum addresses the push and pull effect of globalization: universal values that underlie the uniting force toward interdependency contrasted with the particularistic, culturally specific values that are part of the differentiating force of multiculturalism.

Combining the axes in a matrix yields the four categories for a typology of citizenship education that responds to globalization: (1) cross-cultural sensitivity, (2) glocal service, (3) international understanding, and (4) global justice (see Table 7.1). We illustrate each of these categories with a citizenship education program. These programs were selected purposefully to match the characteristics of each category. Furthermore, we looked for programs that provided a unique curriculum or project and that was not merely a site to warehouse other resources.

Category 1: Cross-cultural Sensitivity

The citizenship education programs in the first category concentrate on the need for intercultural dialogue and understanding between diverse peoples. Based on principles of multicultural education, these programs seek to foster social cohesion by reducing stereotypes and prejudices of diverse groups and helping youth acquire the knowledge and skills for cross-cultural interactions. Information communication technologies (ICTs) drive much of the work in this area as virtual exchanges leveraging face-to-face video meetings between students and real-time translation have replaced older forms of communication to allow for dynamic interactions between distant peoples.

Program Example for Category 1: Cross-Cultural Sensitivity

Since its founding in 1998, the nonprofit Global Nomads Group (www.gng. org) is at the forefront of virtual cultural exchange programming for schools. The organization seeks to connect students across the world by "bridging culture gaps and shattering misconceptions" through interactive video-conferencing (www.gng.org/join-our-team). This approach aims to help students identify with someone like them and to understand the personal dimension of stories about world events told by young people their age. Global Nomads works with youth across the world, presently with established sites in 15 countries that are identified as having the largest cultural gap with young people in North America in order to target stereotypes, with special attention to the Middle East, North Africa, and Sub-Saharan Africa. Schools are selected in these countries that do not have access to advanced video-conferencing equipment and other communication technologies, which Global Nomads then provides. One program, Campfire, combines an activity-based curriculum that promotes online sharing of students' culture and ideas to work on projects in collaboration with a companion class in another country. Another, Youth Voices, focuses on live dialogue between students through interactive videoconferencing in combination with shared projects. A third, Pulse, is described as a "virtual town hall meeting" that provides a live, broadcasted forum about the ways that youth around the world experience world events and allows for interactive questioning. The primary focus of all of the programs is to promote cross-cultural sensitivity and understanding through interactive dialogue.

Category 2: Glocal Service

Citizenship education programs in this category promote deep understanding of cultures and people across the world through participatory service and study projects in other countries. The goals are to develop intercultural competency with local community partners and to examine one's own cultural beliefs and assumptions, both in respect to the promotion of human equality. Programs in this quadrant seek to achieve these goals by providing students with immersive experiences with cultures different from their own that extend beyond the traditional focus of study abroad on language and culture by building in social responsibility, critical reflection, and analysis of global issues.

Program Example for Category 2: Glocal Service

Amizade, a nonprofit global service-learning organization, was founded in 1994 to provide grassroots community service and cultural awareness across the world (amizade.org). Program commitments have evolved to focus on empowering local communities through volunteer service that the communities identify and regulate. Each of Amizade's programs has a thematic focus. For example, an established program is Community Health in Brazil, which partners with a local community partner, Fundação Esperança, to set up a series of experiences in public health facilities with local professionals. Students also learn about issues in local health care in the context of ideas of sustainable development and working closely with professionals during the program to provide health services to rural communities that lack services. All of the programs involve cultural immersion as a key component, which is achieved through these service activities, field trips, and social interactions during participation in the daily life of the community. Service experiences as a component of global citizenship is a persistent theme across Amizade's programs.

Category 3: International Understanding

Efforts to teach students to understand significant controversial public issues are a central goal of citizenship education. These programs take a variety of pedagogical approaches that emphasize the need for citizens in the globalizing world to be well-informed about world events, peoples, and places. Limited emphasis, if any, is generally placed on political activism. There are a number of university-based programs in this category that are often associated with international or global studies programs, which influence the selection and organization of the curriculum content by national case studies or global issues for middle and high schools. Some prominent examples include Facing the Future at Western Washington University (www.facingthefuture.org), SPICE (Stanford Program on International and Cross-Cultural Education) of the Freeman Spogli Institute for International Studies (spice.fsi.stanford.edu/), and the Choices Program of the Watson Institute for International Studies at Brown University (www.choices.edu). These programs emphasize alignment with state and national standards, a curriculum-based approach, and professional development for teachers.

Program Example for Category 3: International Understanding
ICONS (International Communication and Negotiation Simulation) is a prominent and popular model in this category used at the higher education and secondary levels. The program was created at the University of Maryland in 1982 and is presently part of the Center for International Development and Conflict Management. The focus is on international simulations "to advance participants' understanding of complex problems and strengthen their ability to make decisions, navigate crises, think strategically, and negotiate collaboratively" (icons.umd.edu/education/mission). Student teams are placed in the roles of international leaders and local actors to find solutions to major political issues. They research issues, design policies, and negotiate with other groups in an online platform. Topics often include roles

for multiple countries' representatives, social movement actors, and international organizations. For example, in a simulation entitled Globalization and Nigerian Oil, students learn about the conflicts that develop as natural resources are extracted with the involvement of international actors. There are eight team roles that included government, Indigenous people, activist groups such as Greenpeace and Human Rights Watch, a multinational corporation (Shell Oil), and the International Monetary Fund (IMF). The simulation takes the form of a conference during which teams negotiate online a "memorandum of understanding" to resolve security, investment, human rights, and political participation.

Category 4: Global Justice

Citizenship education programs in this category foster political participation in causes that focus on issues of social justice and equality as well as the recognition of difference that extend beyond the scope of a single nation. Such programs may be linked to a social movement, nongovernmental organization, or global institution, or rely on grassroot efforts. Programs empower students to have a voice by developing them as activists who work on campaigns outside of the formal political system. Learning about the related issues in depth within a larger global context serves to support these campaigns.

Program Example for Category 4: Global Justice

Oxfam, a leading global justice organization that works to find solutions to worldwide problems such as poverty, sustainable development, and human rights, produces educational resources for schools and teachers to promote global citizenship (www.oxfam.org.uk/education/global-citizenship/global-citizenship-guides). Since 1997 it has produced a schoolwide curriculum guide centering on the study of contemporary global issues that supports efforts to improve the world, which states that "alongside a rigorous development of global understanding and multiple perspectives, an education for global citizenship should also include opportunities for young people to develop their skills as agents of change and to reflect critically on this role" (Oxfam Development Education Programme, 2006, p. 5). Although Oxfam was developed for the United Kingdom context and focuses its resources there, its global influence in promoting citizenship education for global justice is evident in the popularity of its resources. The teaching materials are based on a variety of active learning strategies, such as discussion, role plays, and inquiry. The starting point for student activism in the Oxfam curriculum is typically a global issue that has an impact beyond the school's locality. The most unique aspect of the materials are the activities focused on thinking, planning, and decision-making skills, which follow a "learn-think-act" teaching model: examining an issue (*learn*), reflecting on how the issue could be addressed (*think*), and taking action on the issue (*act*).

CONCLUSION

Globalization poses new challenges for the content and delivery of citizenship education. New and revised approaches are necessary to engage local, national, and global aspects of citizenship and identity. They are also necessary to prepare youth for participation in more diverse and transnational societies as well as in more globally interconnected economies, institutions, and workplaces. To address these challenges, this chapter provides an overview of globalizing trends that are leading to shifting conceptions of citizenship and national identity, with particular attention given to the impact that these are having on civic identities and values, social issues, and political participation. This chapter also discusses implications for the curriculum and teaching of citizenship education in formal and informal settings, and includes a typology that takes into consideration their civic purposes and values.

To revisit the question that we posed earlier in the chapter, Do we need a new civic education?, we believe that there is a strong case for new practices in K–12 schooling. The strategies and programs described above illustrate glocalized opportunities for students to navigate between culturally specific and universal values and in ways that develop knowledge, skills, and dispositions necessary for civic engagement within more globally interdependent communities. Hopefully, these may serve as a guide to what citizenship education in a globalizing age may become, with each pushing the boundaries of state-centric citizenship education (Fischman & Haas, 2014) with innovative practices. However, for meaningful citizenship education practices to benefit all students, particularly those of immigrant origin, a fundamental rethinking of what it means to be a citizen needs to inform the public school curriculum.

REFERENCES

Abu El-Haj, T. R. (2007). "I was born here, but my home, it's not here": Educating for democratic citizenship in an era of transnational migration and global conflict. *Harvard Educational Review, 77*(3), 285–316.

Alba, R., & Nee, R. (1999). Rethinking assimilation theory for a new era of immigration. In C. Hirschman, P. Kasinitz, & J. DeWind (Eds.). *The handbook of international migration: The American experience* (pp. 137–160). New York, NY: Russell Sage Foundation.

Appadurai, A. (1996). *Modernity at large: Cultural dimensions of globalization.* Minneapolis, MN: University of Minnesota Press.

Baker, D. P. (2014). *The schooled society: The educational transformation of global culture.* Stanford, CA: Stanford University Press.

Banks, J. A. (2004). Introduction: Democratic citizenship education in multicultural societies. In J. A. Banks (Ed.), *Diversity and citizenship education: Global perspectives* (pp. 3–15). San Francisco, CA: Jossey-Bass.

Banks, J. A. (2008). Diversity, group identity, and citizenship education in a global age. *Educational Researcher, 37*(3), 129–139.

Banks, J. A. (2015). Failed citizenship, civic engagement, and education. *Kappa Delta Pi Record, 51*(4), 151–154.

Beck, U. (2002). The cosmopolitan society and its enemies. *Theory, Culture, and Society, 19*(1–2), 17–44.

Bender, T. (2000). *The La Pietra Report: A report to the profession.* Bloomington, IN: Organization of American Historians.

Bender, T. (2006). *A nation among nations.* New York, NY: Hill & Wang.

Bourdieu, P. (1986). The forms of capital. In J. Richardson (Ed.), *Handbook of theory and research for the sociology of education* (pp. 241–58). New York, NY: Greenwood Press.

Bromley, P., Meyer, J., & Ramirez, F. (2011a). Student-centeredness in social science textbooks, 1970–2008: A cross-national study. *Social Forces, 90*(2), 547–570.

Bromley, P., Meyer, J., & Ramirez, F. (2011b). The worldwide spread of environmental discourse in social studies, history, and civics textbooks, 1970–2008. *Comparative Education Review, 55*(4), 517–545.

Brubaker, R. (1996). *Nationalism reframed: Nationhood and the national question in the New Europe.* New York, NY: Cambridge University Press.

Caldas-Couthard, C. R., & Iedema, R. (Eds.). (2010). *Identity trouble: Critical discourse and contested identities.* London, United Kingdom: Palgrave McMillan.

Callahan, R. M., & Muller, C. (2013). *Coming of political age: American schools and the civic development of immigrant youth.* New York, NY: Russell Sage Foundation.

Castles, S. (2004). Migration, citizenship, and education. In J. A. Banks (Ed.), *Diversity and citizenship education: Global perspectives* (pp. 17–48). San Francisco, CA: Jossey-Bass.

Castles, S., & Miller, M. J. (2009). *The age of migration: International population movements in the modern world* (4th ed.). New York, NY: Guilford Press.

Cohen, C. J., Kahne, J., Bowyer, B., Middaugh, E., & Rogowski, J. (2012). *Participatory politics: New media and youth political action* (YPPSP Research Report). Retrieved from ypp.dmlcentral.net/sites/default/files/publications/Participatory_Politics_Report.pdf

Davies, I., & Issitt, J. (2005). Reflections on citizenship education in Australia, Canada and England. *Comparative Education, 41*(4), 389–410.

Donald, J. (2007). Internationalisation, diversity and the humanities curriculum: Cosmopolitanism and multiculturalism revisited. *Journal of Philosophy of Education, 41*(3), 289–308.

Driver, S., Hensby, A., & Sibthorpe, J. (2012). The shock of the new? Democratic narratives and political agency. *Policy Studies, 33*(2), 159–172.

Fischman, G. E., & Haas, E. (2014). Moving beyond idealistically narrow discourses in citizenship education. *Policy Futures in Education, 12*(3), 387–402.

Flanagan, C. (2009). Young people's civic engagement and political development. In A. Furlong (Ed.), *Handbook of youth and young adulthood: New perspectives and agendas* (pp. 293–300). New York, NY: Routledge.

Fuhrman, S., & Lazerson, M. (2005). Introduction. In S. Fuhrman & M. Lazerson (Eds.), *The public schools* (pp. xxiii–xxxvi). New York, NY: Oxford University Press.

Gaines, K. (2008). The civil rights movement in world perspective. In G. Reichard & T. Dixon (Eds.), *America on the world stage: A global approach to U.S. history* (pp. 190–216). Urbana: University of Illinois Press.

Galston, W. A. (2007). Civic knowledge, civic education, and civic engagement: A summary of recent research. *International Journal of Public Administration, 30*(6–7), 623–642

Gibson, C., & Levine, P. (2003). *The civic mission of schools.* New York, NY: The Carnegie Corporation of New York.

Glazer, N., & Moynihan, D. P. (1970). *Beyond the melting pot: The Negroes, Puerto Rican, Jews, Italians, and Irish of New York City* (2nd ed.). Cambridge, MA: MIT Press.

Gordon, M. M. (1964). *Assimilation in American life: The role of race, religion, and national origins.* New York, NY: Oxford University Press.

Gould, J. (Ed.). (2011). *Guardians of democracy: The civic mission of schools.* Silver Spring, MD: Campaign for the Civic Mission of Schools. Retrieved at civicmission.s3.amazonaws.com/118/f0/5/171/1/Guardian-of-Democracy-report.pdf

Gutmann, A. (2005). Afterword: Democratic disagreement and civic education. In S. Fuhrman & M. Lazerson (Eds.), *The public schools* (pp. 347–360). New York, NY: Oxford University Press.

Hahn, C. L. (2008). Education for citizenship and democracy in the United States. In J. Arthur, I. Davies, & C. Hahn (Eds.), *The Sage handbook of education for citizenship and democracy* (pp. 263–278). Thousand Oaks, CA: Sage.

Hess, D. E. (2009). *Controversy in the classroom: The democratic power of discussion.* New York, NY: Routledge.

Hirschman, C., Kasinitz, P., & DeWind, J. (Eds.), (1999). *The handbook of international migration: The American experience* (pp. 127–136). New York, NY: Russell Sage Foundation.

Ito, M., Soep, E., Kligler-Vilenchik, N., Shresthova, S., Gamber-Thompson, L., & Zimmerman. A. (2015). Learning connected civics: Narratives, practices, infrastructures. *Curriculum Inquiry, 45*(1), 10–29.

Kahne, J., & Middaugh, E. (2008). *Democracy for some: The civic opportunity gap in high school* (CIRCLE Working Paper, No. 59). College Park, MD: Center for Information and Research on Civic Learning and Engagement.

Kasinitz, P., Mollenkopf, J. H., Waters, M. C., & Holdaway, J. (2008). *Inheriting the city: The children of immigrants come of age.* New York, NY: Russell Sage Foundation.

Krogstad, J. M., & Fry, J. (2014). *Dept. of Ed. projects public schools will be "majority-minority" this fall.* Retrieved from www.pewresearch.org/fact-tank/2014/08/18/u-s-public-schools-expected-to-be-majority-minority-starting-this-fall/

Kymlicka, W. (1998, Fall). American multiculturalism in the international arena. *Dissent, 45*(4), 73–79.

Kymlicka, W. (2004). Foreward. In J. A. Banks (Ed.). *Diversity and citizenship education: Global perspectives* (pp. xiii–xviii). San Francisco, CA: Jossey-Bass.

Ladson-Billings, G. (2004). Culture versus citizenship: The challenge of racialized citizenship in the United States. In J. A. Banks (Ed.), *Diversity and citizenship education: Global perspectives* (pp. 99–126). San Francisco, CA: Jossey-Bass.

Lawless, J. L., & Fox, R. L. (2015). *Running from office: Why young Americans are turned off to politics.* Oxford, United Kingdom: Oxford University Press.

Lee, W. O. (2002). The emergence of new citizenship: Looking into the self and beyond the nation. In G. Steiner-Khamsi, J. Torney-Purta, & J. Schwille (Eds.). *New paradigms and recurring paradoxes in education for citizenship: An international comparison* (pp. 37–60). New York, NY: Elsevier Science Ltd.

Levinson, M. (2012). *No citizen left behind.* Cambridge, MA: Harvard University Press.

Levy, F., & Murnane, R. (2004). *The new division of labor: How computers are creating the next job market.* Princeton, NJ: Princeton University Press.

Marshall, T. H. (1992). Citizenship and social class. In T. H. Marshall & T. Bottomore, *Citizenship and social class.* London, United Kingdom: Pluto Press. (Original work published 1950)

Martin, P. (2013, November). The global challenge of managing migration. *Population Bulletin, 68*(2), pp. 1–16.

Martin, P., & Zurcher, G. (2008, March). Managing migration: The global challenge. *Population Bulletin, 63*(1), pp. 1–20.

Massey, D. (1999). Why does immigration occur? A theoretical synthesis. In C. Hirschman, P. Kasinitz, & J. DeWind (Eds.), *The handbook of international migration: The American experience*, (pp. 34–52). New York, NY: Russell Sage Foundation.

Meyer, J., Bromley, P., & Ramirez, F. (2010). Human rights in social science textbooks: Cross-national analyses, 1970–2008. *Sociology of Education, 83*(2), 111–134.

Mintrop, H. (2002). Teachers and civic education instruction in cross-national comparison. (pp. 61–84). In G. Steiner-Khamsi, J. Torney-Purta, & J. Schwille (Eds.), *New paradigms and recurring paradoxes in education for citizenship: An international comparison.* New York, NY: Elsevier Science.

Mittelman, J. H. (2005). What is critical globalization studies? In R. P. Appelbaum & W. I. Robinson (Eds.), *Critical globalization studies* (pp. 19–29). New York, NY: Routledge.

Myers, J. P. (2007). Citizenship education practices of politically active teachers in Porto Alegre, Brazil, and Toronto, Canada. *Comparative Education Review, 51*(1), 1–24.

Myers, J. P., McBride, C., & Anderson, M. (2015). Beyond knowledge and skills: Discursive construction of civic identity in the world history classroom. *Curriculum Inquiry, 45*(2), 198–218.

Myers, J. P., & Zaman, H. A. (2009). Negotiating the global and national: Immigrant and dominant culture adolescents' vocabularies of citizenship in a transnational world. *Teachers College Record, 111*(11), 2589–2625.

National Academy of Sciences, National Academy of Engineering, & Institute of Medicine. (2010). *Rising above the gathering storm, revisited: Rapidly approaching category 5.* Washington, DC: National Academies Press.

National Center for Education Statistics (NCES). (2014). *National Assessment of Educational Progress (NAEP): Civics assessment.* Washington, DC: United State Department of Education, Institute of Education Sciences, National Center for Education Statistics. Retrieved from nces.ed.gov/nationsreportcard/civics/

National Research Council. (2011). *Assessing 21st century skills: Summary of a workshop.* Washington, DC: National Academies Press.

Nederveen Pieterse, J. (2013) What is global studies? *Globalizations, 10*(4), 499–514.

Niemi, R. G., & Junn, J. (1998). *Civic education: What makes students learn.* New Haven, CT: Yale University Press.

Oxfam Development Education Programme. (2006). *Education for global citizenship: A guide for schools.* Oxford, United Kingdom: Oxfam GB.

Park, R., & Burgess, E. (1921). *Introduction to the science of sociology.* Chicago, IL: University of Chicago Press.

Parker, W. C. (2011). International education in U.S. public schools. *Globalisation, Societies and Education, 9*(3–4), 487–501.

Parker, W. C. (2014). Citizenship education in the United States: Regime type, foundational questions, and classroom practice. In L. P. Nucci, D. Narvaez, & T. Krettenauer (Eds.), *The handbook of moral and character education* (2nd ed., pp. 347–367). New York, NY: Routledge.

Partnership for 21st Century Learning. (2016). Retrieved from www.p21.org/about-us/p21-framework

Ramirez, F. (2006). From citizen to person? Rethinking education as incorporation. In A. Wiseman, & D. Baker (Eds.), *The impact of comparative educational research on neoinstitutional theory* (pp. 367–88). Oxford, United Kingdom: Elsevier Science.

Ramirez, F., Bromley, P., & Russell, S. G. (2009). The valorization of humanity and diversity. *Multicultural Education Review, 1*(1), 29–54.

Reichard, G., & Dickson, T. (Eds.) (2008). *America on the world stage: A global approach to U.S. history.* Urbana: University of Illinois Press.

Rippberger, S. J., & Staudt, K. A. (2003). *Pledging allegiance: Learning nationalism at the El Paso-Juárez border.* New York, NY: Routledge Falmer.

Ritzer, G. (2007a). *The globalization of nothing.* Thousand Oaks, CA: Sage.

Ritzer, G. (2007b). Introduction to part 1. In G. Ritzer, (Ed.). *The Blackwell companion to globalization* (pp. 16–28). Malden, MA: Blackwell.

Ritzer, G. (2008). *Modern sociological theory.* New York, NY: McGraw Hill.

Robertson, R. (1992). *Globalization: Social theory and global culture.* London, United Kingdom: Sage.

Robertson, R. (1995). Glocalization: Time–space and homogeneity–heterogeneity. In M. Featherstone, S. Lash, & R. Robertson (Eds.), *Global modernities* (pp. 25–44). London, United Kingdom: Sage.

Rumbaut, R. (1999). Assimilation and its discontents: Ironies and paradoxes. In C. Hirschman, P. Kasinitz, & J. DeWind (Eds.), *The handbook of international migration: The American experience* (pp. 172–195). New York, NY: Russell Sage Foundation.

Sassen, S. (2006). *Territory, authority, rights: From medieval to global assemblages.* Princeton, NJ: Princeton University Press.

Schlesinger, A. (1991). *The disuniting of America: Reflections on a multicultural society.* New York, NY: Norton.

Schwille, J., & Amadeo, J. (2002). The paradoxical situation of civic education in schools: Ubiquitous and yet elusive. In G. Steiner-Khamsi, J. Torney-Purta, & J. Schwille (Eds.), *New paradigms and recurring paradoxes in education for citizenship: An international comparison* (pp. 105–136). New York, NY: Elsevier Science.

Soysal, Y. N. (1996). Changing citizenship in Europe: Remarks on postnational membership and the nation state. In D. Cesarani & M. Fulbrook (Eds.), *Citizenship, nationality, and migration in Europe* (pp. 17–29). London, United Kingdom: Routledge.

Stearns, P. N. (2007). American students and global issues. *World History Connected, 4*(2). Retrieved from worldhistoryconnected.press.uiuc.edu/4.2/stearns.html

Stearns, P. N. (2009). *Educating global citizenship in colleges and universities: Challenges and opportunities.* New York, NY: Routledge.

Suárez-Orozco, C. (2004). Formulating identity in a globalized world. In M. M. Suárez-Orozco & D. B. Qin-Hilliard (Eds.), *Globalization: Culture and education in the new millennium* (pp. 173–202). Berkeley: University of California Press.

Suárez-Orozco, M., & Sattin-Bajaj, C. (2010). *Educating the whole child for the whole world: The Ross School model and education for the global era.* New York, NY: New York University Press.

Suárez-Orozco. M., & Suárez-Orozco, C. (2009). Globalization, immigration, and schooling. In J. A. Banks (Ed.), *The Routledge international companion to multicultural education* (pp. 62–76). New York, NY: Routledge.

Tilly, C. (Ed.). (1996). *Citizenship, identity, and social history.* New York, NY: Press Syndicate of the University of Cambridge.

Torney-Purta, J., Barber, C. H., & Wilkenfeld, B. (2007). Latino adolescents' civic development in the United States: Research results from the IEA civic education study. *Journal of Youth and Adolescence, 36*(2), 111–125.

Torney-Purta, J., Lehmann, R., Oswald, H., & Schulz, W. (2001). *Citizenship and education in twenty-eight countries: Civic knowledge and engagement at age fourteen.* Amsterdam, Netherlands: IEA.

United Nations Department of Economic and Social Affairs, Population Division. (2016). *International migration report 2015: Highlights* (ST/ESA/SER.A/375). Retrieved from www.un.org/en/development/desa/population/migration/publications/migrationreport/docs/MigrationReport2015_Highlights.pdf

Wells, C. (2010). Citizenship and communication in online youth civic engagement projects. *Information, Communication and Society, 13*(3), 419–441.

Willinsky, J. (1998). *Learning to divide the world: Education at empire's end.* Minneapolis: University of Minnesota Press.

Zhou, M. (1999). Segmented assimilation: Issues, controversies, and recent research on the new second generation. In C. Hirschman, P. Kasinitz, & J. DeWind (Eds.), *The handbook of international migration: The American experience* (pp. 196–211). New York, NY: Russell Sage Foundation.

CHAPTER 8

Education in a Globalized World

Challenges, Tensions, Possibilities, and Implications for Teacher Education

Sonia Nieto

Given the increasing and unrelenting movement of people around the world, the growing interdependence among nations, and ongoing international tensions concerning social and cultural differences, a book that gives serious consideration to the role of education in preparing young people for civic inclusion is welcome indeed. But it is no easy matter to address these complex issues. As the chapters in this impressive book confirm, although a worthwhile goal, educating students of diverse backgrounds to become responsible and active citizens in our globalized world is full of contradictions and challenges. This is especially true when some of these young people are not accepted as worthy participants, nor do they relate in positive ways to their societies.

In the preceding chapters, the authors describe the state of affairs of civic inclusion in a number of societies. They document the growing number of people residing outside their nations of origin, and they demonstrate how immigration and globalization are affecting national priorities and actions, local educational policies and practices, and countless individual lives. Throughout, they present a picture of education for civic inclusion that is complex, thorny, at times promising, but not always optimistic.

Although the chapter authors address numerous issues in global education, few of them mention in any depth the role of teachers in the enormous task of educating students for civic inclusion, focusing instead on broader sociopolitical issues. These broader issues are, of course, a necessary framework for understanding schools and public education, yet the role of classroom teachers—those on the front lines—seems a particularly relevant topic to include in a book on civic inclusion. Consequently, while I will comment briefly on the other chapters in this book. I will also address in more detail what it means to prepare teachers for our globalized world. I begin by reviewing some of the challenges, tensions, and possibilities of educating young people for civic education and inclusion. Next, I explore the role of teachers in our globalizing world and the implications for teacher education. I describe some promising strategies to promote civic inclusion, focusing on two, ethnic studies and Youth Participatory Action Research (YPAR). I end with several implications for the preparation of teachers and the future of civic education and inclusion in highly diverse societies, providing a small number of examples of teachers who exemplify a global perspective.

GLOBALIZATION

Globalization is a fact that cannot be denied, ignored, or contained. While not the focus of this chapter, it is nevertheless important to mention that globalization is not beneficial for everyone (Apple, 2013). In their chapters, several authors address both the problems and the benefits of globalization. Though it can bring about enormous advantages, particularly in terms of technological advances, globalization also can, and indeed has, exacerbated inequality and oppression. Multinational corporations, for example, reap substantial financial benefits from globalization, but the same is not true for most ordinary citizens. On the contrary, globalization is wreaking havoc on people in many societies by intensifying inequality, particularly in those institutions most affecting the poor and dispossessed.

The numbers are enormous. The United Nations estimates that migrants number some 244 million around the world (United Nations, 2016). In societies characterized by inequality, Nail (2015) argues that "history and the society it has built is off-limits to the migrant" (p. 191). Today's migrant is, according to him, "the collective name for all the political figures in history who have been territorially, politically, juridically, and economically displaced as a condition of the social expansion of power" (p. 193). Hence, recognizing the role that power plays in the continued exclusion of migrants and other groups disenfranchised in societies is crucial. As cogently argued by Nail (2015), global migration poses a serious threat to the stated commitment of most nations for political equality. He explains that this is the case because migrants with no status are subject to a permanent inequality with no voting or labor rights, and with the threat of deportation, among other problems. These conditions, according to Nail, are impossible to reconcile with almost any political theory of equality, universality, or liberty.

Globalization is affecting public education in school systems around the world in a variety of ways. Some of the challenges and tensions, as well as possibilities, of global education are articulated below. Before discussing these challenges and possibilities, a brief definition of *global education* is in order. According to Pike (2000, 2008), because the term is used in so many different ways, it can be a slippery concept. He suggests, however, that most theoretical frameworks of global education include the following: global connections and interdependence; global systems; global issues and problems; cross-cultural understanding; human beliefs and values; and awareness of choices for the future. In terms of actual classroom practice, Pike found that teachers in Canada, the United States, and the United Kingdom shared several common threads of global education. These included interdependence; connectedness; a global perspective; and multiple perspectives (Pike, 2000). Nevertheless, Pike (2008) also suggests, "Beneath this bland visage, however, lie variations of global education, in both theory and practice, that span a spectrum of ideological positions and which, in some cases, have given rise to considerable controversy" (p. 469). Some of these controversies are embedded in the challenges and tensions of the field as articulated below.

CHALLENGES AND TENSIONS OF CIVIC EDUCATION AND INCLUSION IN A GLOBALIZED WORLD

In public education, macrolevel neoliberal policies including privatization, marketization, and standardization are examples of how globalization is negatively affecting school systems around the world (Apple, 2013; Darder, 2015; Nieto, 2013b, 2014). These policies include rigid accountability for both students and teachers, the deprofessonalization of teachers, dramatically increased levels of testing of students, and standardized curricula (Darling-Hammond et al., 2015). These policies also have an impact at the microlevel of classrooms and schools attended by children living in poverty because they have been among the most negatively affected by neoliberal educational policies. This is the case because immigrant children and long-term residents different from the mainstream population often live in poverty. Neoliberal microlevel policies inevitably lead to a narrowing of the curriculum, an eroding of teachers' autonomy and creativity, and a pedagogy that Haberman (1991) famously called "the pedagogy of poverty": a basic pedagogy used with children living in poverty that consists primarily of asking questions, giving directions, making assignments, and monitoring seatwork. It is, according to Haberman, a pedagogy that rather than promote teaching and learning impedes both. In addition, the students most affected by global macro- and microlevel policies are young people who have a hard time seeing themselves as significant members of their society, especially immigrants and domestic racial, ethnic, and religious minorities.

In contemplating the influence of globalization on public education in the United States and other societies, Darder (2015) has concluded that while neoliberal policies have their own logic, they have little to do with educational justice. In prioritizing profits over educational goals, neoliberal policies such as profit-making testing regimes, for-profit schools, and the deprofessionalization of the teaching profession contradict the goals of social justice and equity in education. Darder explains:

> Educational justice cannot echo the logic of the market place and educational success cannot be reduced to an efficiency language of quantification and expediency, which strips away our humanity from the process of teaching and learning. (p. xii)

Young people represent a significant portion of migrants, and schools and nonschool educational institutions are responsible for the incorporation of these youngsters into society. In order to work toward meaningful civic engagement, the structural inclusion of all young people is necessary. But while structural inclusion may be articulated as a goal toward which all nations should strive, it needs to be reconceptualized to include the affirmation of people's identities and their basic human rights. Without the recognition of young people's essential humanity, their structural inclusion in schools is a sham.

In what follows, I briefly describe three tensions that make civic inclusion hard to achieve, particularly for disenfranchised youths. These include the suspicion and rejection of difference, as well as the fear of loss of influence on the part of the most powerful in society, whether they are in the majority or not.

Suspicion of Difference

Though immigration is, and has always been, a historical reality as comprehensively documented in this volume, it is now more widespread than ever, with consequences for both receiving nation-states and nation-states losing residents. From the negative reactions of many nations and citizens, particularly (but not exclusively) in Western countries, it is obvious that most new immigrants are neither wanted nor welcomed. They are often considered too foreign and too different from the mainstream population to be accepted as equals. This is especially true for impoverished immigrants who are not highly educated, do not speak the national language, and differ in culture, race, native language, or in other ways from the majority of residents of the receiving country (see chapter by Suárez-Orozco & Marks in this volume). As a result, such immigrants are typically defined as problems: They are viewed as causing all sorts of difficulties, from increasing the crime rate to squandering the resources of the receiving nation, and even of participating in terrorist activities. In terms of schooling, immigrants are frequently blamed for lowering the quality of education in the communities in which they settle. They are often seen, according to Bekerman (see chapter in this volume), as "existential threats" to the nation.

Despite the fact that this book focuses on immigrants, it is necessary to insist that it is not only immigrants who are viewed in negative ways. The example of some Muslim youths in European countries, in spite of being born and raised in those countries, is visible proof that even citizens, when marginalized by policies, practices, traditions, and even laws in their societies, can become radicalized (Meer, Pala, Modood, & Simon, 2009). Also, recent headlines in the United States have documented that Black men are often viewed with great suspicion, sometimes killed by police officers simply because of their race (McFadden, 2006). In these cases, a nation's residents, some of whose forebears have been in a nation for many generations and sometimes for hundreds of years, are excluded from the definition of "citizen" due to their race, ethnicity, or religion. As a result, for many White citizens, this difference from the mainstream White majority makes these individuals suspect. A similar situation occurs with Caribbean Blacks in Great Britain (Gillborn, 2008), Palestinians in Israel (see chapter by Agbaria in this volume), and Indigenous and Roma people in many nations (Kyuchukov, 2009), as well as other groups throughout the world (Banks, 2009a).

Rejection of Difference

A major way in which some students are marginalized in schools is through the partial or complete invisibility of their backgrounds, histories, and cultures in the curriculum. Although the violence students experience as a result may not be direct and physical, the absence of their lives in the day-to-day policies and practices of schools has the effect of discounting their lives. That is, when the identities, histories, and realities of certain young people are not reflected in curricula or other school policies, *symbolic violence* is the result (Bourdieu, 1984). In English-speaking countries, for example, as Valdés (see chapter in this volume) has asserted, exclusionary language ideologies discourage the use of other languages besides English in instruction, even as a temporary strategy for immigrants and their children as they adapt to their new society.

Attempts to develop civic identities among minoritized and racialized youths in some nations are thwarted in other ways as well. As Bekerman (see chapter in this volume) suggests, hegemonic forces often result in rendering the lives (and in the case he discusses, the religious affiliations) of some youths as inconsequential or invisible. Consequently, the separation of religion from politics (commonly known as "church and state" but in this case, "mosque and state"), though it may be expressed as a national value, might be impossible to attain. Religious differences are thus treated as aberrant rather than as simply different.

When immigrants and others are excluded from belonging to the citizenry of a nation because of their racial, cultural, linguistic and other differences, there is little chance they can become part of the larger polity. In the United States, for example, the white skin of European immigrants continues to trump their "foreign" accents and other differences, particularly because the children and grandchildren of European immigrants can "become White" after being in the nation for just a few years and dropping their native languages and accents (Ignatiev, 2008; Roediger, 2005). The same is generally not the case for immigrants of color, even if they are highly educated, speak the national language, and have lived in the country for many generations. This situation is not limited to the United States. As several of the authors in this volume point out, some immigrants, even if they accept the values and traditions of their new country, may nonetheless not be accepted as legitimate citizens.

Fear of Loss of Power

Power underlies a society's traditions, goals, laws, and institutions. It is no surprise then, that a third tension related to promoting civic education in a globalized world is the fear of loss of power of those groups most powerful in society. Education, too, is inevitably about power—who has it, and how it is used or abused.

Foucault conceptualized what he termed the "regimes of truth" (1980, p. 113) that is, the discourses promoted by a society as truth, and produced, transmitted, and kept in place by systems of power such as universities, the military, and the media. A society's regimes of truth help perpetuate the status quo even when the status quo is unjust, or perhaps especially when that is the case. The result of these regimes of truth is that perspectives and realities different from those officially sanctioned by a society are likely to remain invisible.

How power is produced and maintained by societal vested interests can be explained by Gramsci's (1971) theory of *hegemony,* that is, the process by which dominant groups create and maintain social control over others. It is as a result of hegemony that individuals from dominated groups learn to believe they are naturally inferior in culture, language, and experience to those from dominant groups (Gramsci, 1971). In the case of education, hegemony is created through schools' policies and practices, particularly the curriculum, pedagogy, segregation in separate and unequal schools, testing policies, outreach (or lack of outreach) to marginalized families and communities, special programs and so-called "ability group tracking" (Oakes, 2005), and others. In addition, as Freire (1985) has insisted, power is implicated in *every* educational decision, practice, and policy, whether at the state, local, or classroom level.

When the curriculum changes to include the experiences and perspectives of those previously excluded, the reaction from powerful groups can be swift and vehement, with questions about the legitimacy of previously excluded knowledge and perspectives, and claims that the changes will diminish the quality of education for everyone. Such was the case, for example, after the introduction of bilingual and multicultural education in public schools in the United States (Gándara & Hopkins, 2010; Sleeter, 1995) and ethnic studies in higher education (Bloom, 1987; Hirsch, 1987).

The example of bilingual education in the United States is a case in point—despite overwhelming and worldwide evidence of the benefits of this approach, it has been a hotly contested issue for decades primarily because it challenges the notion that an "English-Only" policy is the best way to learn English, a notion that has been disproven time and again (Cummins, 2000; O. García, 2009; Macedo, Dendrinos, & Gounari, 2003; Wright, Boun, & García, 2015). Clearly, in such cases, the issue of power trumps solid research evidence. The same can be said of multicultural education, ethnic studies, and other approaches, some of which I consider below.

HOPEFUL POSSIBILITIES FOR CIVIC INCLUSION

Given the realities explored above, what hope is there to educate young people for civic education? Banks (see chapter in this volume) suggests that civic education can work toward what he defines as "a sustainable version of social cohesion" through education that advances civic equality, recognition, and structural inclusion. Not as sanguine that this will happen, Blum (2014) nevertheless insists that to be meaningful, education in highly diverse nations must consist of three overarching goals: recognizing differences, national cohesion, and equality. Yet as exemplified by most of the chapters in this volume, in many nation-states with diverse populations, none of these goals have been fully realized. The result is that if differences are not recognized and affirmed, equality may be impossible to achieve.

Despite the three major problems articulated above, the possibility of engaging a broad range of students for productive lives in diverse societies is nevertheless a goal worth pursuing. As Ben-Peretz and Aderet-German (see chapter in this volume) assert, given the right conditions, meaningful civic education can be achieved. One possibility is what Banks (see chapter in this volume) has termed "multiple acculturation" that can happen when young people learn from, participate in, share, and transform their own identities as well as popular culture. However, without the explicit inclusion of the history, languages, and perspectives of people other than the majority in schools' curriculum and pedagogy, multiple acculturation would be difficult, if not impossible, to attain. In this regard, ethnic studies, multicultural education, bilingual education, and other iterations of education for diversity (such as culturally responsive pedagogy, social justice education, dual language immersion, peace education, and education for human rights) are hopeful developments that can address the challenges to civic education discussed in previous sections of this chapter. Many volumes and thousands of articles have been published on the benefits of these approaches around the world, but in spite of their relatively long history in theory, classroom practice has not kept up with theory (Banks, 2009a; O. García, 2009; Gay, 2004; Wright et al., 2015).

Below, I identify two among a number of promising trends, namely, ethnic studies and Youth Participatory Action Research (YPAR), both of which have received growing attention in the past several years among researchers and educators. They are offered as the kinds of approaches that might help toward achieving the goal of multiple acculturation suggested by Banks.

Case One: Ethnic Studies

As a result of their invisibility and alienation in schools because of the symbolic violence they suffer, many immigrant and other marginalized students are disengaged from school, as well as from identifying with the nation in which they reside. The field of ethnic studies, which has a fairly long history as an inclusive educational process, can help ameliorate this situation (Banks, 2009b). According to Banks (2012), ethnic studies is an important way to help students become effective and productive citizens in a global world. An ethnic studies curriculum can present a more inclusive narrative to help young people identify as significant members of their societies.

Originally conceived and demanded by students of color on U.S. college and university campuses as a direct outgrowth of the 1960s civil rights movement, ethnic studies programs are still found primarily on college campuses. Yet given the many challenges it has faced, particularly from neoconservative critics, ethnic studies has not developed a strong foothold in many public school classrooms. Nonmajority students are not oblivious to the exclusion of their people in the curriculum. As Sleeter (2011) points out, in the United States, "by the time they reach high school, students of color are not only aware of a Euro-American bias in curriculum, but they can describe it in some detail, and view it as contributing to their disengagement" (p. 4).

In a research review of the benefits of ethnic studies, Sleeter (2011) found numerous studies that documented how both marginalized and majority groups became more engaged with schools as a result of exposure to an ethnic studies curricula. She concludes, "Ethnic studies, by allowing for multiple voices to enter dialog constructing the narrative of this country, is critical to the development of a democracy that actually includes everyone" (p. 5). In a later review of how ethnic studies is embedded in curricula in Canada, New Zealand, and the United States, Sleeter (2015) concluded that "national political contexts matter for how ethnicity and curriculum are framed and who does the framing. Who is involved, which groups lead efforts, and who has power to shape curriculum?" (p. 232). Nevertheless, she also found that incorporating ethnic studies into the curriculum has been both popular and successful with students. In spite of its success, however, ethnic and Indigenous studies "are usually regarded by the dominant society with deep suspicion and fear" (Sleeter, 2015, p. 240).

It is instructive to present the case of a high school program as a model for what ethnic studies can do for students of all backgrounds at the high school or even younger levels. One recent and significant study concerns the much-maligned and ill-fated Mexican American Studies (MAS) program at Tucson High School in New Mexico (Cabrera, Milen, Jaquette, & Marx, 2014). When started in the 1990s, it was reportedly the only ethnic studies program at the high school level in the United States. The teachers and staff members of the MAS program defined it as based on a "critically compassionate pedagogy" (Cammarota & Romero, 2006), that is, a philosophy that both affirmed students' identities and also encouraged them to question received wisdom. The classes became a place where the identities of the Chicano/a students were made visible and affirmed, but also where students of all backgrounds learned to think critically.

Given the demographics of Tucson High School—about 90% Mexican American—a major goal of the program was to represent Mexican American culture and perspectives more fully and honestly in the curriculum, thus engendering a sense of pride and affirmation in Mexican American students. Another goal of the program was to recruit students of other backgrounds as well. In the process, some of the latter became the biggest supporters of the program when it was under attack. For example, in an article about the foundation and goals of the program, Curtis Acosta, one of the program's teachers, and Asiya Mir, a Pakistani American student in the program (Acosta & Mir, 2012), described the rationale for the MAS, stating:

Our classes were products of the Chican@ Movement in the 1960s and a further grass-roots effort in the 1990s to build an educational experience for our youth founded on the premise that the experiences, history, literature, and art of Chican@s/Latin@s were a necessary and valid area for rigorous academic exploration. (p. 16)

The MAS program proved to be successful with both Mexican American and other students not only in cultural affirmation and historical knowledge, but also in achievement. Because of the curriculum, pedagogy, and strong relationships with program staff, students' academic skills flourished and many went on to postsecondary education. In a study of the 2008–2011 academic years, the peak years of MAS enrollment, the results for graduation rates were impressive, with MAS students significantly more likely to graduate than their non-MAS peers. According to the report's authors (Cabrera et al., 2014), "Taking MAS classes is consistently, significantly, and positively related to increased student academic achievement, and this relationship grows stronger the more classes students take" (p. 1107).

In spite of its success, the MAS program proved to be controversial. Conservatives decried it as divisive, subversive, and even un-American. The initial attacks came from outside politicians, including Tom Horne, the State Schools Superintendent, and other high-level state politicians. These were followed by internal attacks, with two members of the district school board actively working to eliminate the MAS program. One of the teachers in the program, Maria Federico Brummer, who is featured in a book on culturally responsive teachers (Nieto, 2013a), described how all but two of her MAS courses were taken away from her. Instead, she was assigned to teach three general education American history courses, and an assistant principal who had never been involved in the program was reassigned as her supervisor. By 2012, all the Mexican American courses were eliminated from the school district and the ethnic studies program was dismantled.

Some of the books used in the program's curriculum—including Paulo Freire's *Pedagogy of the Oppressed* (1970) and William Shakespeare's *The Tempest* (1623/1998)—were banned, even though they are regularly used in other schools around the nation. More than ever, the teachers were under constant surveillance. As María Brummer explained, "Our lesson plans had to be approved and we were provided 'training' from administration and other teachers on how to 'tease out' any MAS curriculum" (cited in Nieto, 2013a, p. 113). It became clear that the perceived loss of power of the dominant group dictated the dismantling of the program.

In acknowledging that an ethnic studies approach could be a significant way for schools to educate young people while also helping them become bicultural, an important opportunity was lost. It was, as the title of an article concerning research on the program states, a failure to miss "the (student achievement) forest for all the (political) trees" (Cabrera et al., 2014).

Case Two: Youth Participatory Action Research (YPAR)

Another promising practice for engaging young people for civic involvement is Youth Participatory Action Research (YPAR), an approach that has especially captured the imagination of researchers working with young people of diverse backgrounds in the United States (Cammarota & Fine, 2008; Morrell, 2008). There are numerous examples of how YPAR is helping young people of disenfranchised backgrounds engage more successfully in their education and, in the process, challenge taken-for-granted educational policies and practices. Nicole Mirra, Danielle Filipiak, and Antero Garcia (2015) call YPAR "a powerful practice that reimagines the *who, what, why,* and *how* of research" (p. 49). In their book on the topic, Nicole Mirra, Antero Garcia, and Ernest Morrell (2016) define YPAR more specifically in the following way:

> At its most basic level, YPAR refers to the practice of mentoring young people to become social scientists by engaging them in all aspects of the research cycle, from developing research questions and examining relevant literature to collecting and analyzing data and offering findings about social issues that they find meaningful and relevant. (pp. 1–2)

The authors go on to caution, however, that YPAR is about much more than producing mini-researchers. It also has implications for reimagining the very nature of teaching and learning, the way that policymakers think about the capabilities and aspirations of young people, and the purpose and ethics of educational research. In YPAR, relationship building is conceptualized as a *pedagogical strategy,* not simply as a "feel-good" way to make schools more palatable to students who have been turned off by too many years of indifferent, cold, and callous schooling (Mirra et al., 2016).

A number of researchers have used YPAR to motivate young people to be civically engaged by becoming invested in solving problems in both their schools and their broader communities. For example, Irizarry (2011) worked with Latin@ youngsters to help them become researchers of their own education. While most of these young people had never before considered college as a possibility, and most did not even know what was required to pursue higher education, as a result of their active involvement in a YPAR project, some of them did indeed decide to continue their education.

In a more recent example, an article by Garcia, Mirra, Morrell, Martinez, and Scorza (2015) explores the relationship between critical literacy practices, digital media production, and civic agency. Making the case that literacy is more than simply reading and writing or passing high-stakes tests, the authors articulate a vision of literacy that is tied to power structures and this knowledge can motivate students to become active rather than passive learners. In their recent book, Mirra, Garcia, and Morrell (2016) chronicle one year of the UCLA Council of Youth Research, a 15-year project that has seen an astounding 100% of its high school participants go on to postsecondary education, this in a community where a college education is often unattainable for many reasons, including the poor quality of its schools. With a compelling mix of theory, method, stories, and insightful interludes, the researchers—from high school students to veteran professors—paint a picture of engaged, enthusiastic participants cocreating spaces of hope and empowerment. These and a growing number of examples of YPAR projects demonstrate that inspiring activities and relevant curricula can lead to more successful civic schooling and brighter futures for all students.

Given the success of both ethnic studies and YPAR, the question then becomes how teachers can be prepared with the knowledge, skill, and enthusiasm to use these approaches, among others, in their classrooms. The answer, of course, lies in appropriate teacher preparation, an issue to which we now turn.

GLOBALIZING EDUCATION AND TEACHER PREPARATION

The purpose of schooling young children has never been simply to teach them literacy and numeracy. Depending on the place and historical context, other goals have taken on even greater importance, many of them having to do with acculturation and nationalism. These have included assimilating immigrants to their new culture and language, preparing them for "their place" in society, promoting patriotism, defining the society's national character, writing or rewriting its history, and other such concerns. The policies to promote these values have sometimes been heavy-handed, even brutal; at other times, they have been less so. But whether explicit or not, the policies have been inculcated in teachers as well. The question becomes, then, how can teachers learn practices that are more aligned with civic inclusion than is currently the case?

Needed are explicit policies and practices in teacher education that prepare preservice teachers to properly educate young people for diverse and democratic societies and for our globalizing world. This is, after all, a major stated goal, though not the practice, of many nation-states today. Nevertheless, the preparation of teachers is the so-called elephant in the room of global and civic education. That is, if we are serious about preparing young people for productive lives in multicultural societies, then more care and attention must be given to teacher education.

Despite the proven benefits of ethnic studies, multicultural education, bilingual education, and YPAR, among other inclusive approaches for educating both majority and nonmajority students, most teachers regardless of background have not been adequately prepared to teach ethnic studies or use a YPAR pedagogy, or even to adequately teach students not yet fluent in the national language (see chapter by Valdés in this volume). Yet this should be the responsibility of all teachers regardless of specialization or racial, ethnic, or linguistic background.

Part of the problem is that many teacher educators themselves have not had the personal experience or knowledge to prepare young people for living in a globalized world. As a result, many teacher educators do not have the capacity to do this work. In a study of 80 teacher educators recognized for their success in preparing teachers in both multicultural and global education, Merryfield (2000) found that personal experiences with people different from themselves, experiences with discrimination, and outsider status were among the reasons the teacher educators gave for their commitment to multicultural and global education. For the most part the teacher educators of color drew on personal experiences with diversity and discrimination, whereas the White teacher educators had their most profound experiences with diversity when they traveled and lived outside the United States. Merryfield (2000) concluded that, given the demographics of U.S. teacher educators, there are limits to how well the nation's universities can prepare teachers in multicultural and global education.

In a handbook on citizenship and education, Merryfield and her colleague Duty (2008) explore what young people need to know and be able to do to become civically engaged global citizens. This is not simply about "appreciating" or "celebrating" diversity, but rather about giving young people the information they need to understand our complex world, as well as the tools to improve it. They write,

> If we want students to create a more just and equitable world, citizenship education must address the realities of global power and methods for overcoming poverty and oppression. Students need to understand how power is exerted globally, the effects of global actors on social, economic, cultural, environmental, and political inequities and injustice, and the ways in which people have resisted oppression and worked to gain rights and self-determination. (p. 86)

Merryfield and Duty here are suggesting nothing short of a call to action for global education, one that demands a great deal from both teachers and students. For example, they stress that students need to study not only mainstream academic knowledge but also the "transformative, contrapuntal knowledge that gives voice and agency to people and issues largely ignored by those in power" (p. 87).

Clearly, however, young people cannot create these understandings or tools on their own; they need competent teachers to help them become globally minded and empowered citizens who will make a difference in the world. This is where teacher education comes in. Before discussing needed changes in teacher education, it must be recognized that the conditions for teaching must also be changed because even the highest-quality teacher education programs cannot be successful if teachers are thrust into schools that rely on tired, unimaginative policies such as an overreliance on high-stakes tests and other punitive approaches that have defined educational reform in numerous nations in the past several decades. For one, teaching needs to be made a more rewarding and consequential profession, one in which teachers are treated like the professionals they are meant to be. Until that happens, and unless structural changes take place in the profession as a whole, the multiple roles demanded of teachers can result in more of them leaving the classroom.

In their book on teacher education in several nations around the world, Linda Darling-Hammond and her colleagues (2015) reviewed conditions that have led to successful teaching and learning in a number of nations. They concluded that such conditions require, among other changes, creating systems that respect teachers and that make teaching an attractive profession, investing in continuous learning on the part of teachers, and providing the needed resources to make such structural changes meaningful.

A number of implications for teacher education follow, with examples from a small number of teachers. Though all of the latter are from the United States and thus reflect particular sociocultural and sociopolitical realities that differ in many respects from teachers in other nations, they nonetheless represent models of what teacher educators can learn from classroom teachers.

RECRUITING AND RETAINING TEACHERS OF NONMAJORITY BACKGROUNDS FOR DIVERSE CLASSROOMS

In most nations, educators of minority-group backgrounds are greatly underrepresented among the general population of teachers. Having more teachers who reflect the backgrounds and experiences of their students is a benefit both for students and for other teachers who can learn from them (Clewell, Puma, & McKay, 2001; Dee, 2000; Tintiangco-Cubales et al., 2015). Doing so can have many benefits as Irvine and Fenwick (2009) found in a review of the positive impact that teachers of nonmajority backgrounds can have on the learning of all students. They write: "Teachers of color do more than teach content. They dispel myths of racial inferiority and incompetence and serve as surrogate parents, guides, and mentors to their students" (p. 5).

Teachers who share, or those who learn about, the lived realities of their students can promote the civic inclusion of marginalized youths. In a chapter on immigrant youths in the United States, C. Suarez-Orozco and Marks (see chapter in this volume) document some of the many challenges these young people face, especially when their parents are unfamiliar with the language and culture of their new land. As a result, children and their parents often switch roles, with children becoming the translators and experts and parents feeling helpless and incompetent. Having teachers and administrators who reflect the ethnic and cultural backgrounds of students can be particularly helpful by making the adaptation and inclusion process for entire families less stressful.

There are other situations in which exclusion is built into the educational system, even for students born and raised in those societies. Glaring examples of the alienation of Muslim and Roma students in European countries, and Indigenous and long-term minority communities in other nations such as Australia, New Zealand, and the United States make it clear that these problems are not specific to one nation or society (besides some of the examples in this text, see others from various countries around the world in Arthur, Davies, & Hahn, 2008; Banks, 2009b).

Agbaria (see chapter in this volume) uses the example of Palestinian youths in Israel to provide a glaring case of exclusion. Even in this case, however, the author describes how Palestinian teachers of citizenship education use what he calls *counterknowledge* to offset the indoctrination of Palestinian youths "in favor of moralizing and justifying an exclusive definition of the state as a Jewish

state." Thus we see how the tenets of another recent approach, Critical Race Theory (CRT), including *counter-storytelling*, are used in educational contexts in various nations (Ladson-Billings, 2004). Agbaria argues that teachers of Palestinian
youths in Israel have a dual role: to educate students about their objective reality in
oppressive conditions, while at the same time preparing them to pass the nation's
matriculation exam in civics, a requirement for entrance into higher education.
This balancing act, no easy feat, is actually practiced by many teachers in nations
around the world who teach disenfranchised youths (Banks, 2009b).

An example of a teacher whose background is congruent with those of her
students comes from María Rosario (2015), an elementary school teacher in a
Chicago public school. In an essay about why she continues to teach in spite of
conditions that make it difficult to do so, Maria effectively articulates the need for
students to have teachers who share their backgrounds:

> Young people deserve to see people who look like them, have had the same experiences
> as they have, and who can be their advocates when no one else is willing to do the ex-
> ceptionally hard work that must be done when a child is suffering. Teachers need to be
> willing to be that advocate when all other people have failed them. (p. 200)

Though María Rosario (2015) could not as a child articulate her feelings of
alienation in the classroom, she writes, "I felt unable to connect with anything
going on at school because nothing that we studied or learned reflected me, told
the story of my history, or was about my lived experiences" (p. 194). It was not
until 5th grade that María had a teacher who "saw the potential in me and affirmed
my talents" (p. 196). Having experienced both alienation and affirmation in her
own education, María developed a sense of social justice very early. As a result,
she made the decision to become a teacher. She was determined to be the kind of
teacher who would honor all of her students by creating spaces of inclusion and
solidarity in her classroom. But it is not only cultural affirmation that María wants
to effect; it is also academic achievement. She writes,

> Academic achievement does not belong to one race or social group, and teachers need
> to be aware and vigilant of the messages they send to their students by closely selecting
> topics, people, and themes that reflect positive messages about who students are and
> who they can expect to become in the future. (Rosario, 2015, p. 197)

An important implication for teacher education programs is to use the experiences of teachers of diverse backgrounds in their courses. Through personal narratives, invited speakers, and in numerous other ways, teacher education
programs can make it clear to prospective teachers that students of marginalized
backgrounds are significant members of a community and must be treated as such.
Until that happens, too many young people who feel alienated and resentful will
continue to be failed by schools. It is not only they who are jeopardized; it is also
the communities and the society in which they live that lose out.

While there is a great need to recruit teachers of nonmajority backgrounds to the profession, it is not only teachers who reflect the backgrounds and experiences of their students who should take responsibility for teaching them, or for learning about them. On the contrary, majority-group teachers have a special responsibility to learn about and connect with their nonmajority group students. This means preparing all teachers to be social justice educators, an especially significant role for those who prepare a nation's teachers.

PREPARING SOCIAL JUSTICE TEACHERS OF ALL BACKGROUNDS

What does it mean for classroom teachers to prepare students for a globalized world? In one study, Merryfield and her colleagues Joe Tin-Yau Lo and Masataka Kasai (2008) documented how teachers in Hong Kong, Japan, and the United States prepared students to become what they call "worldminded citizens." According to the authors, worldmindedness "begins as global awareness and grows as individuals begin to appreciate the viewpoints, experiences, and worldviews of others, especially those quite different from themselves" (p. 7). Worldmindedness increases the opportunities students have to become civically engaged on issues from human rights to environmental justice, among many others. Based on rich case studies and vignettes of teachers' practices, Merryfield, Lo, and Kasai suggest five elements of global education used successfully by the teachers they studied: a knowledge of global interconnectedness; inquiry into global issues; skills in perspective consciousness; habits of mind such as open-mindedness and recognition of bias, stereotypes, and exotica; and providing cross-cultural experiences to develop students' intercultural competence.

Preparing teachers to teach worldmindedness also means exposing them to the realities of the students they will teach so that they become not only their teachers, but also their mentors and advocates. If they have already developed a social consciousness by the time they begin their preparation as teachers, so much the better. But many of the young people who enter the teaching profession, given their own lack of experience with people different from themselves, have to learn to relate to their students of diverse backgrounds, to learn about their lives, and to have high expectations for them. These crucial aptitudes and behaviors can be promoted through course content, extracurricular experiences in diverse communities, and practicum experiences in classrooms with diverse populations of students.

Becoming a social justice teacher cannot be taught directly, but that does not mean it cannot be learned. Teacher education programs can set a climate for inclusion and respect in many ways. For example, they can provide curricula that inform prospective teachers about the students in their society. In too many cases, programs rely on a one-course approach to prepare teachers for the enormous diversity they will face when they step into a classroom. A single course in "diversity" often includes a multitude of issues—culture, race, language, special needs, and other topics—clearly too many to cover with any degree of comprehensiveness. The approach is rarely successful, especially if it consists mainly of generalizations about marginalized groups that can quickly become damaging stereotypes. Even teaching prospective teachers about students' cultural backgrounds can be a slippery slope unless accompanied by critical conversations about racism, ethnocentrism, power, and privilege. This has certainly been the case with the work of Ruby Payne (2005) in "understanding poverty," work that has been harshly criticized for leading to deficit perspectives about cultural differences (e.g., see Gorski, 2013).

If teachers are to become knowledgeable and competent in ethnic studies, YPAR, multicultural education, and bilingual education, among other promising approaches, the curriculum to which they are exposed needs a radical transformation. A promising approach is to create curricula that include histories of a nation's diverse communities. Curricula that encourage outreach to diverse communities, including home visits, can also be more powerful than simply reading about difference. But home visits without the appropriate kind of preparation can become voyeuristic and can even perpetuate negative stereotypes. In her chapter in the *Handbook of Research on Teacher Education* (2008), Sleeter reviews some community-based learning strategies that can help disrupt preservice teachers' preconceived notions about families different from themselves. Just walking in the neighborhood to become acquainted with the people, businesses, social service providers, and the general character of the community can help dispel stereotypes and biases about the students they will teach. Absent this kind of preparation, teachers are left to their own devices to figure out who their students are and the daily struggles they might face.

Though becoming knowledgeable about the subject matter they will teach and the pedagogical strategies to accompany the content are essential, prospective teachers also need to learn that teaching is especially about the relationships they will develop with their students. These relationships can, in fact, make the difference between student success and failure. A good example comes from Matt Hicks (2015) who wrote an essay for a book about his experiences as an English teacher in Athens, Georgia. Until the past two decades, "diversity" in the Southeast region of the United States had been described primarily in Black and White terms, but this changed as an influx of Mexican American and Central American immigrants drastically changed the nature of the towns, cities, and even the entire region. Matt and his colleagues have had to learn to expand their understanding of diversity. In his essay, Matt described his transformation from knowing very little about his students to becoming a major advocate for them.

Part of Matt Hicks's transformation came about as a result of his understanding that he was not simply a teacher of literacy. His dawning awareness of the limited educational opportunities faced by his immigrant students changed him as a teacher and as a person. Because many were undocumented—that is, they had entered the United States without proper documentation, most as young children—they were not entitled to postsecondary education in most of the state's colleges and universities. Through his experiences with them as both a teacher and a soccer coach, Matt began to learn about their lives and daily struggles. He became an advocate for his undocumented students, creating spaces of inclusion through his curriculum and also through extracurricular activities. For instance, he and one of his students developed a guide for undocumented students. With information about college admission policies, the names of colleges to which they could apply, and the scholarships for which they were eligible, the guide was shared with guidance counselors and other advocates around the state. He then created a class at the high school, giving it a vague-sounding name, in which he brought together aspiring college-bound undocumented students to teach a class from the guide. At the end of the year, many of the students had gained admission to college, and several were awarded scholarships and financial aid.

Slowly, Matt became an advocate not just for his individual students, but also an activist for the rights of all undocumented students. He attended rallies to protest punitive state laws against the immigration of undocumented people into Georgia, even testifying against such restrictive and exclusionary legislation. His actions led him, he explained, to come into "full humanity," explaining that the work "was no longer an abstraction or intellectual pursuit." Instead, he wrote, "It was close to my heart each night as I prepared for school. It was what brought me there each day" (Hicks, 2015, p. 135).

Teacher education programs can help prospective teachers become advocates like Matt through both curricular and extracurricular opportunities. Courses on ethnic studies, multicultural education, bilingual education, and YPAR can all have practicum components so that from the beginning prospective teachers learn to work with, and in, the communities in which they will eventually teach. Teacher educators can also invite teachers such as Matt to be guest lecturers, to coteach courses with faculty, or to teach entire courses on these topics. Teacher education programs or individual faculty members can partner with social service agencies and school districts so that preservice teachers learn the fundamentals of YPAR, as in the examples given above; they can also become interns and teaching assistants in such endeavors. Though not always a comfortable alliance for either schools or universities because the result can be that students and teachers begin to challenge the policies and practices of both, such partnerships also result in public school students becoming empowered, critical learners who begin to demand more of education than it had previously delivered.

Of course, preparing preservice and practicing teachers with a global perspective is more complicated than these strategies would suggest. No set of strategies can do the job, particularly in sociopolitical contexts where exclusion and racism are rampant or where educators of all stripes—teacher educators, classroom teachers, school district administrators, and policymakers—have not been exposed to a global perspective. In addition, simply adding courses in diversity, hiring teacher educators of diverse backgrounds, or even incorporating community-based perspectives into teacher education programs can become tokenistic if not accompanied by both broad-based structural changes and respect for, and understanding of, diverse communities. That said, incorporating some of these practices into teacher education programs might help pave the way for creating more inclusive and global teacher preparation.

FINAL THOUGHTS

According to the chapter authors of this volume, the future of civic education is murky and complex. On the one hand, according to White and Myers (see chapter in this volume), due to globalization, the entire field is being redefined, repackaged as "21st-century skills aimed at preparing students with cross-cultural communication and problem-solving skills to more effectively compete in a global economy." If this is the case, the nobler goals of civic engagement and productive citizenship that previously defined the field have been abandoned. More idealistic than some of the current articulations of civic education, the former goals were more about engagement and collective commitment, less about functionalism, individual gain, and national security. We are left with a critical question: Is globalization about becoming world citizens, or is it about economic preparation for the workplace? As White and Meyer rightly point out, this turn in the field augurs a further decline in political knowledge and civic participation, particularly for disenfranchised youths.

Given the so-called education reform movement now sweeping the globe (what Sahlberg, [2011] has aptly termed GERM, the Global Education Reform Movement; see Sahlberg; and Valdés in this volume), where teachers have been stripped of autonomy because of rigid mandates and accountability requirements, we might well ask: How can the role of classroom teachers change to promote civic engagement? How can they help rescue civic inclusion from a wholly functionalist future?

Bringing civic education back to its more community-minded goals will take sustained structural changes in schools, universities, and society in general. At the same time, doing so will take consistent work on the part of scholars, policymakers, administrators, and, in the end, teachers. That is, it will take concerted action not only on the part of teachers—who on their own have insufficient power—but also policymakers, teacher educators, and entire communities to promote change that can lead to civic inclusion. Change usually comes slowly, and promoting civic engagement in a globalized world may prove a difficult and bumpy road ahead. Nevertheless, it is worth the struggle if what we—everyone from individuals to nations—claim to believe about equity, justice, and diversity is ever to have a chance.

REFERENCES

Acosta, C., & Mir, A. (2012). Empowering young people to be critical thinkers: The Mexican American Studies Program in Tucson. *Voices in Urban Education, 34,* 5–26.

Apple, M. W. (2013). Thinking internationally and paying our debts: Critical thoughts on diversity, globalization, and education. *Kappa Delta Pi Record, 49*, 118–120.

Arthur, J., Davies, I., & Hahn, C. (Eds.). (2008). *The Sage handbook of education for citizenship and democracy.* Thousand Oaks, CA: Sage.

Banks, J. A. (Ed.). (2009a). *The Routledge international companion to multicultural education.* New York, NY: Routledge.

Banks, J. A. (2009b). *Teaching strategies for ethnic studies* (8th ed.). New York, NY: Pearson.

Banks, J. A. (2012). Ethnic studies, citizenship education, and the public good. *Intercultural Education, 23*(6), 467–473.

Bloom, A. (1987). *The closing of the American mind.* New York, NY: Simon & Schuster.

Blum, L. (2014). Three educational values for a multicultural society: Difference recognition, national cohesion and equality. *Journal of Moral Education, 43*(3), 332–344.

Bourdieu, P. (1984). *Distinction: A social critique of the judgment of taste* (R. Nice, Trans.). Cambridge, MA: Harvard University Press.

Cabrera, N. L., Milen, J. E., Jaquette, O., & Marx, R. W. (2014). Missing the (student achievement) forest for all the (political) trees: Empiricism and the Mexican American studies controversy in Tucson. *American Educational Research Journal, 24* (6), 1084–1118.

Cammarota, J., & Fine, M. (Eds.). (2008). *Revolutionizing education: Youth participatory action research in motion.* New York, NY: Routledge.

Cammarota, J., & Romero, A. (2006). A critically compassionate pedagogy for Latino/a youth. *Latino/a Studies, 4*(3), 305–312.

Clewell, B. C., Puma, M., & McKay, S. A. (2001). *Does it matter if my teacher looks like me? The impact of teacher race and ethnicity on student academic achievement.* New York, NY: Ford Foundation.

Cummins, J. (2000). *Language, power, and pedagogy: Bilingual children in the crossfire.* Clevedon, United Kingdom: Multilingual Matters.

Darder, A. (2015). Foreword. In K. M. Sturges (Ed.), *Neoliberalizing educational reform: America's quest for profitable market-colonies and the undoing of the public good* (pp. ix–xvii). Rotterdam, the Netherlands: Sense.

Darling-Hammond, L., Rothman, R., Sahlberg, P., Pervin, B., Campbell, C., & Choo, T. L. (2015). *Teaching in the flat world: Learning from high-performing systems.* New York, NY: Teachers College Press.

Dee, T. S. (2000). *Teachers, race, and student achievement in a randomized experiment.* Cambridge, MA: National Bureau of Economic Research.

Foucault, M. (1980). Truth and power. In C. Gordon (Ed.), *Power/knowledge: Selected interviews and other writings 1972–1977* (pp. 107–133). Brighton, United Kingdom: Harvester Press.

Freire, P. (1970). *Pedagogy of the oppressed.* New York, NY: Seaview.

Freire, P. (1985). *The politics of education: Culture, power, and liberation.* South Hadley, MA: Bergin & Garvey.

Gándara, P., & Hopkins, M. (2010). *Forbidden language: English learners and restrictive language policies.* New York, NY: Teachers College Press.

Garcia, A., Mirra, N., Morrell, E., Martinez, A., & Scorza, D. (2015). The Council of Youth Research: Critical literacy and civic agency in the digital age. *Reading and Writing Quarterly, 31*(2), 151–167.

García, O., with Beardsmore, H. B. (2009). *Bilingual education in the 21st century: A global perspective.* Malden, MA: Wiley–Blackwell.

Gay, G. (2004). Curriculum theory and multicultural education. In J. A. Banks & C. A. M.

Banks (Eds.), *Handbook of research on multicultural education* (2nd ed., pp. 30–49). San Francisco, CA: Jossey-Bass..

Gillborn, D. (2008). *Racism and education: Coincidence or conspiracy?* London: Routledge.

Gorski, P. (2013). *Reaching and teaching students in poverty: Strategies for erasing the opportunity gap.* New York, NY: Teachers College Press.

Gramsci, A. (1971). *Selections from the prison notebooks* (Q. Hoare & G. Nowell Smith, Eds. & Trans.). New York, NY: International.

Haberman, M. (1991). The pedagogy of poverty versus good teaching. *Phi Delta Kappan, 73,* 290–294.

Hicks, M. (2015). Coming into full humanity through teaching, sharing, and connecting. In S. Nieto (Ed.), *Why we teach now* (pp. 131–137). New York, NY: Teachers College Press.

Hirsch, E. D. (1987). *Cultural literacy: What every American needs to know.* Boston, MA: Houghton Mifflin.

Ignatiev, N. (2008). *How the Irish became White.* New York, NY: Routledge.

Irizarry, J. (2011). *The Latinization of U.S. schools: Successful teaching and learning in shifting cultural contexts.* Boulder, CO: Paradigm.

Irvine, J. J., & Fenwick, L. T. (2009). *Teachers and teaching for the new millennium: The role of HBCUs.* Washington, DC: U.S. Department of Education and National Board for Professional Teaching Standards.

Kyuchukov, H. (2009). Diversity and citizenship in Bulgaria. In J. A. Banks (Ed), *The Routledge international companion to multicultural education* (pp. 360–369). New York, NY: Routledge.

Ladson-Billings, G. (2004). New directions in multicultural education: Complexities, boundaries, and critical race theory. In J. A. Banks & C. A. M. Banks (Eds.), *Handbook of research on multicultural education* (2nd ed., pp. 50–65). San Francisco, CA: Jossey-Bass.

Macedo, D., Dendrinos, B., & Gounari, P. (2003). *The hegemony of English.* Boulder, CO: Paradigm.

McFadden, R. D. (2006, November 28). Police kill man after a Queens bachelor party. *The New York Times.* Retrieved from www.nytimes.com/2006/11/26/nyregion/26cops.html?_r=0

Meer, N., Pala, V. S., Modood, T., & Simon, P. (2009). Cultural diversity, Muslims, and education in France and England: Two contrasting models in Western Europe. In J. A. Banks (Ed.), *The Routledge international companion to multicultural education* (pp. 413–424). New York, NY: Routledge.

Merryfield, M. (2000). Why aren't teachers being prepared to teach for diversity, equity, and global interconnectedness? A study of lived experiences in the making of multicultural and global educators. *Teaching and Teacher Education, 16*(4), 429–443.

Merryfield, M., & Duty, L. (2008). Globalization. In J. Arthur, I. Davies, & C. Hahn (Eds.), *The Sage handbook of education for citizenship and democracy* (pp. 80–91). Thousand Oaks, CA: Sage.

Merryfield, M., Lo, J. Y.-T., & Kasai, M. (2008). Worldmindedness: Taking off the blinders. *Journal of Curriculum and Instruction, 2*(1), 6–20.

Mirra, N., Filipiak, D., & García, A. (2015). Revolutionizing inquiry in urban English classrooms: Pursuing voice and justice through Youth Participatory Action Research. *English Journal, 105*(2), 49–57.

Mirra, N., García, A., & Morrell, E. (2016). *Doing youth participatory action research: A methodological handbook for researchers, educators, and youth.* New York, NY: Routledge.

Morrell, E. (2008). *Critical literacy and urban youth: Pedagogies of access, dissent, and liberation*. New York, NY: Routledge.

Nail, T. (2015). Migrant cosmopolitanism. *Public Affairs Quarterly, 29*(2), 187–199.

Nieto, S. (2013a). *Finding joy in teaching students of diverse backgrounds: Culturally responsive and socially just practices in U.S. classrooms*. Portsmouth, NH: Heinemann.

Nieto, S. (Ed.). (2013b). Diversity, globalization, and education: What do they mean for teachers and teacher educators? *Kappa Delta Pi Record, 49*(3), 105–107.

Nieto, S. (Ed.). (2014). Introduction to "Diversity, globalization, and education." *Educational Forum, 78*(1), 3–6.

Oakes, J. (2005). *Keeping track: How schools structure inequality* (2nd ed.). New Haven, CT: Yale University Press.

Payne, R. (2005). *A framework for understanding poverty* (4th ed.). Highlands, TX: Aha! Process.

Pike, G. (2000). Global education and national identity: In pursuit of meaning. *Theory Into Practice, 39*(2), 64–73.

Pike, G. (2008). Global education. In J. Arthur, I. Davies, & C. Hahn (Eds.), *The Sage handbook of education for citizenship and democracy* (pp. 468–480). Thousand Oaks, CA: Sage.

Roediger, D. R. (2005). *Working toward Whiteness: How immigrants became White: The strange journey from Ellis Island to the suburbs*. New York, NY: Basic Books.

Rosario, M. (2015). Teaching on the frontline. In S. Nieto (Ed.), *Why we teach now* (pp. 192–201). New York, NY: Teachers College Press.

Sahlberg, P. (2011). *Finnish lessons: What can the world learn from educational change in Finland?* New York, NY: Teachers College Press.

Shakespeare, W. (1998). *The tempest (Signet updated edition)*. New York, NY: Penguin. (Original work published 1623)

Sleeter, C. E. (1995). An analysis of the critiques of multicultural education. In J. A. Banks & C. A. M. Banks (Eds.), *Handbook of research on multicultural education* (pp. 81–94). New York, NY: Macmillan.

Sleeter, C. E. (2008). Preparing White teachers for diverse students. In M. Cochran-Smith, S. Feiman-Nemser, D. J. McIntyre, & K. E. Demers (Eds.), *Handbook of research on teacher education: Enduring questions in changing contexts* (3rd ed., pp. 559–582). New York, NY: Routledge.

Sleeter, C. E. (2011). *The academic and social value of ethnic studies: A research review*. Washington, DC: National Education Association.

Sleeter, C. E. (2015). Ethnicity and the curriculum. In D. Wyse, L. Hayward, & J. Pandya (Eds.), *The Sage handbook of curriculum, pedagogy, and assessment* (pp. 231–246). New York, NY: Sage.

Tintiangco-Cubales, A., Kohli, R., Sacramento, J., Henning, N., Agarwal-Rangnath, R., & Sleeter, C. E. (2015). Toward an ethnic studies pedagogy: Implications for k–12 schools from the research. *Urban Review, 47*, 104–125.

United Nations, Department of Economic and Social Affairs, Population Division. (2016). *International migration 2015* (ST/ESA/SER.A/376). Retrieved from www.un.org/en/development/desa/population/migration/publications/wallchart/docs/MigrationWallChart2015.pdf

Wright, W. E., Boun, S., & García, O. (Eds.). (2015). *Handbook of bilingual and multilingual education*. New York, NY: Wiley.

About the Contributors

Tali Aderet-German has an MA in curriculum planning, with distinction, from the School of Education at Tel Aviv University and is a doctoral candidate at the Department of Learning, Instruction, and Teacher Education at the Faculty of Education at the University of Haifa, where she is a teaching assistant. She is working on her dissertation, "School Self-Evaluation: A Case Study," under the supervision of Professor Miriam Ben-Peretz. She was the coordinator of a research team studying the education of immigrant students and currently coordinates the editing process of two books on teacher education.

Ayman K. Agbaria is a scholar, human rights activist, and senior lecturer in education policy and politics at the University of Haifa and the head of educational research at the Mandel Leadership Institute in Jerusalem. Currently, he serves as a visiting scholar at the Centre for Research and Evaluation in Muslim Education, UCL Institute of Education in London. He specializes in education among ethnic and religious minorities, and is also a widely anthologized poet and playwright.

James A. Banks holds the Kerry and Linda Killinger Endowed Chair in Diversity Studies and is the founding director of the Center for Multicultural Education at the University of Washington–Seattle. His research focuses on multicultural education and diversity and citizenship education in a global context. His books include *Educating Citizens in a Multicultural Society* (2nd ed., 2007, Teachers College Press), and *Cultural Diversity and Education: Foundations, Curriculum, and Teaching* (6th ed., Routledge, 2016). He is the editor of *Diversity and Citizenship Education: Global Perspectives* (Jossey-Bass, 2004) and the *Encyclopedia of Diversity in Education* (Sage Publications, 2012).

Zvi Bekerman teaches anthropology of education at the School of Education and the Melton Center, Hebrew University of Jerusalem, and is a faculty member at the Mandel Leadership Institute in Jerusalem. His main interests are the study of cultural, ethnic, and national identity, including identity processes and negotiation during intercultural interactions. He is particularly interested in how concepts such as culture and identity intersect with issues of social justice, intercultural and peace education, and citizenship education. His books include *The Promise of Integrated Multicultural and Bilingual Education: Inclusive Palestinian–Arab and Jewish Schools in Israel* (Oxford University Press, 2016).

Miriam Ben-Peretz is professor emerita at the faculty of education at the University of Haifa. She is past chair of the department of teacher education and former head of the School of Education at the University of Haifa. She is the founder and head of the Center for Jewish Education in Israel and the Diaspora. Her main research interests are curriculum, teacher education and professional development, policy-making, and Jewish education. Her publications include *Learning from Experience: Memory and the Teacher's Account of Teaching* (SUNY Press, 1995) and *Policy-Making in Education: A Holistic Approach in Response to Global Changes* (Rowman & Littlefield, 2009).

Amy K. Marks is an associate professor of psychology at Suffolk University. Her scholarship focuses on risk and resilience processes among minority youth. Her books include: *Transitions: The Development of Immigrant Children* (coeditor, NYU Press, 2015), *The Immigrant Paradox in Children and Adolescents: Is Becoming American a Developmental Risk?* (coeditor, APA Press, 2012), and *Immigrant Stories: Ethnicity and Academics in Middle Childhood* (coauthor, Oxford University Press, 2009). She was awarded a Jacobs Foundation Young Scholar Award for her research on academics and ethnic identity among immigrant youth.

Minas Michikyan is a doctoral student at the University of California–Los Angeles (UCLA), and a researcher at the Institute for Immigration, Globalization, and Education (UCLA), at the Children's Digital Media Center @ LA, (UCLA/ Cal State LA), and at the Center for Multicultural Research (Cal State, LA). He is a lecturer in the Department of Psychology and Biological Sciences at California State University–Los Angeles. Minas's research interests focus on the psychosocial, cognitive, and cultural aspects of multiple and intersecting identities of youth from diverse backgrounds in offline and online contexts and their implications for development and well-being.

John P. Myers is an associate professor in the School of Teacher Education at Florida State University and coordinator of the social sciences education program. His research examines the consequences of globalization for how youth think about the complexities of the modern world. He is especially interested in classroom practices that foster global citizenship and identities as students come to understand core world history and social science concepts. His work has been published in journals such as *Curriculum Inquiry, Teachers College Record, The American Journal of Education,* and *Comparative Education Review.*

Sonia Nieto has devoted her professional life to questions of diversity, equity, and social justice in education. With research focusing on multicultural education, teacher education, and the education of students of culturally and linguistically diverse backgrounds, she has written or edited 11 books and dozens of book chapters and journal articles, as well as a memoir, *Brooklyn Dreams: My Life in Public Education* (Harvard Education Press, 2015). She has received numerous awards for her scholarly work, activism, and advocacy, including six honorary doctorates. Elected as a Laureate of Kappa Delta Pi (2011), and a Fellow of AERA (2011), in 2015 she was elected a member of the National Academy of Education.

Carola Suárez-Orozco is a professor of human development and psychology at the University of California–Los Angeles (UCLA). Her books include *Learning a New Land: Immigrant Students in American Society* (coauthor, Harvard University Press, 2008) as well as the recently released *Transitions: The Development of the Children of Immigrants* (coeditor, NYU Press, 2015). She has been awarded an American Psychological Association (APA) Presidential Citation for her contributions to the understanding of the cultural psychology of immigration and has served as chair of the APA Presidential Task Force on Immigration. She is the editor of the *Journal of Adolescent Research* and a senior program associate for the W. T. Grant Foundation.

Marcelo M. Suárez-Orozco is the Wasserman Dean, UCLA Graduate School of Education and Information Studies. He is the award-winning author and coauthor of multiple books published by university presses such as Harvard University Press, Stanford University Press, University of California Press, and Cambridge University Press. The recipient of the Mexican Order of the Aztec Eagle—Mexico's highest honor bestowed on a foreign national—he was Special Advisor to the Chief Prosecutor, The International Criminal Court, The Hague, and has authored multiple texts for Pope Francis's Pontifical Academies. At Harvard, he was the Victor Thomas Professor of Education and co-director of the Harvard Immigration Projects.

Guadalupe Valdés is the Bonnie Katz Tenenbaum Professor of Education at Stanford University. Her research has focused on the bilingualism of Latinos in the United States. Her current NSF-funded research is concerned with the design of New Generation Science Standards materials for students who are in the process of acquiring English. Her recent publications include *Common Core and ELLs/Emergent Bilinguals: A Guide for All Educators* (coauthor, Caslon Publishing, 2015) and "Latin@s and the Intergenerational Continuity of Spanish: The Challenges of Curricularizing Language," (in *International Multilingual Research Journal*, 2015).

Gregory White serves as executive director of the National Academy of Education and is a doctoral candidate in sociology at the University of Maryland, College Park. He has previously served in various roles with civic and education-focused organizations, including City Year, United Way, and the American Psychological Association Center for Psychology in Schools and Education. His research interests include civic education, the social and organizational context of learning, and educational inequality.

Index

227